SHAKESPEARE AND VIOLENCE

Shakespeare and Violence connects to current anxieties about the problem of violence, and shows how similar concerns are central in Shakespeare's plays. In the early histories and tragedies he took delight in outdoing Christopher Marlowe and other dramatists in spectacular stage violence for its entertainment value. His later plays on English history led him to consider violence in relation to rule, and in the context of the much debated question as to whether war can be just. The almost continual wars of the 1580s and 1590s no doubt affected him and led to scepticism about their value, a theme picked up in the classical plays. In these plays and in his major tragedies he also explored the construction of masculinity in relation to power over others, to the value of heroism, and to self-control. Shakespeare's last plays present a world in which human violence appears analogous to violence in the natural world, and both kinds of violence are shown as aspects of a world subject to chance and accident. This book is the first to examine the development of Shakespeare's representations of violence and to explain their importance in shaping his career as a dramatist.

R. A. FOAKES is Professor Emeritus at the Department of English, University of California, Los Angeles. His publications include *A Midsummer Night's Dream* (Cambridge, 1984), *Illustrations of the English Stage 1580–1642* (1985), *Coleridge's Criticism of Shakespeare* (1989), *Hamlet versus Lear* (Cambridge, 1993), *King Lear* for the third Arden series (1997), and, with Mary Foakes, *The Columbia Dictionary of Shakespeare Quotations* (1998). In 2002 he published the second edition of *Henslowe's Diary* (first edition Cambridge, 1961).

SHAKESPEARE AND VIOLENCE

R. A. FOAKES

CAMBRIDGE
UNIVERSITY PRESS

PUBLISHED BY THE PRESS SYNDICATE OF THE UNIVERSITY OF CAMBRIDGE
The Pitt Building, Trumpington Street, Cambridge CB2 1RP, United Kingdom

CAMBRIDGE UNIVERSITY PRESS
The Edinburgh Building, Cambridge, CB2 2RU, UK
40 West 20th Street, New York, NY 10011-4211, USA
477 Williamstown Road, Port Melbourne, VIC 3207, Australia
Ruiz de Alarcón 13, 28014 Madrid, Spain
Dock House, The Waterfront, Cape Town 8001, South Africa

http://www.cambridge.org

First published 2003

Printed in the United Kingdom at the University Press, Cambridge

Typeface Baskerville Monotype 11 / 12.5 pt   *System* LaTeX 2ε [TB]

A catalogue record for this book is available from the British Library

Library of Congress Cataloguing in Publication data

Foakes, R. A.
Shakespeare and Violence / R. A. Foakes.
p.   cm.
Includes bibliographical references and index.
ISBN 0-521-82043-X – ISBN 0-521-52743-0 (pb.)
1. Shakespeare, William, 1564–1616 – Views on violence.   2. Shakespeare, William,
1564–1616 – Views on war.   3. Violence in literature.   4. War in literature.   I. Title.
PR3069.V55   F63   2002
822.3′3 – dc21   2002067610

ISBN 0 521 82043 X hardback
ISBN 0 521 52743 0 paperback

I could hardly be persuaded, before I had seen it, that the world could have afforded so marble-hearted and savage-minded men, that for the only pleasure of murder would commit it; then cut, mangle, and hack other members in pieces: to rouse and sharpen their wits, to invent unused tortures and unheard-of torments; to devise new and unknown deaths and that in cold blood, without any former enmity or quarrel, or without any gain or profit; and only to this end, that they may enjoy the pleasing spectacle of the languishing gestures, pitiful motions, horror-moving yellings, deep fetched groans, and lamentable voices of a dying and drooping man.

Michel de Montaigne, 'Of Cruelty', *Essays* (1580), Second Book, Chapter xi, as translated by John Florio in 1603.

Contents

Illustrations

Preface

This is a book about a problem that troubled Shakespeare and his age as much as it does our own world, namely, how to relate to and cope with human violence. Much recent criticism has been devoted to repudiating any idea that Shakespeare's works can speak directly to our time or have any transhistorical meaning. Deconstructive critics insist on the instability of meaning, and argue that the plays are 'not intelligible by commonsensical notions of coherence, since they are constituted by historical contingencies of the stage, conventions, location, and audience',[1] so that they would say there are no authorially validated meanings. Materialist critics also tend to treat the literary text 'as an enactment or production' of a historical context or 'cultural system'.[2] The author disappears, to be reinvented 'not indeed as the origin and owner of meaning beloved by nineteenth-century literary biography, but as a cultural construct determined by the representational practices of a particular historical era'.[3] Authority is transferred to the reader or critic, who is conceived as creating the meaning of a work. No doubt we can interpret Shakespeare's plays only in the light of our own experience; but as we are reading a text or watching a play performed, common sense may well find something peculiar in the notion of incoherent and unstable works written by a cultural construct.

It is true that 'interpretation responds to the moment of their representation, the moment of reading or of onstage enactment',[4] so that we negotiate Shakespeare's plays in relation to our own age and perceptions. Violence as manifested in our society in murder, rape, and casual street attacks, in the activities of serial killers, and in acts of terrorism is deeply troubling at the present time, and it is in an awareness of this problem that I consider Shakespeare's treatment of violence in this book. At the same time the plays remain vitally alive, coherent, and rich in embodied meanings for millions of playgoers and readers. Theoretical debates about the status of the author and the text have their own fascination, but on the whole theorists speak to other theorists.[5] Editors, indeed, impose their own choice and arrangement of the text, and printers and publishers design the format of an edition, but the texts of the plays have for long been basically established, and variations and revisions have been pretty thoroughly analysed. Stage directors and actors impose their own style and shaping in productions, and performance is never a mere repetition of the work. But the plays survive our scrutiny, and I think will survive current efforts to destabilize them. In this book I shall treat Shakespeare as the author of his plays, and as the originator in them of perceptions that resonate across the centuries and take on new life and meaning in the context of our own time.

I am grateful to many friends, colleagues, and members of my family who have helped me in discussion to clarify my thinking about violence. The University of California has aided me with research funding, and I have relied heavily on the Folger Shakespeare Library in Washington, DC, the libraries of the Shakespeare Institute and Shakespeare Centre in Stratford-upon-Avon, the Huntington Library in San Marino, and the Young Research Library at UCLA. I owe thanks to Peter Wright, Kate Falzareno, and especially to Curt Whitaker, whose aid as a research assistant proved invaluable. The advice of the readers for the Press has also been very helpful. Chapter 6, on *Hamlet*, is reworked and expanded from my essay 'Hamlet's Neglect of Revenge', published in Arthur Kinney, ed., *Hamlet: New Critical Essays* (New York and London: Routledge, 2001), 85–99; I have also used some material from another essay, 'Coleridge, Violence and "The Rime of the Ancient Mariner"', *Romanticism*, 7 (2001), 41–57. Line references for quotations from Shakespeare are to *The Arden Shakespeare Complete Works*, ed. Richard Proudfoot, Ann Thompson, and David Scott Kastan (London: Thomas Nelson, 1998).

NOTES

1. Susan Zimmerman, ed., *Shakespeare's Tragedies* (New Casebooks. Basingstoke: Macmillan; New York: St Martin's Press, 1998), 2.
2. Ivo Kamps, ed., *Materialist Shakespeare: a History* (London and New York: Verso, 1995), citing the Introduction by Kamps, 5.
3. Richard Wilson, *Will Power: Essays on Shakespearean Authority* (London and Detroit: Harvester Wheatsheaf, 1993), 18.
4. Citing W. B. Worthen, *Shakespeare and the Authority of Performance* (Cambridge University Press, 1997), 60. Worthen goes on to say that the plays 'can only

speak in the idiom of the present', which I think untrue. Shakespeare's language is for the most part accessible to modern audiences, if only because so much of it has passed into common usage or is known by quotation – and performance often clarifies meaning through action.

5. See R. A. Foakes, 'Shakespeare Editing and Textual Theory: a Rough Guide', *Huntington Library Quarterly*, 60 (1999), 425–42.

CHAPTER I

Introduction: 'Exterminate all the brutes'

Our world is deeply troubled by the problem of violence, as manifested, for instance, in violent crime, in terrorism, in war, in prolonged feuds between neighbouring groups (as in Northern Ireland), and in territorial battles such as those between street-gangs in inner cities. The horrific acts of terrorism on 11 September 2001 that demolished the World Trade Center in New York provoked, understandably, an instant response in the American bombing of Afghanistan, with calls for the extirpation of terrorism throughout the world. The aim is laudable, but history suggests that it is also impracticable. Human beings, especially males, have been addicted to violence since myths and legends first circulated and recorded history began. Terrorism has long been practised in many forms, and often in the name of a religious cause. It is hard to understand why 'bad things are done by people who otherwise appear to be good – in cases of religious terrorism, by pious people dedicated to a moral vision of the world',[1] unless violence is natural to men. A morality that categorizes forms of behaviour as good or evil may be seen as one means by which societies attempt to exert pressure on their members to conform, but no moral vision has yet had much effect in controlling violence. What Americans wanted instantly in the wake of the destruction in New York was retaliation, countering violence with more violence. Here may be glimpsed the basic problem of violence – it appears that we have instinctual drives that prompt us to defend ourselves when attacked, to use violence if necessary to protect family, tribe, or nation, as well as to maintain or improve status.

If violence is natural to human beings, then we need to come to terms with this issue, and seek understanding from the stories and enduring works of literature that have dealt with it. My particular concern is with Shakespeare, who must have been aware of the most spectacular act of terrorism in his time, the Gunpowder Plot, the attempt by a group of Catholics to blow up the House of Lords and King James I in 1605. His plays may be seen as following a trajectory that begins with a delight in representing violence for entertainment, continues in a series of plays that explore various aspects of the problem of violence, and ends with a searching study of human aggression in relation to self-control in *The Tempest*. Although Shakespeare's world was very different from that of the present day, and advances in technology have made available weapons he could not imagine, the basic issues remain the same.

In Joseph Conrad's *Heart of Darkness*, Marlow, the narrator, tells a story about taking a rickety steamboat up a river through jungles in Africa to find and collect the ivory gathered by Mr Kurtz, the most spectacularly successful trader of the company that has hired him. Mr Kurtz had written a report for the 'International Society for the Suppression of Savage Customs' which strikes Marlow as splendid: 'It gave me the notion of an exotic Immensity ruled by an august Benevolence.'[2] But when Marlow reaches the decaying house where Mr Kurtz lives, he notices it is surrounded by posts with what look like ornamental carvings at the top; only on a nearer view does he discover that they are not carvings, but human heads with their faces turned towards the house of Kurtz. Mr Kurtz, it turns out, had found the natives treated him as a supernatural being, and he had come to accept and use that ascendancy ruthlessly in controlling the natives and in acquiring ivory. The heads, Marlow is told, are the 'heads of rebels' (75), and to Marlow it seems as if Mr Kurtz invaded the wilderness, and the wilderness has taken a terrible vengeance on him by invading him. But that is Marlow's reading. The novel goes further in taking us not only into the heart of darkness and violence in the depths of the jungle, but also into the darkness and violent propensities of the human heart. Mr Kurtz had added a postscript to the fine sentiments of his report, 'scrawled evidently much later' (66): 'Exterminate all the brutes.' Both impulses, the desire to exert benevolence, and the desire to exterminate, are prompted by that heart of darkness, and can exist in the same person.

Conrad's powerful novel focuses in this way on an issue that has repeatedly troubled societies and their writers and artists through the centuries in western culture. It is the problem of how to deal with the human propensity, especially among males, to violence. Its recurrence in various forms from ancient epic and the Bible to the modern novel supports the view that there is such a thing as human nature, giving us instincts and modes of behaviour that are still affected by the deep-rooted urges to claim territory, defend the tribe, protect women and children, and use violence to fight for and maintain possessions. This view has been dismissed as reactionary by cultural materialists, who assert that the 'subject' or individual is a construction, and who reject the 'belief that in its essence the subject does not change, that liberal humanism itself expresses a human nature which, despite its diversity, is always at the most basic, the most intimate level, the same'.[3] Such categorical formulations, which stress terms such as 'essence' and 'always', are rhetorically suspect, and have deservedly been criticized, and the notion that 'Man's nature' should be seen simply 'as the product of forces external to him' is being questioned by literary theorists.[4] The matter has been much debated by anthropologists and psychologists, some of whom take the evolutionary view that aggression is instinctive in males especially, or programmed into human DNA.[5] Others, who may be anxious to ensure that those who commit violent acts are held responsible, claim that aggression is socially constructed and depends on the values of a specific society at a given time.[6] A third group avoids such dogmatism by allowing for the influence of both nature and nurture, while recognizing the extent to which theorists 'have displaced and complicated the origin of constitutive violence from male agency to patriarchal structures of economic and ideological domination'.[7] This last seems to me the best view to take, since the origins of human behaviour are inevitably speculative. The history of human violence, I think, shows that males have always had to cope with an urge to violence in a variety of circumstances, and that western societies have always been concerned with ways of channelling or controlling that urge. The proneness to violence, to lash out, is both a part of what constitutes the nature of human beings, especially men, and is also culturally constructed. Hence it can erupt in different ways at any time, and the problem continues to haunt our own age as much as it did that of Homer, or of Shakespeare, the principal concern of this book.

At the present time most people in Britain and America appear to regard violence as a major problem in society, specifically in relation to violent crime and violence in the media. We cling to the notion, fostered by the Romantics, that children are innocent creatures who enter the world 'trailing clouds of glory' in Wordsworth's words, and that human beings are basically good, or ought to be. Thus a great many people who see themselves as representative of a norm regard violence as a deviation from that norm, and believe it should be punished with severity. Governments, reflecting popular voting patterns, have responded to widespread concerns about violent crime by increasing police forces and building more prisons, moves which appear to give satisfaction to a majority who believe that violence may be controlled and distanced by such means. In 1993 Michael Howard, Home Secretary in Britain at that time, claimed in a government White Paper that what he called 'the war against crime' could be won. There is, in fact, little evidence that what the police do has 'much more than a very marginal impact on crime levels', according to research done in Britain.[8] Many state legislatures in America have introduced or brought back the death penalty in recent times, seemingly in a belief that it will give potential killers pause; and more than two million people are incarcerated in the United States. But though the amount of violent crime fluctuates year by year, it does not decrease in proportion to these measures, which may please voters, but which have little effect on criminal violence.

One reason people can continue to take unfounded assumptions for granted and follow policies that fly in the face of the evidence is that we are still to some extent conditioned by the belief, given wide currency in the nineteenth century, in what Wordsworth called 'a progress in the species towards unattainable perfection'.[9] Coleridge's vision of the 'progressive amelioration of mankind' and of continued 'advances in civilization' has effectively narrowed in modern times into the concept of economic 'progress' as measured by the gross national product. Terms such as 'progress' and 'development' are comforting, and fit the image of winning the war on crime. At the same time, paradoxically, the desire for more police and prisons is driven by fear, fear of violence, which might seem more in tune with the Hobbesian idea of men as preserved from mutual destruction only by a power that keeps them in awe. It is also paradoxical that putting criminals in prison does not serve to change them or deter others from violence. Michel Foucault argued that shutting a criminal away in prison has the effect of making him seem 'a villain, a monster, a madman, perhaps, a sick and before long "abnormal" individual', so encouraging the idea that criminal violence is a deviation from the norm.[10] There is evidence, in fact, that punishment by incarceration 'does not lower the rate or frequency of acts of violence. Punishment stimulates violence; punishment causes it.'[11]

The most debated and publicized form of violence in western society now is associated with crime, but there are various other kinds. Social historians and evolutionary psychologists suggest an alternative origin for violence in the tendency of alpha-males to seek dominance, form hierarchies, and regard those outside their group as inferior. A desire for status operates at all levels, and among the street-gangs of large cities a teenager may be driven to violence, even to kill, if he feels he has been 'dissed', or treated with disrespect; his standing may depend upon establishing a credible threat of violence. So violence may have a subsidiary origin in social conditions; where poverty, lack of education, and other conditions that deny people status exist, violence may provide a way to achieve some kind of prestige.[12] Prosperous societies seek to preserve their structures and the safety of the better-off by means of police and the use of institutionalized violence through the law, often while neglecting welfare for the deprived. One form of safety-valve is to channel hostility against those outside the frontiers. Enormous sums are spent on defence budgets to provide for a military establishment that can protect a country's interests elsewhere in the world. In this way the use of terrible forms of violence in making war against demonized others, as in Vietnam, Iraq or Chechnya, is tolerated, even applauded. Violence that would not be permitted within a society is regarded as legitimate when practised against other countries, especially if it can be presented, in the words of John Keegan, as a form of 'civilized warfare'.[13]

The self-contradictory beliefs of those who think violence is what others do, not themselves, and yet vote for the death penalty or punishment by institutionalized violence, and the equally conflicted views of those of us who are appalled by violence at home, in our streets or country, but applaud the use of military violence against other countries, become understandable if violence originates in instinctual urges to defend the self and the tribe, or in the construction of masculinity in a society that fosters the desire for status and respect. Aggressiveness is associated with achievement, and can help people compete for positions of authority. In prosperous societies physical violence has been to some extent replaced by other kinds, most obviously verbal violence, as used to humiliate others, to put people down, as we say. Aggression is thus now acceptable if it contributes to the functioning of a competitive society, and to dealing with enemies outside the borders, but it is unacceptable and regarded as criminal when practised by those demonized by laws designed to protect possessors of property and wealth. The contradictions built into common attitudes to violence may help to explain why viewers in America and Britain are fascinated by news reports of criminal or accidental violence, by crime fiction, and by films and TV series about murders, especially serial killings. Wendy Lesser has argued persuasively that in films such as *The Silence of the Lambs* we identify with both the detective and the murderer: she claims, 'the detective is in some way the murderer. Not only must one imagine oneself to be the murderer in order to find him . . . one must also admit to the existence in one's own core of unknown and generally inaccessible violence.'[14] There is something of Mr Kurtz in all of us.

There are politicians and commentators who like to blame the media, especially the Hollywood movie industry, for exploiting violence, and producing 'nightmares of depravity' that encourage antisocial behaviour 'with devastating consequences for our civilization' resulting from its 'addiction to graphic violence'.[15] If watching violence or reading about it in the media encouraged people to be violent themselves, millions would be on a killing spree every day. Our fascination with violence has much more to do with the beast in each of us,[16] with deep-seated fears about the animal instincts we strive to control. If all humans are capable of violence, of striking out to protect, defend, or retaliate against an attacker or someone who has given offence, then one reason we are fascinated by violence on TV or movie screens may be because watching and identifying with it harmlessly releases impulses everyone has and normally represses. Anthropological theories about human origins and evolution have lent support to the idea that impulses to violence are natural to human beings, especially males, and originate in the genes we share with the primates.[17] This idea in turn has led to the development of theories about the origin of religious practices. Religion may have arisen as a 'device for aiding social cohesion' in the face of enemies or wild beasts by stimulating group confidence through forms of play and ritual. Add a felt need to propitiate the mysterious forces of nature that cannot be controlled by humans, and which bring earthquakes, floods, plagues, fire, dearth, etc., and a plausible explanation can be found for the origins of the widespread practice of sacrifice. So René Girard identified violence with the sacred, arguing that in sacrifice violence is deflected away from the members who seek protection and on to a victim or scapegoat. The sacrificial victim can then be 'exposed to violence without fear of reprisal'. Religious rites, Girard claims, preceded any formation of a judicial system as a way of preventing the eruption of conflict and the 'recurrence of reciprocal violence'[18] provoked by the urge to retaliate. In a post-Darwinian world an anthropological perspective on the origins of violence, religion, and sacrifice is commonplace, so that it seems appropriate that the section on the story of creation in Genesis 1–11 in The *Cambridge Companion to the Bible* (1997) should be headed, 'The Nature and Functions of Myth', and begin, 'The origin stories of the ancient Near East helped societies of those times to cope with the difficult and puzzling world in which they had to live.'[19]

Anthropology has offered explanations of the origins of humanity and of religion inconceivable to a pre-Darwinian Christian society which relied on Genesis for an account of the beginning of the world and of human beings. Thus it would seem at first sight that current anxieties about violence emerge from conditions radically different from those prevailing in Shakespeare's age. Technology has developed a range of killing weapons, unimaginable in past centuries, in guns, missiles, bombs, and gas-chambers. The media can now provide immediate photographic records of acts of violence throughout much of the world. In spite of these enormous changes, the fundamental questions why civilized humans are prone to violence and how we can deal with this problem have remained a powerful concern in major literature from Homer to the present day. Just as now many people maintain paradoxical or self-contradictory attitudes to human violence, so in earlier ages there have always been conflicting views, if only because values we prize in some circumstances may seem appalling in other ways; what is good on the battlefield may be outrageous in peacetime. Underlying all considerations of violence is the issue that has troubled many great writers, namely how it is that an individual, usually a man since violence has always been primarily associated with males, can for no adequate reason commit terrible acts of violence. Such acts can have enormous consequences for a society, especially where the individual holds power of some kind. It is, I think, an issue that concerned Shakespeare, whose plays explore it in ever greater depth as his career developed. In the chapters that follow, I consider Shakespeare's treatment of violence in his history plays, tragedies, and late romances. The most substantial sections are on *Hamlet*, where I take the centre-point to be not Hamlet's revenge, but his sudden act of violence in killing Polonius, and on *The Tempest*, a play in which the uneasy suppression by Prospero of his own impulses to violence and of murderous attempts by others leads to an ambivalent ending that leaves open the prospect of a renewal of violence in Milan and Naples.

I do not deal with the comedies, which typically involve threats of violence if not violent acts, such as Orlando's overthrow of Charles the wrestler in *As You Like It*, but find a means to release the audience from the threat in such a way as to enhance the harmony of the marriages with which they conclude. Even those in which violence is most prominent achieve this escape, if at some cost. In *The Merchant of Venice*, Shakespeare added a whole act after the final exit of Shylock from the stage in order to help the audience dismiss him temporarily from their minds and attend to the byplay with wedding rings. The ending of *Measure for Measure* also seems difficult after the explosion of Angelo's sexual violence, and the threat of a death sentence on Claudio, for its action is deeply involved with issues of justice and mercy. However, Shakespeare seems to have developed ways of exploiting violence in these and other comedies in order to enrich our sense of the fragility of happiness, as notably in *Twelfth Night*, in which Sir Toby with his bloody coxcomb, Malvolio crying revenge, and the wistfully melancholy final song of Feste, all contribute a counterpoint to an ending that celebrates a 'golden time' that marks the unions of Orsino and Viola, Sebastian and Olivia, as well as Sir Toby and Maria. The use of violence here is much more complex than in early farces such as *The Comedy of Errors*, in which the two Dromios are beaten time and again for no fault of their own without any sign that they are ever hurt; such apparent violence, typical of farce, is fun for an audience, apparently as a vicarious release of impulses they have repressed.

violence in comedy

The uses of violence in comedy deserve attention, especially in relation to Nicholas Brooke's claim that 'horrid laughter' in Jacobean tragedy is essential to tragic form, and that 'the tradition of English tragedy, then, springs from violent farce', as a spin-off from morality plays. Tragedy, he argues, deals with 'extreme emotions' which, because they are extreme, 'are *liable* to turn over into laughter'.[20] If this is true, nevertheless some important distinctions need to be made. He discusses six non-Shakespearean tragedies in which laughter is indeed exploited in various ways. In some the controlling perspective is that of a savage satirist, such as Vindice in *The Revenger's Tragedy*; in others, such as *The Changeling*, the laughter is confined to the subplot. Brooke does not consider the purpose of laughter in these plays, which may be to distance and qualify an action that would otherwise evoke horror, or more narrowly, to provide a temporary release from emotional tension, a kind of breathing-space or safety-valve, which I take to be a function of the Porter in *Macbeth*. In Shakespeare's tragedies, comic interventions generally serve this limited purpose. Only in his earliest history plays and in *Titus Andronicus* are there moments when violent action topples, perhaps, into farce.

My concern is with the representations of violence in Shakespeare's histories, tragedies and romances, violence associated mostly with killings, humiliations or tortures that determine the shape of a play's action and the fate of its characters.[21] These plays, considered here in rough chronological order, I believe show Shakespeare's exploration of issues linked to the propensity for violence that seems natural to human beings. The plays, indeed, reveal a continuing development in his treatment of violence from an early delight in sensational stage violence for its theatrical excitement to his late works in which violence is represented as an inescapable aspect of human experience that can only be comprehended in the long perspective of time. I pay special attention in what follows to what I call the primal scene of violence, the deed that seems spontaneous and to have no meaning until we build interpretations into it later, for it is violence of this kind, initiated in the murder of

"the primal scene of violence"

Abel by Cain, that especially troubled Shakespeare's imagination. He was not alone in being fascinated by acts of violence that seem to have no cause, to be unmotivated or inadequately motivated, and there are notable works by some of his contemporary dramatists that focus on such deeds, such as John Webster's variant of the Cain and Abel pattern in *The Duchess of Malfi*. In this play Ferdinand remorselessly persecutes, tortures, and arranges the murder of his twin sister the Duchess, and only after her death looks for a reason, when he says he must have been out of his mind ('distracted of my wits', 4.2.278), though it is ironically later on that he does indeed go mad. Shakespeare is a special case in that during a long career he dramatized changing perspectives on representations of violence that show a maturing of his thinking about this matter, culminating in the perspective of the late plays in which human violence is portrayed as analogous to violence in the natural world.

I began this introduction with a brief account of present-day attitudes to violence, and the first chapter offers a description of a different but analogous culture of violence in which Shakespeare came to maturity, one that raised many of the issues that remain current, in spite of a different frame of reference, in which, to put it crudely, the Bible and classical literature had the kind of importance now assigned to Darwin and Freud. I then comment on what I call the Rose spectaculars, the *Henry VI* plays and *Titus Andronicus*, plays that appear in Philip Henslowe's lists as performed at his theatre, and which show Shakespeare competing with the spectacular representations of violence in plays by other dramatists of the time, especially Marlowe. This is followed by a study of modern film versions of two early tragedies, *Richard III* and *Romeo and Juliet*, by directors who have shown how fundamentally the action of these popular plays relates to current anxieties about violence. The next chapter is concerned with Shakespeare's later English history plays mainly in terms of war, in a sequence that runs from *King John* (rather than from *Richard II*) to *Henry V*. After completing this section I came across Middleton Murry's perceptive observation, made in 1936, that Falstaff and Hotspur are 'the Bastard's direct descendants',[22] meaning the Bastard Faulconbridge in *King John*; he did not, however, develop this idea, which is central to my reading of these plays.

Hamlet has a chapter to itself, as a play that marks a deepening of *Hamlet* Shakespeare's exploration of violence, in war and in peace, revisiting the Cain and Abel story that framed his early histories in another play that involves brother killing brother, and subordinating revenge in the end to the unpremeditated slaying of Polonius. The next two chapters consider the later tragedies and the Roman plays, paying particular attention to their concern with what it is to be a man, and with power. *Coriolanus* figures in both chapters as a play that contains Shakespeare's most incisive critique of the idea of the heroic and of manliness, and also his perception that human violence is inescapable in peace as well as in war. The last chapter is much concerned with the importance of natural violence as manifested in storms, shipwrecks, and the like, and its relation to human violence. *The Tempest* receives a more extended treatment, since it seems in many ways a kind of summing up, in dealing with so many aspects of violence: natural (the storm at sea), personal (Prospero's difficulty in controlling his own urges), and violence involved in struggles for power (the various attempts to gain power by murder). I see Shakespeare's use of costume as especially important for a full appreciation of what he was about in this play, and argue that the ending is deeply ambivalent in taking the characters back to the uncertain corridors of power in Italy.

Since my primary focus is on representations of violence in the plays, I am more concerned with action than with character and language. The complexity of Shakespeare's language and wordplay has proved inexhaustibly productive of meaning, and his major characters seem open to endless investigation, so that inevitably these have drawn most critical attention. Stage productions have to settle for one way of doing a play, and are ephemeral, so have had as yet relatively little impact on literary criticism. Attending not merely to the language, but to the action, to what the text tells us happens on stage, I hope redresses the balance somewhat. The viewpoint from which these chapters begin may seem strange, as in the case of *Hamlet*, for instance, where I have little to say about the prince's soliloquies, but am very interested in the significance of the presence on stage of the bleeding body of Polonius during Hamlet's scene with his mother. I think an investigation of the plays that focuses more on violence in action helps to account for important aspects of Shakespeare's growth as a dramatist. Violence has always been associated chiefly with masculinity, and although Shakespeare created some remarkably tough and violent female characters in his history plays and in Lady Macbeth, for example, I am inevitably much more concerned with his male figures.

NOTES

1. Mark Juergensmeyer, *Terror in the Mind of God: the Global Rise of Religious Violence* (Berkeley and Los Angeles: University of California Press, 2000), 7.

2. Ross C. Murfu, ed., *Joseph Conrad's Heart of Darkness*. Case Studies in Contemporary Criticism (New York: Bedford Books of St Martin's Press, 1996), 66; further page references are to this edition.

3. Catherine Belsey, *The Subject of Tragedy: Identity and Difference in Renaissance Drama* (London and New York: Methuen, 1985), ix.

4. See John Lee, *Shakespeare's Hamlet and the Controversies of Self* (Oxford: Clarendon Press, 2000), 25–33 and 84–7; the quotation is from 27; also Brian Vickers, *Appropriating Shakespeare: Contemporary Critical Quarrels* (New Haven, Conn. and London: Yale University Press, 1993), especially 214–15 and 224–5.

5. See, for example, Martin Daly and Margo Wilson, *Homicide* (New York: Aldine de Gruyter, 1988); Desmond Morris, *The Naked Ape* (New York: McGraw-Hill, 1967); and Michael P. Ghiglieri, *The Dark Side of Man: Tracing the Origins of Male Violence* (Reading, Mass.: Helix Books, 1999).

6. See Richard Rhodes, *Why They Kill: the Discoveries of a Maverick Criminologist* (New York: Alfred A. Knopf, 1999); Ashley Montagu, *Man and Aggression* (New York: Oxford University Press, 1968); and Lt Colonel Dave Grossman, *On Killing* (Boston: Little, Brown and Co., 1995).

7. Citing Arthur F. Redding, *Raids on Human Consciousness: Writing, Anarchism, and Violence* (Columbia: University of South Carolina Press, 1998), 173; see also Gerard G. Neuman, ed., *Origins of Human Aggression: Dynamics and Etiology* (New York: Human Sciences Press, 1987); Walter Benjamin, 'Critique of Violence', in *Reflections*, transl. Edmund Jephcott (New York: Schocken Books, 1986), 277–300; and Robert Wright, 'The Biology of Violence', *New Yorker* (13 March 1995), 69–77.

8. Rod Morgan and Tim Newburn, *The Future of Policing* (Oxford: Clarendon Press, 1997), 9.

9. 'Answer to Mathetes', in Samuel Taylor Coleridge, *The Friend*, ed. Barbara Rooke (2 vols., *Collected Works*, Bollingen Foundation Series LXXV. Princeton University Press; London: Routledge, 1969), 1.392.

10. *Discipline and Punish. The Birth of the Prison*, transl. Alan Sheridan (London: Penguin Books, 1979), 101.

11. James Gilligan, *Violence. Reflections on a National Epidemic* (New York: Random House, 1996; Vintage Books, 1997), 163–87, citing 184; see also Matthew Silberman, *A World of Violence. Corrections in America* (Belmont, Calif.: Wadsworth, 1995), 183.

12. Morgan and Newburn, *The Future of Policing*, 26, comment on crime as a 'feature of the culture of poverty' in poor areas in Britain.

13. John Keegan, *A History of Warfare* (1993; London: Pimlico Books, 1994), 4.

14. Wendy Lesser, *Pictures at an Execution. An Inquiry into the Subject of Murder* (Cambridge, Mass.: Harvard University Press, 1993), 18.

15. Bob Dole, speaking as candidate for the presidency of the United States in 1995, cited in Laurent Bouzereau, *Ultra Violent Movies from Sam Peckinpah to Quentin Tarantino* (Secaucus, N.J.: Citadel Press, 1996), 231–2; and Michael Medved, *Hollywood vs America. Popular Culture and the War on Traditional Values* (New York: HarperCollins, 1992), 183.

16. See Denis Duclos, *The Werewolf Complex. America's Fascination with Violence* (1994), transl. Amanda Pingree (Oxford University Press; New York: Berg, 1998), 133–43. He shares Sigmund Freud's gloomy view, put forward in *Civilization and its Discontents*, transl. James Strachey (1930; New York: W. W. Norton and Co., 1961), 59, that because of the 'primary mutual hostility of human beings, civilized society is perpetually threatened with disintegration'.

17. See Jared Diamond, *The Third Chimpanzee. The Evolution and Future of the Human Animal* (New York: HarperCollins, 1992), 15–31 and 284–98; he points out that we share with chimpanzees the practice of genocide; and Barbara Ehrenreich, *Blood Rites. Origins and History of the Passions of War* (Metropolitan Books. New York: Henry Holt and Co., 1997), especially 52–7.

18. René Girard, *Violence and the Sacred*, transl. Patrick Gregory (Baltimore: Johns Hopkins University Press, 1977), 13, 55.

19. Howard Clark Kee, Eric M. Meyers, John Rogerson, and Anthony J. Saldarini, *The Cambridge Companion to the Bible* (Cambridge University Press, 1997), 43.

20. Nicholas Brooke, *Horrid Laughter in Jacobean Tragedy* (London and New York: Barnes and Noble, 1979), 130, 8, 3; compare Michael Neill's comments on what he calls the macabre in the tragedies of this period in *Issues of Death: Mortality and Identity in English Renaissance Tragedy* (Oxford: Clarendon Press, 1999), 59–93.

21. The violence in Shakespeare's plays was exploited in the spoof horror film *Theatre of Blood* (1973), in which an actor turns into a serial killer who revenges himself on theatre critics by murdering them using methods derived from the plays in which his performances were condemned. Deborah Cartmell, in *Interpreting Shakespeare on Screen* (Basingstoke: Macmillan; New York: St Martin's Press, 2000), 9–11, notes that the violence in Shakespeare's plays has perhaps not been given much attention because 'there appears to be a need to preserve the myth of a non-violent, family-viewing Shakespeare, that is, to protect Shakespeare's cultural status'.

22. John Middleton Murry, *Shakespeare* (New York: Harcourt Brace, 1936), 125.

CHAPTER 2

Shakespeare's culture of violence

This book focuses mainly on Shakespeare's treatment of violence, a topic I was led to by prolonged study of *Hamlet* and *King Lear*, initially for a critical study, and later for an edition of the latter play. Both of these plays stage wanton acts of violence, most notably in the killing of Polonius and the blinding of Gloucester. For long the blinding of Gloucester in *King Lear* was omitted, carried out offstage, or concealed from the audience, as, in Dr Johnson's words,[1] 'an act too horrid to be endured in dramatic exhibition'; but did Shakespeare want his spectators to face up precisely to the horrid nature of the deed? Since Peter Brook directed a famous production in 1962, in which Cornwall used a spur to gouge out an eye in full view of the audience, performances have often emphasized the violence at this point.[2] This deed is especially horrid because it is pointless. Cornwall and Regan have nothing to learn from interrogating Gloucester; they are aware that he has sent the old King to Dover, for, as Regan tells him, 'we know the truth' (3.7.43). The blinding appears an act of gratuitous cruelty and, since Gloucester is already impotent, it defies explanation. Later in the action Edgar fights with and kills Oswald, who has attempted to seize his father, the blind Gloucester, as a traitor. In the 1993 production at the Royal Shakespeare Theatre, Edgar was 'so traumatized by the blinding of his father that he repeatedly sought to revenge it, blinding Oswald with his staff as he killed him'.[3] In fact, Oswald was not present when Cornwall and Regan gouged out Gloucester's eyes, so that blinding Oswald was not an act of revenge, but rather, like the blinding of Gloucester, meaningless; the reviewer has supplied a meaning, which is what we tend to do when coping with gratuitous violence. In this production Edgar could be seen as taking out on Oswald his anger and bitterness at what has happened to his father. In a similar way an audience may enjoy Kent's wanton beating up of Oswald when they meet outside Goneril's house in 2.2 because they are glad to see him letting off steam, as we say, and to think of Goneril and

Figure 1 Cain striking Abel with a mattock while kicking him down with one foot. From the frieze sculpted round the interior of the Chapter House at Salisbury Cathedral, thirteenth century.

Regan as indirectly put down; but, again, they are attributing a meaning to a gratuitous deed.

During his career as a playwright, Shakespeare, I believe, was increasingly interested in exploring the nature of violence, and especially acts of violence that are apparently spontaneous, and that seem to have no motive, or no adequate motive. He appears to have brought an unusual range of sympathies and to have applied an unusual intelligence to what has been a recurrent issue since the killing of Abel by Cain as recorded in the Bible. God's acceptance of Abel's offering and rejection of Cain's appears arbitrary, and Cain is angry with God; but his killing of his brother is given no explanation in Genesis 4, where it is narrated simply as an event that 'came to pass'. Shakespeare alludes a number of times to the Cain and Abel story, and fratricide or attempted fratricide recurs in his plays from his early histories to *The Tempest*. Later commentators attributed motives, such as envy, to Cain (see below, p. 25), and the desire to explain, to try to understand, seems natural. But in the course of his career Shakespeare becomes more interested in the inadequacy of motives to account for murders and acts of violence. In his mature tragedies he creates characters such as Brutus, who persuades himself against reason ('I know no personal cause') to assassinate Caesar, and Iago, a great inventor of unconvincing motives.

Violence in Shakespeare's plays has drawn little attention. In a recent 'preliminary survey' Jonas Barish wrote that 'a civilized and civilizing Shakespeare' gradually lost interest in violence for its own sake, though, as will be seen, the plays hardly bear out this conclusion.[4] Representations of violence in Shakespeare's drama have been considered chiefly in relation to society and order in his age, that is to say, as 'produced by a social code which valorizes order as a social value'. In other words, violence has been seen as a product of patriarchal structures in society, and as deployed to 'fulfil the imperatives of the political and ideological structure' within which the characters are created: 'Acts of violence belong to patriarchy as surely as fathers do.'[5] A more nuanced account of the culture of violence in Shakespeare finds him to be deeply conservative in assuming that 'the king is the prophylaxis against violence' in the tragedies, which promulgate 'the inexorable truth that domination is natural and even benign'.[6] In *The Culture of Violence*, Francis Barker goes on to deal at length with *Titus Andronicus* in an effort to show that its representation of violence occludes the actual violence of Shakespeare's time, as manifested in the 'execution by hanging of huge numbers of the common people'. The thought that possibly as many as an average of 370 men and women were hanged annually in England and Wales horrifies him, and Shakespeare's failure to bring this out is interpreted as deliberate concealment; but this is to respond with a modern sensibility to modes of punishment that may have seemed acceptable at the time, and less horrific than burnings at the stake. Barker's main interest is in the extent to which, as he sees it, Shakespeare's theatre underwrites the 'signifying practices of the dominant culture' and its structures of power.[7]

The most incisive commentary on the wildness that erupts at the heart of civilization in Shakespeare's plays is that by Richard Marienstras in his book, *New Perspectives on the Shakespearean World*. He rightly, in my view, stresses that the violence in *Titus Andronicus* is not, as some claim, distanced 'by the preciosity of the language. That is to underestimate the theatrical force of the murders committed before the very eyes of the spectators.'[8] He is especially interested in the idea of sacrifice, and the way Shakespeare exploits this theme in some later plays, especially *Julius Caesar* and *Macbeth*. His analysis supports my contention that while particular forms of violence may be socially produced at different times in relation to structures within society and changes in technology, the urge to violence is deeply embedded in the human psyche, and creates recurring problems whatever political formations are dominant. Shakespeare became interested, I believe, in this underlying problem of violence, and his plays provide an increasingly complex exploration of issues relating to it.

The mode of violence that has attracted most critical attention is revenge, which, in transferring a desire for retribution from a murdered character to survivors, raises questions of 'duty, justice, and loyalty'.[9] Revenge has thus provided a stimulus to dramatists from Aeschylus to the present day. Yet revenge is limited because it is always secondary, a reaction to an initial act of violence, and the predicament of the revenger is imposed on him. However ingenious the means of revenge may be, the situation of revengers is always the same, and there are few plays that can fairly be called revenge plays. In Shakespeare's own time, two masterpieces stand out: *Hamlet*, and *The Revenger's Tragedy*, and it is misleading, as I argue later, to think of *Hamlet* simply as another revenge tragedy in this way. Revenge has a function in many plays, but in the most compelling tragedies it has a subsidiary role. I think Shakespeare was much more deeply interested in what I call the primary act of violence, or primal scene, especially violence that has no motive, or is inadequately motivated, violence that may appear to arise spontaneously, and to be essentially meaningless, until meaning is attributed to it after the event.

Violence is culturally constructed in different ways in different ages, as the spear gives way to the gun, and warrior tribes are replaced by businessmen, but there is another unruly dimension that cannot be contained by concepts of culture, and that may be related to the deepest instincts in human beings, especially in males. In what follows the focus is nearly always on men, and mainly on the violence they do to one another. The matter of violence to women, especially in rape, is a topic others are investigating.[10]

The problem of violence has haunted the imagination of writers and artists throughout recorded history, and has become more complicated as civilization has developed, populations have grown, and means of killing or maiming have proliferated. It seems that public exhibitions of violence, whether in executions, sacrifices, natural disasters or accidents, have always fascinated people. Those who once turned up in crowds to see a beheading or hanging now enjoy watching violence displayed in films or on television screens, and slow their cars down on motorways to stare at the carnage whenever there is a nasty accident. Violent sports remain popular, and fantasies of eliminating enemies are continually reinvented in versions of the thriller, the detective story, the star wars of science fiction, and other media forms. Violence at once repels and attracts us, above all gratuitous violence such as the random murders carried out by serial killers. Representations of such violence in films, as in *The Silence of the Lambs*, raise afresh the perennial question whether they incite viewers to go and do likewise, or vicariously satisfy and neutralize the urges to violence everyone may have. It is apparent that such representations appeal to millions of people, but hardly any of them become killers in their turn.

Violence is identified now in Britain and America with violent crime, terrorism, and war, and our society continually struggles, with only limited success, to find ways of coping with it. In Shakespeare's less complex and crowded world the problem of violence was perceived differently, but in ways that still relate to the present time, as the reworking of some of his plays as films set in the twentieth century shows, in, for example, *Romeo and Juliet* and *Hamlet* reconfigured in terms of corporate warfare and street-gangs, and *Richard III* refashioned as the rise and fall of a fascist dictator. Shakespeare's treatment of violence relates to his perception of history and of war, but also grows out of his cultural conditioning through the founding myths of his culture. One of these myths was expressed in the accounts of the Trojan War in Homer and Virgil, which lay behind the legend of a nephew of Aeneas named Brutus sailing on from Rome to found 'Brutain' and the city of New Troy, or London. Another takes its origin from the biblical story of the killing of Abel, which left Cain as at once a murderer and the only begetter of civilization. Shakespeare's plays reflect his double inheritance of the classical values he encountered in his schooling, and the Christian values promulgated in his own society. In the rest of this chapter I outline some of the ways in which Shakespeare was exposed to representations of violence in his cultural background and in the kinds of literature available to him.

Shks dual inheritance: classical mythology + Christian

SHAKESPEARE AND CLASSICAL VIOLENCE

Shakespeare made much use of Ovid, and he was acquainted with Homer's *Iliad* and Virgil's *Aeneid*. His knowledge of these epics has been studied chiefly in relation to his creation of heroic figures in his plays: 'It is part of Shakespeare's originality and greatness as a dramatist that he is able to combine the inwardness of the Virgilian hero with the outward independence of the actors of Homer.'[11] The extent to which Shakespeare modelled heroic characters in his plays on Aeneas, Achilles or Hercules is important in recovering for his and our time a sense of human grandeur and magnificence. In focusing on the hero, however, it is easy to lose sight of an aspect of the epic that I think affected Shakespeare just as deeply. In Homer's epics a ruler or king having quasi-priestly status and, perhaps claiming descent from a god, leads his people in sacrifices and in making offerings to propitiate various gods and seek their aid. The gods behave in arbitrary ways nonetheless; Odysseus, for example, incurs the anger of Poseidon, who ruthlessly punishes the seafaring Phaeacians, most generous in their help to Odysseus, by piling mountains round their harbour (*Odyssey*, XIII.158–70). The ruler exerts power by his heroic stature as warrior, like Odysseus, 'sacker of cities'. The early Greek world depicted in this epic is one of small societies, 'not a coherent nation, but tiny pockets of people who pushed and jostled each other for centuries',[12] dominated by a warrior class and prone at any moment to quarrels, wars, and outbreaks of violence.

Homer

Virgil

In the *Iliad* Homer 'made poetry of the sufferings and deaths of brave men, and of the blind but majestic passions that prompted them; he sang the glory of human suffering and especially of the violent deaths of heroes'.[13] The gods mingle with the heroes and cannot easily be distinguished from them. They share the same blindnesses and passions as human beings, so that their interventions in human affairs appear capricious. The heroes know their pecking order, with Achilles the best, but the outcome of any fight is unpredictable, and the better man may be defeated by the inferior fighter. The heroes seek fame through their achievements in battle, and are prepared for death at any time. Their world is permeated by violence, which is elevated into heroism: so Hector knows that Ilium will be destroyed and his wife Andromache carried off to slavery after his death, but he still chooses to go into battle,

To stand up bravely
Always to fight in the front ranks of Trojan soldiers,
Winning my father great glory, glory for myself.
(*Iliad*, vi.527)

Man's business is warfare and winning fame.

The *Iliad* celebrates the violence of men, and at the same time provides a kind of rationalization for it. Those of high rank, the heroes, gain stature by their acts of violence and leadership in hand-to-hand combat. They are treated as supermen, and their prowess in the front line of battle seems godlike: 'our people look on us like gods' (xii.362). The gods, indeed, constitute a society parallel to that of the warrior culture of the Achaeans and Trojans. Although immortal, they feast like humans, make love to and have children by human women, quarrel and fight among themselves (xx.80–90), and at one point launch into 'total war' (xxi.437) to the entertainment of Zeus, their king, who is amused to see this chaos erupt. They have their favourites among the heroes, and protect them up to a point, but even Zeus cannot preserve his own son, Sarpedon, from death, from 'his doom sealed long ago' (xvi.524). The world of the gods is basically a reflection of the world of human beings as they might wish it to be if they were immortal. Many of the gods represent natural forces that are violent (thunder, storms, earthquakes), or that provoke violence in people (Ares the god of war, Aphrodite the goddess of love or lust). They shadow and intervene in the progress of a war fought by men seeking fame through violence, and the cruelty and horror of the carnage of warfare are brought home in realistic details of brains scattering or intestines spilling and uncoiling as spears strike home. At the burial of his friend Patroclus, Achilles mercilessly hacks to pieces 'a dozen brave sons of the proud Trojans' (xxiii.200). Even Achilles has a moment when he wishes things could be different, 'If only strife could die from the lives of gods and men' (xviii.126), but in the main it is true that 'The Iliad is a poem that lives and moves and has its being in war, in that world of organized violence in which a man justifies his existence most clearly by killing others. The violence is Achilles' native element.'[14]

Homer

In Homer (as in Shakespeare's *Troilus and Cressida*) Achilles' reasons both for initially refusing to fight, and later on for returning to battle, are personal, to do with his desire for Briseis and his grief for the death of Patroclus. He has no larger allegiance. Hector uniquely carries a burden of responsibility for the survival of the city of Troy, though he knows he is doomed to die in battle. The city of Troy had been sacked by Heracles while Priam's father Laomedon was king (v.733–8). Two cities are depicted on the shield Hephaestus makes for Achilles, one in which a quarrel among kinsmen has led to a murder, and the other a city besieged and under attack, with the corpses of the dead piling up (xviii.1572–92). The word 'city' gives a false impression of small citadels such as Troy, which sheltered 'a few hundred people with perhaps a thousand or so living around it',[15] and which was destroyed and rebuilt many times in the course of its long history. The destruction of 'cities' seems to have been a common outcome of disputes; Zeus 'has lopped the crowns of a thousand cities' (ii.138), and one of the usual epithets attached to Ulysses is 'sacker of cities'. Coming from such tribal fortresses, nothing like the later cities of Athens or Rome, the warlords in the *Iliad* fight as individuals for glory. Violence is their way of life, and their code encourages them to yield to their impulses to give way to rage, as when Achilles draws his sword thinking to slay Agamemnon (i.224–57). Even as they acknowledge the cruelty and misery that war brings, the heroes elevate violence as the means by which heroism is defined in the courage to outface any adversary, and in the acceptance of an early death. The epic still fascinates readers, and Bernard Knox's eloquent explanation is persuasive:

The *Iliad* accepts violence as a permanent factor in human life, and accepts it without sentimentality, for it is just as sentimental to pretend that war does not have its monstrous ugliness as it is to deny that it has its own strange and fatal beauty, a power which can call out in men resources of endurance, courage, and self-sacrifice that peacetime, to our sorrow and loss, can rarely command. Three thousand years have not changed the human condition in this respect; we are still lovers and victims of the will to violence, and so long as we are, Homer will be read as its truest interpreter.[16]

However, this account skips too easily over three thousand years in which human societies have changed enormously, not least in a continuing effort to find ways of controlling violence. In Homer's world fighting is a way of life among men, women are chattels to be seized as booty (Achilles and Agamemnon quarrel over the girl, Briseis, whom Agamemnon prefers to his wife, 1.132), and there is no social order outside the citadel, so that only the self matters in the end.

I think we remain engaged by Homer's epic not because it is the 'truest interpreter' of the will to violence, but rather because it displays human aggressiveness powerfully in a technologically primitive world in which men fight and kill one another as individuals face to face. At the same time, it reveals and clarifies for us the force of impulses and instincts we have to learn to manage, and one of the issues underlying the rest of this book is whether the 'human condition' has not changed even though we live in a radically different kind of society, or whether, as many now argue, all our beliefs and attitudes are culturally constructed. Certainly men have always been at war somewhere in the world, and the epic unsparingly depicts the cruelty of fighting and of deaths in combat, inviting us to measure the horrors of warfare against the fortitude demanded of the hero. The tender scene of Hector acknowledging the anxieties of his wife Andromache and explaining why he cannot shrink from battle anticipates the dilemma of many a military officer in later times. The brilliant image of his little son screaming in terror at the sight of his father's 'flashing bronze' helmet also makes us realize that the heroic posturing of the warrior lords in the poem is culturally constructed, and momentarily exposes the limitations of a way of life dedicated to violence.

In Shakespeare's time chroniclers still perpetuated the legend that Britain was named after Brutus, a nephew of Aeneas who sailed on after the founding of Rome to establish New Troy or Troynovant on the bank of the Thames. The story of Troy certainly interested Shakespeare, in whose early poem, *The Rape of Lucrece*, his protagonist, meditating on her condition after she has been violated by Tarquin, calls to mind a painting of 'Priam's Troy' (1367). This painting, described in detail for almost two hundred lines, represents the fall of Troy as analogous to Lucrece's fall, as she identifies especially with the distress of Hecuba staring at her dead husband Priam, slaughtered by Pyrrhus (1443–9). In his reading of Virgil's *Aeneid*, or parts of it, in the original or perhaps in translation, it was this story, of the fall of Troy as narrated in Book 11, that Shakespeare stored in his imagination. In the poem Aeneas tells the story, and speaks as an eyewitness, as one who suffered through the events described, so that his narration conveys a depth of personal feeling that differentiates him from the Homeric heroes. The *Iliad* registers the horrific details of butchery on the battlefield, but simply as events, as what happens in war. When Aeneas recounts the destruction of Troy to Dido, he does so as one who finds it painful to recall the misery of that time when he participated in the pain and terror (11.559). He reports what especially moved him, and invites Dido to share his emotion: 'Perhaps you would like to know what was Priam's fate' (11.506). This sense of the hero's inwardness seems to have appealed to Shakespeare, who recreated the scene of the death of Priam in the Player's speech in *Hamlet*, which draws tears from the Player and a passionate outburst from Hamlet.

Shakespeare does not seem to have had much interest in the *Aeneid* as a whole. In his wanderings Aeneas resembles Odysseus more than Hector or Achilles, but he differs from all of them in being driven by a mission laid on him by fate to found a city in Latium. His sense of duty, of imperatives that thwart his personal desires, and of failings and weaknesses that threaten to divert him from his mission, give him an inner life and a sense of mental struggle that was no doubt suggestive for the dramatist. However, the story of Dido and the fall of Troy most notably affected Shakespeare, and partly because the savagery of violence for its own sake is rendered with such feeling by Virgil, who recreates something of the Homeric world of violence as a way of life in the later part of his epic. Turnus is an Achillean figure, who, wounded in the thigh, yields to Aeneas in the final lines of the poem, and reminds him of his care for his father, Anchises, whom he carried on his back from the ruins of Troy. An embittered Aeneas hesitates for a moment, then angrily buries his sword in the defenceless Turnus, so giving way at the end to passion he has tried to control. So Aeneas ends as he began, driven by a kind of frenzy, as he had been, by his own account, when the Greeks overwhelmed Troy, and in his affliction he wanted to rush into battle and die gloriously in arms (11.314–17).[17] Here he invokes the Homeric acceptance of an early death bringing fame, and indeed he fights boldly for a time, but his task is to endure the burden of suffering as he journeys on to Italy, a burden made literal as he carries his old father Anchises away from the ruins of Troy. In his account of the destruction of Troy Aeneas expresses a quite different attitude to dying when he describes the killing of Priam, his head chopped from his shoulders, and his body lying on the shore, a corpse without a name ('sine nomine corpus', 11.558). His horror and desolation at this violent end to a life is accompanied by sadness at the loss of identity, at the possibility of death as mere oblivion. This aspect of Virgil's treatment of the fall of Troy appealed to Shakespeare, who was also much possessed by a similar anxiety about death.[18]

Shakespeare was more familiar with Ovid's *Metamorphoses*, especially in the translation by Arthur Golding (1567), and found inspiration in

Virgil

the very idea of change, especially in many of his comedies, in which 'The gaze will be allowed to rest on an exotic, erotic, poetic worlds, on strange transformations and experiences far removed from the audience's quotidian experience.' But Shakespeare transforms Ovid too in these plays, in which 'drastic violence is always forestalled and those who intend it are converted or expelled'[19] – or the violence is converted by parody into laughter, as in the staging of Pyramus and Thisbe by the rude mechanicals in *A Midsummer Night's Dream*. Metamorphosis of a sufferer into a tree, a flight of birds, a nightingale, a rock, or into a god, as in the case of Hercules, in Ovid's retelling of classical myths typically provides a release from some act of terrible violence: 'Adonis is gored, Actaeon dismembered, Io raped, Daphne saved from rape only by being dehumanized.'[20] If local recollections of Golding or Ovid can be found scattered throughout Shakespeare's works, three episodes had a larger influence. One is the story of Venus and Adonis (x.519–739), the latter of whom is gored to death by a boar and changed into a flower; another is the story of the rape of Philomel by Tereus, her terrible revenge when she feeds him with the flesh of his own son Itys, and the transformation of her into a nightingale as he pursues her with drawn sword (vi.438–674). The rape and mutilation of Lavinia in *Titus Andronicus* is explicitly related to this tale. Her tongue cut out, she makes known what has happened by drawing the attention of Titus to a book that proves to be Ovid's *Metamorphoses*: she is 'Ravished and wronged as Philomela was' in a gloomy wood such as the poet Ovid describes, 'By nature made for murders and for rapes' (4.1.51–8).[21]

The third episode is the story of the Trojan War as retold in Books xii and xiii. Ovid's treatment of the end of Troy is very different from that of Virgil or Homer. The deaths of Hector and Achilles are narrated briefly in Book xii, and Book xiii begins with a quarrel between Ajax and Ulysses, each claiming the weapons of Achilles in a boasting speech to the Grecian captains. Ajax brags that he is such a great warrior that the arms of Achilles seek him to share his glory (xiii.96–7), while Ulysses argues that his cleverness gave the Greeks victory and that he conquered Troy (xiii.349). In his translation Golding brought out what is perhaps implicit in Ovid's account by representing Ajax as a 'dolt' and Ulysses as crafty and sly. Shakespeare developed further a satirical image of both Greek heroes in *Troilus and Cressida*, and while, like Ovid, he uses Ulysses to ridicule 'the heroism of brute force'[22] displayed by Ajax, he also debunks the craftiness of Ulysses, whose grand speeches are undercut by the petty schemes he devises in an effort to get the inactive Achilles to fight. In one other episode Ovid deals at length with the sufferings of Hecuba over the loss of Hector, the sacrifice of her daughter Polyxena to appease the ghost of Achilles, and the death of her youngest son Polydorus, butchered by Greek spears. In *The Rape of Lucrece* 'Time's ruin, beauty's wrack, and grim care's reign' (1451) are depicted in the wrinkled figure of the aged Hecuba as she stares at the death-wounds inflicted on Priam by Pyrrhus; in her Lucrece sees an image of her own sorrows. Ovid dwells on Hecuba's misery in old age, and makes her wish to die (XIII.516–20), whereas Virgil describes the death of Priam in the presence of Hecuba. Shakespeare drew on both Ovid and Virgil in *The Rape of Lucrece*, and also in the Player's speech in *Hamlet*, where the Player elaborates, as Ovid does, the suffering of Hecuba, but in relation to the malice of Pyrrhus in 'mincing with his sword her husband's limbs' (2.2.514) as described by Virgil in the *Aeneid* (II.552–3).

Shakespeare refers to many more of the 'vast repertory of tales in which extremity of suffering or desire brings about transformation' in the *Metamorphoses*,[23] and turns them to comic use by parody (as in *A Midsummer Night's Dream*), or by allusion (to Actaeon, for instance, in the 'transformation' of Falstaff in *The Merry Wives of Windsor*).[24] But from his encounters with classical myths as retold by the ancient Greek and Roman poets Shakespeare recalled in his weightier plays stories of violence, most notably the Trojan War, the fate of Priam, the rape and mutilation of Philomel, and the death of Hercules (in *Antony and Cleopatra*). These stories, which spring from a culture of violence, or which deal in excessive violence involving torment or malice beyond the occasion, fed Shakespeare's imagination, as also did the works of Seneca, whose tragedies, as Thomas Nashe said, yield 'many good sentences' or *sententiae*, pithy phrases, cited in some plays of the period in Latin; 'and if you entreat him fair in a frosty morning, he will afford you whole Hamlets, I should say handfuls of tragical speeches'.[25] Nashe was writing in 1589, and so not referring to Shakespeare's *Hamlet*. However, Shakespeare, like other playwrights of the time, was struck by the capacity for emotional violence of Seneca's characters, their *furor* or rage, as well as their capacity for stoicism in the face of suffering. In plays like *Thyestes*, *Agamemnon*, and *Medea* Seneca relishes the savage cruelty of the murders carried out off-stage by his protagonists. The extent of Seneca's impact on Shakespeare has been much debated, for it has less to do with direct reference than with motifs and sentiments, with a relish for wickedness (*scelus*) and extreme passion (*furor*), and for characters such as Richard III who are willing 'to say the unspeakable and do the unthinkable'.[26]

SHAKESPEARE AND CHRISTIAN VIOLENCE

The stories and spectacles of violence that have played a vital role in the development of Christianity provided another fund of motifs for Shakespeare's plays. The first translations of the Bible into English appeared during the sixteenth century, and Shakespeare was familiar with both the Geneva version (1560), with its marginal commentary sympathetic to Calvinism, and the Bishops' Bible (1568), designed to counteract the influence of the Geneva version; his plays quote or refer to these versions frequently. He also seems to have known Cranmer's *Book of Common Prayer*, which was revised under Queen Elizabeth in 1559. The cultural traditions represented by the Greek and Roman classics on the one hand, and the Bible on the other, were major formative influences on Shakespeare's development.

The killing of Abel by Cain may be regarded as a founding legend of Christianity. The biblical story of man begins in an act of wanton violence for which no motive is given. God sets a mark on Cain which both separates him from other men and protects him from them; through his son Enoch, Cain becomes the founder of civilization, for it is he who builds the first city (Genesis 4.17). Cain as a human thus embodies both a capacity for violence and a love of order, the conflicting impulses that have driven humanity ever since. The story, narrated simply as an event in the Bible, has allowed varying interpretations. For St Paul, Abel had faith and offered a 'more excellent sacrifice' (Hebrews 11.4). Philo saw Abel rather as an ideal of right conduct and Cain as a model of depravity. St Augustine attributed the motive of envy to Cain, and aligned him with the earthly city, while Abel represented the heavenly city. A marginal note in the Geneva Bible (1560) provides Cain with a bad character as 'an hypocrite' who 'offered only an outward show without sincerity of heart'. Cain might be regarded as an outcast, driven out from mankind, and the source of evils in the world, whose descendants included monsters, ogres, and giants, according to *Beowulf*, 99–114. In the Corpus Christi mystery plays Abel prefigures Christ, while Cain is concerned for profit. An idea begins to emerge of Cain as representative of an earthly civilization that is centred on the city as a place of violence. Cain could be related to many other examples of fratricidal conflict in myth and history, and seen both as initiator and as scapegoat, if the murder of a brother is what it takes to establish the city, so Jeremiah (9.4) laments, 'Take ye heed every one of his neighbour, and trust ye not in any brother: for every brother will utterly supplant, and every neighbour will walk with slanders.' All such legends of conflict between brothers (for example, that of Jacob and Esau, Eteocles and Polyneices, or Romulus killing his twin brother Remus in founding Rome) are seen by René Girard as transfigurations of 'sacrificial crises'.[27]

In later times the story of Cain was reinterpreted in ways more sympathetic to him, as in Salomon Gessner's *Death of Abel* (1760), which was translated into English in 1762 and circulated widely in many popular editions.[28] In this prose poem Cain is motivated by envy, but he is allocated barren fields to till, while Abel has an idle life watching his flocks of sheep grow fat. Abel is soft and effeminate, like his father Adam, in contrast to the firmness of temper shown by Cain. When Adam falls sick, Abel weeps and prostrates himself in prayer; Adam recovers, and Abel offers thanks with the sacrifice of a lamb, which is accepted. Cain has only sparse 'fruits of the field' to offer, and these are blown away in a whirlwind. Cain despairs, and an evil spirit, Aminelech (a name echoing that of Abimelech, who murdered his seventy brothers to be made King of Shechem in Judges 9.1–5), appears to tempt Cain to violence by causing him to dream that his descendants will be enslaved by the children of Abel. He awakens to find Abel clasping his knees and offering love, but Cain crushes his skull with a club, after which, tortured by remorse, he wanders off, with wife and children, into 'desert regions' never trodden by man. This sentimental version emphasizes the arbitrary nature of God's preference for Abel, and goes some way towards excusing Cain. Such revisionary interpretations offering a more sympathetic image lie behind the figure of the Wandering Jew who turns up in novels such as M. G. Lewis's *The Monk* (1796) in the late eighteenth century.

In such reinterpretations a new Cain could be glimpsed as a man who affirms a principle of individuation, and a right to self-determination. He could thus be recuperated as a revolutionary or even regenerative figure, whose violence contributes to social change and a new unity. Byron recreated a Cain who acts in rebellion against a tyrannical God who demands blood sacrifice. Such a Cain could appear superior to Abel as one who, as Schopenhauer said, 'through guilt acquired a knowledge of virtue by repentance, and so came to understand the meaning of life'.[29] It is a Cain recast in this way that lies behind the lawman or the upright lone gunman who is caught in a conflict in many Western films. Cain could become associated with the idea of masculine identity. The deliberate echo of his name in Will Kane, the marshal who is driven by his inner compulsion to face a group of outlaws on his own in *High Noon*, suggests the source of his authority; as he says, pointing to his marshal's badge,

[margin note: Cain reinterpreted]

'I'm the same man, with or without this.'[30] Cain is echoed again in the eponymous hero of *Shane*, the lone gunman who has learned, through his own violence and guilt in killing, an understanding of the need for social harmony. Shane succeeds in restoring wholeness, but only by a further act of violence that forces him to wander off as an outcast at the end of the film. Civilization, it might seem, begins in violence, and its conflicts continually have to be resolved by further violence.

If the Romantics first transformed Cain into a sympathetic rebel, the anxiety shown in various earlier reactions to his story indicates that there has always been something troubling about the arbitrariness of God's preference for Abel. The violence of Cain against his brother 'comes to represent necessary physical and psychical fact of individuation, the flight from undifferentiated communion'.[31] Cain shows independence and initiative, while Abel remains passive, a conformist who obeys the rules. Shakespeare found a power in this tale, which raised a question about the nature of authority and who should best wield it. References to Cain and Abel frame his early history plays, and the rivalry of brothers is a recurrent theme in other works, most notably in the fratricide that triggers the action of *Hamlet*. The story of Cain and Abel seems simple and straightforward as told in Genesis, but raises a complex of issues, some of which are brought out in another well-known biblical story: that of Esau, the elder brother, the hairy hunter and 'man of the field', and Jacob, the plain man of the tents or city. In this tale God arbitrarily informs Rebecca, their mother, that 'the elder shall serve the younger'. Jacob twice cheats Esau, first out of his birthright, and then out of his father's dying blessing, but achieves authority and God's favour to become the founder of the tribe of Israel (Genesis 25–7). Shakespeare's plays on English history are much concerned with the rivalry between siblings, only one of whom can have authority and be king.

The Old Testament offers a history of early civilization as one of more or less continual wars and atrocities, and God partakes of this violence. He is a punisher who causes others to suffer, sometimes arbitrarily, as in the afflictions of Job. He is also a god of war, supporting the Israelites, who are under constant threat, and seek God's help to defend them. The psalms, which had a prominent place in church services, are full of pleas for help against enemies: 'Deliver me from mine enemies, O my God: defend me from them that rise up against me' (Psalm 59). Many of the most prominent images in the New Testament are associated with the passion and crucifixion of Christ. The pain and suffering associated with his sacrifice, as imagined in the crown of thorns, the flagellation,

A true defcription of the racking and cruell handeling of
Cutbert Simfon in the Tower.

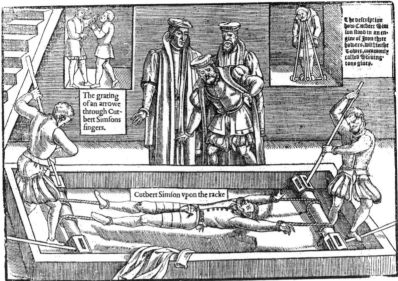

The grating of an arrowe through Cutbert Simfons fingers.

The defcription how Cutbert Simfon ftood in an engine of Iron three holdes, with the the Tower, commonly called Scauingtons gluea.

Cutbert Simfon vpon the racke

Figure 2 Forms of torture in the sixteenth century. From John Foxe, *Acts and Monuments* or *Book of Martyrs* (Fifth printing, 2 vols., 1596), 11.1843.

the carrying of the cross, the nails driven through feet and ankles, were graphically rendered in numerous medieval and Renaissance works of art, and the agonies of martyrdom were vividly recaptured in the illustrations to John Foxe's *Acts and Monuments*, or *Book of Martyrs*, placed in every cathedral by government order in 1570, and in many churches. Both Old and New Testament scenes of violence and pain were featured in the medieval cycles of Mystery plays, so much so that a recent book on French cycles is entitled *The Medieval Theater of Cruelty*.[32] The emphasis on the body and on suffering in the late medieval English cycle plays may well have 'authorized the portrayal of violence and physical brutality' on the Elizabethan and Jacobean stage, their legacy being a 'theater of cruelty' in Shakespeare's age too.[33] The Christian country in which Shakespeare grew up was accustomed to public displays of cruel violence that would now not be tolerated, for example in hangings of convicted criminals and the hanging, drawing, and quartering of traitors, or in bear- and bull-baiting. The classical world as depicted by the ancient poets and the Christian world, both as portrayed in the Bible and as experienced in sixteenth-century England, were steeped in violence.

¶ A lamentable fpectacle of three women, with a fillie infant brafting out of the mothers wombe, being firft taken out of the fire, and caft in againe, and fo all
burned togither in the Ifle of Garnfey. 1556, Iuly. 18.

Figure 3 Burning at the stake in 1556. From John Foxe, *Acts and Monuments* (1596),
11.1764.

The most prominent form of organized violence was warfare, which was troubling to Christians who worried whether it was morally permissible to fight. As Elaine Scarry pointed out, power relations in the Old Testament are determined by the fact that men have bodies, while God does not. God can punish or destroy in many ways, by war, by fire, by plague, by causing the earth to swallow hosts of men, and He does so in order to confirm faith and eliminate doubt. God forbids men to kill, yet they do so repeatedly, since among men, too, power relations can only be maintained by control of bodies, by inflicting pain or punishment, or by fighting and wars. In the New Testament God assumes a human body in Christ, whose torments at the hands of others establish him as a willing scapegoat who carries off the sins of the world, and at the same time confirms a human addiction to the violence shown in the crucifixion. How could accommodation be found for the conflicting testimony found in the Bible: 'Thou shalt not kill' follows hard on the destruction of the Egyptians in the Red Sea and the exultant cry of Moses, 'The Lord is a man of war' (Exodus 15.3). The moral laws pronounced by Jesus, love

War

God and love thy neighbour as thyself, are qualified by his and St Paul's insistence that rulers are ministers of God and must be obeyed (Romans 13). St Augustine found in the Old Testament reason for arguing that a just war could be waged in order to bring about peace, and might be construed as a punishment by divine judgement for the crimes and sins of peoples. Even wicked men could be agents of God's providence in this way. The doctrine of a just war as punishment for sins previously committed left no room for distinguishing between an offensive and a defensive war, and also offered no way to 'prevent a successful war from being treated as a just war'.[34]

The question whether there could be a just war continued to be debated by Christian apologists for centuries, but the rise of professional armies, advances in military technology, and the power struggles and political ambitions that provoked continual wars in Europe throughout much of the reign of Queen Elizabeth I[35] helped to shift arguments into the secular domain. Protestant apologists liked to cite God's aid to Moses in the destruction of the Amalekites (Exodus 17.8–16) as showing that a war 'well undertaken is not only lawful but also necessary' for the glory of God.[36] They argued that a good cause and lawful authority were requirements for a just war, but went on effectively to associate war with patriotism, as a soldier should be expected to fight not only in defence of religion, but also for the good of his country and the credit of his prince.[37] In his sermon, 'The Trumpet of War', delivered in 1598, Stephen Gosson offered a secular justification for war, and in the printed version he added a condemnation of the wars fought by Spain in 'the Indies, in Portingale, in Granada, in the low countries, in France, and against us' as 'uncharitable and unjust'.[38] Wars fought on behalf of England, by contrast, were 'very charitable and just'. If it could be said that 'We are all soldiers, as we are Christians... You bear *Spiritual* Arms against the enemies of your Salvation, and *Material* Arms against the enemies of your country',[39] then any soldier fighting for any Christian country could claim in the name of God that his cause was just.[40] War, indeed, could be treated as a sport for young gentlemen, as in Robert Barret's elaborate manual on *The Theorike and Praktike of Moderne Warres* (1598), with its detailed instructions for the ordering of fights; its only allusion to God comes at the very end, following on a glossary of military terms, and is in French: 'Toute Puissance, gloire & louange, soit à notre bon Dieu éternel.' (All power, glory and praise be to our good, eternal God.)

If war could be defined as 'a kind of execution of public justice',[41] then any war might be defended on these grounds, confirming the pessimism of Erasmus, who long before, in his 'Complaint of Peace' (1517), had condemned as beasts Christian princes who took up arms, while acknowledging that 'perhaps it is the fatal malady of human nature to be quite unable to carry on without wars'.[42] Machiavelli's treatise on war was the only work by him published in an English translation before 1595, and in it he projected a secular idea of war as a form of politics. During the late sixteenth century in England the almost continual wars in which the country was involved, with Spain, in France, in the Netherlands, and in attempts to suppress the Irish, set Protestant against Catholic, but were not fought in the name of God so much as for political and commercial reasons in a struggle for dominance in Europe and on the high seas. In religious terms war might be seen as deplorable, and also defended as necessary, and it offered excitement and action to the bold young men for whom Robert Barret wrote in 1598. It is hardly surprising that war has such a prominent part in the action of many plays of this period.

As war became professionalized, so murder and violent crime began to be associated with the professional assassin, who came to have 'a high public profile in the later sixteenth century'.[43] Like war, violent crime might be treated as God's judgement upon murderers, tyrants, and other sinners, the punishments inflicted on them being a proof of the existence of God, as argued in Thomas Beard's gloomy *The Theatre of God's Judgments* (1597). Published accounts of murders seem more concerned with sensational reporting than with their ostensible purpose, which could be to show 'the vengeance which God inflicteth on murderers', or alternatively to 'restrain and deter us from this bloody Sin'. The agency by which murders are revealed in such accounts is often called miraculous, but turns out to be human, a confession elicited by torture on the rack, or corpses revealed by a farmer's decision to drain a pond. One such account, Thomas Cooper's *The Cry and Revenge of Blood* (1620), based on a trial for murder in Suffolk, deals with the gradual bringing to light of evidence relating to a series of murders. God is said to have given rein to the wicked to harden their hearts, as it took a number of years for justice to be done, and there is little concern for the sufferings of the victims. What makes this account interesting is the presentation of the narrative as a series of scenes in a 'bloody Tragedy', each scene 'more bloody and desperate' than the previous one. Narrative crosses over into drama, as the promise of growing excitement in the build-up of scenes becomes more important than claims for the intervention of providence.

The narratives Shakespeare encountered in the 'Tragedies' versified in the stories of the falls of unfortunate princes in *The Mirror for Magistrates* (1559, expanded in 1563, 1578 and 1587) included accounts of figures of authority drawn from ancient and modern English history, as well as from the lives of Roman emperors. The many violent Italian *novelle* collected in William Painter's *Palace of Pleasure* (1566–7; enlarged 1575, and including the stories of Romeo and Juliet and the Duchess of Malfi), as well as those put together in Geoffrey Fenton's *Certain Tragical Discourses* (1567) and George Turberville's *Tragical Tales* (1574), were presented as tragedies. The translators added a good deal of Protestant moralizing, but describe horrific deeds with considerable relish. The forty-second of Painter's novels, the story of Violenta and Didaco, was rendered separately into verse by Thomas Acheley in 1576, with a prose outline of 'this doleful Tragedy'. In Painter's version, the appropriately named Violenta, daughter of a goldsmith, is pressed into a secret marriage by a wealthy aristocrat, Didaco. When she discovers he has married in public the daughter of a wealthy lord, she plans, with the aid of her maid, to murder him. She lures him to visit her, and when he is asleep she stabs him through the throat, cuts out his eyes, tears out his tongue, rips up his stomach and pulls out his heart, and then mangles his body 'with an infinite number of gashes', before throwing his bodily parts and carcass into the street. The people side with her as she describes what she has done, but, seeking death, she is taken into custody, and beheaded for her 'excessive cruelty'. Painter seems above all interested in the 'sundry kinds of cruelty' his stories display, often carried out by 'fierce and unpredictable women'.[44]

I have outlined various ways in which Shakespeare encountered representations of violence. He may also, of course, have encountered violence on the streets of London, witnessed executions, fought quarrels, gazed at the traitors' heads mounted on the gate of the bridge over the Thames, attended bear- and bull-baitings, seen armed men attack one another in public, shared in the public response to the Gunpowder Plot, and been made aware in many ways of violence practised in his society. The stock-in-trade plays of the professional theatres that developed in an expanding London during this period included many that exploited conflicting attitudes to war and murder in historical pageantry and offered spectacular representations of various kinds of violence, death, and torture on the stage. It may well be that the humanist expansion of cultural horizons forced people to 'learn to live and think from the world rather than from the Bible',[45] and to find ways of understanding war, violence, and death in secular terms.[46] It was a heady time for a young dramatist to launch a career, and Shakespeare's reading as well as the cultural context in which he grew up made issues related to violence vividly present to him.

NOTES

1. H. R. Woudhuysen, ed., *Samuel Johnson on Shakespeare* (London: Penguin Books, 1989), 222.
2. This staging is described in *King Lear*, ed. J. S. Bratton, Plays in Performance (Bristol: Bristol Classical Press, 1987), 157; and Marvin Rosenberg, *The Masks of King Lear* (Berkeley and Los Angeles: University of California Press, 1972), 242–4.
3. Peter Holland, 'Shakespeare Performances in England, 1992–3', *Shakespeare Survey*, 47 (1994), 202.
4. Jonas Barish, 'Shakespearean Violence: A Preliminary Survey', in James Redmond, ed., *Violence in Drama* Themes in Drama, 13 (Cambridge University Press, 1991), 101–21.
5. Derek Cohen, *Shakespeare and the Culture of Violence* (Basingstoke and London: Macmillan, 1993), 1.
6. Francis Barker, *The Culture of Violence: Tragedy and History* (University of Chicago Press, 1993), 89.
7. *Ibid.*, 192, 194–5.
8. First published in French as *Le Proche et le Lointain* (Paris: Editions de Minuit, 1981), and transl. by Janet Lloyd (Cambridge University Press, 1985), 45. Huston Diehl has commented interestingly on 'The Iconography of Violence in English Renaissance Tragedy' in *Renaissance Drama*, New Series XI (1980), 27–44; and John Russell Brown emphasized the performance of violence in Shakespeare's plays in his British Academy Lecture (1994) on 'Violence and Sensationalism in the Plays of Shakespeare and other Dramatists', *Proceedings of the British Academy*, 87 (1995), 101–18.
9. John Kerrigan, *Revenge Tragedy: Aeschylus to Armageddon* (Oxford: Clarendon Press, 1996), 7.
10. See, for example, Marliss Desens, *The Bedtrick in English Renaissance Drama: Explorations in Gender, Sexuality, and Power* (Newark: University of Delaware Press, 1994), and Karen Bamford, *Sexual Violence on the Jacobean Stage* (New York: St Martin's Press, 2000).
11. Reuben Brower, *Hero and Saint: Shakespeare and the Graeco-Roman Tradition* (Oxford: Clarendon Press, 1971), 91.
12. H. D. F. Kitto, *Greek Tragedy* (London: Methuen, 1939; 3rd edn 1973), 198.
13. Walter Kaufman, *Tragedy and Philosophy* (Princeton University Press, 1968), 161–2.
14. Bernard Knox, Introduction to Homer, *The Iliad*, transl. Robert Fagles (New York: Penguin Books, 1990), 35.

15. Michael Wood, *In Search of the Trojan War* (New York and Oxford: Facts on File Publications, 1985), 11–12.
16. Knox, Introduction to Homer, 29.
17. As Michael C. J. Putnam observes in *The Poetry of the Aeneid* (Ithaca: Cornell University Press, 1965, reissued 1988), 'it is not so much the destroyer as the destroyed which moved the poet's fancy' (39).
18. See Robert N. Watson, *The Rest is Silence: Death as Annihilation in the English Renaissance* (Berkeley and Los Angeles: University of California Press, 1994).
19. Jonathan Bate, *Shakespeare and Ovid* (Oxford: Clarendon Press, 1993), 118–19, 120.
20. *Ibid.*, 119.
21. *Ibid.*, 101–17.
22. Brower, *Hero and Saint*, 123.
23. Bate, *Shakespeare and Ovid*, 181.
24. See François Laroque, *Shakespeare's Festive World*, transl. Janet Lloyd (Cambridge University Press, 1991), cited in Bate, *Shakespeare and Ovid*, 164.
25. Preface to Robert Greene's *Menaphon*, in *Works*, ed. R. B. McKerrow (5 vols., 1904–10), III.315–16. For further comment on Seneca in relation to *Hamlet*, see below, pp. 107–8.
26. Robert S. Miola, *Shakespeare and Classical Tragedy: the Influence of Seneca* (Oxford: Clarendon Press, 1992), 85.
27. *Violence and the Sacred* (1972); transl. Patrick Gregory (Baltimore: Johns Hopkins University Press, 1977), 61–4.
28. See Robert M. Maniquis, 'Salomon Gessner's *Der Tod Abels* and the Gentle Death of Sacrifice', in Patrick Coleman, Anne Hofmann, and Simone Zurbruchen, eds., *Reconceptualizing Nature, Science and Aesthetics* (Geneva: Slatkine, 1998), 167–83.
29. Ricardo Quinones, *The Changes of Cain: Violence and the Lost Brother in Cain and Abel Literature* (Princeton University Press, 1991), 116.
30. See Lee Clark Mitchell, *Westerns: Making the Man in Fiction and in Film* (University of Chicago Press, 1996), 217–18. Cain also has some bearing on Orson Welles's *Citizen Kane* and on *The Caine Mutiny*; see Quinones, *Changes of Cain*, chapter 3.
31. Quinones, *Changes of Cain*, 19.
32. Jody Enders, *The Medieval Theater of Cruelty: Rhetoric, Memory, Violence* (Ithaca and London: Cornell University Press, 1996). See also Clifford Davidson's account of 'Cain in the Mysteries: The Iconography of Violence' in his book, *History, Religion, and Violence*, Variorum Collected Studies (Aldershot: Ashgate; Burlington, Vt: Variorum, 2002), 97–123.
33. See Michael O'Connell, *The Idolatrous Eye: Iconoclasm and Theater in Early Modern England* (New York: Oxford University Press, 2000), 87–8. The phrase 'theater of cruelty' is used by him as well as by Jody Enders.
34. Frederick H. Russell, *The Just War in the Middle Ages* (Cambridge University Press, 1975), 306.

35. See Wallace MacCaffrey, *Elizabeth I* (London: Arnold, 1993), Part 5, 'The Waging of War 1585–1603', 235–93; also Nick de Somogyi, *Shakespeare's Theatre of War* (Aldershot: Ashgate Publishing, 1998).

36. A. Leighton, *Speculum Belli Sacri or the Lookingglass War* (1624), 6.

37. *Ibid.*, 28.

38. Gosson, *The Trumpet of War*, B6v and C6r.

39. Thomas Adams, *The Soldiers Honour* (1617), A3r.

40. So in the aftermath of the attack on the World Trade Center in New York (September, 2001), President Bush and millions more in the United States effectively claimed God for their side in war against Afghanistan, as a war of good against evil, enhancing the idea of America as 'one nation under God' and calling 'God bless America', as if there were no other concepts of God than the Christian one in a huge and diverse population. For a study of religious terrorism, see Mark Juergensmeyer, *Terror in the Mind of God: the Global Rise of Religious Violence* (Berkeley and Los Angeles: University of California Press, 2000).

41. William Gouge, *God's Three Arrows: Plague, Famine, Sword, In three Treatises* (1631), 214.

42. *The Erasmus Reader*, ed. Erika Rummel (University of Toronto Press, 1990), 300.

43. Martin Wiggins, *Journeymen in Murder: the Assassin in English Renaissance Drama* (Oxford: Clarendon Press, 1991), 20.

44. See R. W. Maslen, *Elizabethan Fictions: Espionage, Counter-Espionage, and the Duplicity of Fiction in Early Elizabethan Prose Narratives* (Oxford: Clarendon Press, 1997), 86, 91–3.

45. J. R. Hale, *Renaissance War Studies* (London: Hambledon Press, 1983), 338.

46. In *Issues of Death*, 38–41, Michael Neill argues that the Protestant 'denial of Purgatory' swept away traditional consolations for death, which were replaced by memorials and monuments; see also R. N. Watson's account of the fear of oblivion after death in the literature of the period in his *The Rest is Silence* (1994).

CHAPTER 3

Shakespeare and the display of violence

When Shakespeare began to write for the stage the leading dramatist was Christopher Marlowe, who was providing audiences at the Rose Theatre with sensational plays that included spectacular representations of violence. In his early histories (the *Henry VI* plays) and in *Titus Andronicus* Shakespeare was much influenced by Marlowe, and competed in composing plays that invent more and stranger incidents of torture and murder. Dramatists were writing for an audience that enjoyed public spectacles of torture and violence in the execution of criminals and traitors staged as ceremonies validating state power, or in the punishment by whipping until blood flowed that could be inflicted on fornicators by ecclesiastical courts.[1] The professional companies and the first purpose-built arena theatres were at an early point of development, and capitalized on a public fascination with representations of violence that has not diminished to this day: audiences flocked to the film *Hannibal*, about a serial killer, a sequel to *The Silence of the Lambs*, after critics had drawn attention to 'the gruesome nature of the film's violence'.[2] The name Hannibal recalls the legendary Carthaginian warrior and hero whose exploits frightened ancient Rome. In *The Silence of the Lambs* he is imprisoned in a cage, but escapes by murdering his guards. The sight of Bajazeth beating out his brains on his cage in *Tamburlaine*, like that of the imprisoned king horribly murdered with a red-hot poker by hired killers in *Edward II*, must have been similarly exciting when these plays were first performed. In this chapter I aim to show how Shakespeare exploited violence for its own sake in matching Marlowe's Rose spectaculars, and at the same time began to extend the imaginative reach of such plays, notably by his creation of powerful female characters.

MARLOWE AND THE ROSE SPECTACULARS   Tamburlaine

Marlowe was the most innovative of the dramatists who provided the audiences of the 1580s and 1590s with sensational spectacles. He was also
the most influential, notably in the impression he made on Shakespeare.
The two parts of *Tamburlaine* (printed 1590) had the greatest impact of
all the Rose spectaculars, to judge by the numerous allusions to this play
during the following decades. It was innovative not only in its spectacle (in
Part 2 fifteen out of eighteen scenes have processional entries, and stage
effects include a burning town, a father stabbing his own son to death,
and Tamburlaine whipping the two defeated kings who are harnessed to
his chariot), but more importantly in other respects, not least in its geo-
graphical sweep, and in its treatment of war and violence. *Tamburlaine*
is refracted through Marlowe's classical education as related to ancient
epic heroes; the peasant Tamburlaine is surprisingly familiar with classical literature and mythology. So he claims that his boast, 'I hold the Fates
fast bound in iron chains' is more true than 'Apollo's oracles' (1.2.173,
211). Such casual allusions to classical deities run through the text, and
at the end of Part 1 the lovelorn King of Arabia is compared to Turnus
coming against Aeneas at the end of Virgil's epic (5.1.381–3, 394–5).[3]
But the violence of Virgil's epic is transferred to fairly recent history (the
defeat of Bajazeth occurred in 1402); and Tamburlaine conquers and
destroys in seeking world domination rather than the founding of a city.
Tamburlaine now can be understood as a complex play, and the central
figure may be seen in various lights as 'hero, barbarian, liberator, scourge
of God, torturer, Hell-figure, favourite of Jove, rival of Jove'.[4] When first
staged, however, the numerous allusions to the play in the following years
show 'that Tamburlaine was perceived as triumphant, mighty and successful in his rise to power'.[5] The impression the play created at the
Rose was also one of spectacle and noise, '*scenicall* strutting, and furious
vociferation', as Ben Jonson put it in *Timber or Discoveries*.[6] The impact of
Edward Alleyn on the small stage at this theatre, displaying in *Tamburlaine*
'the stalking steps of his great personage', and the creation of sensational
spectacle up close were astonishing when the play was first performed,
perhaps in 1587, and ravished 'the gazing Scaffolders'.[7] Although by
the late 1590s it came to seem old-fashioned as rant to sophisticated
commentators like Ben Jonson, many allusions testify to the power of
its exciting action on stage: such as, for instance, the casual apology in
Middleton's *Blurt Master Constable* (1602), 'We hang out a white flag most
terrible Tamburlaine, and beg mercy'; the reference to Bajazeth beating

out his brains in Thomas Dekker's *Old Fortunatus*; or Dekker's sense in *The Wonderful Year* (1603) that 'Death (like stalking Tamburlaine) hath pitched his tents'. The flags, the tents, Bajazeth in his cage, and Tamburlaine harnessing kings to his chariot made a huge impression.[8]

In Part 1 Tamburlaine's aspirations embrace both the desire for power and the desire for beauty in Zenocrate, but the overwhelming impression given by the play was of the social climb and rise to dominance of a shepherd who becomes a king and mighty conqueror by force and violence. Tamburlaine's claim that birth does not matter challenged audiences used to hierarchy:

Your births shall be no blemish to your fame,
For virtue is the fount whence honour springs.
                    (4.4.130–1)

In his progress towards dominance over Persia, Turkey, and Egypt, Tamburlaine conquers by force of arms and force of personality, and his power is symbolized in making Bajazeth his footstool, and in his peremptory demands enforced by his white, red, and black sequence of colours. In Act 3 of Part 1 Tamburlaine begins to call himself 'the scourge and wrath of God', and insofar as he is slaughtering Muslims and barbarians, the play pays lip-service to the claim of Christian apologists that in war the wicked may serve as instruments of God's punishment of sin. But the series of battles Tamburlaine wins are accompanied by visual atrocities in the deaths of Bajazeth and Zabina, and the killing of the virgins of Damascus, so that 'his honour' in the end has little to do with virtue, but 'consists in shedding blood' (5.1.478). In Part 2 Tamburlaine kills his own son Calyphas, who prefers playing cards to fighting, and he goes on to burn Muslim books while claiming to be 'The scourge of God' (4.1.154). Marlowe plays with the ambiguity of this phrase: Christian apologists could defend waging war by arguing that rulers were the ministers of God to punish those that do evil as well as the enemies of God's true Church,[9] but Tamburlaine's conduct has little to do with the idea of a just war. He delights in torture and atrocity, and the violence in the play culminates in the spectacles of the Governor of Babylon hung in chains and shot, and of Tamburlaine in his chariot which is drawn onstage by two kings bridled and harnessed as if they were horses.

Visually these plays celebrate the achievement and maintenance of power by conquest in war and physical violence. In a period of almost continual wars involving England in some measure, the flamboyance of a theatrical spectacle that made war and violence exciting, and showed that anyone, a mere peasant, might become a hero, had enormous success. Its impact on Shakespeare is apparent in his early histories and in *Titus Andronicus*. Marlowe represents the Other in the rise of the 'Scythian Tamburlaine / Threatening the world with high astounding terms' (Prologue, 5–6), portraying remote countries, exotic settings, and barbaric customs. He came much closer to home in his play *The Massacre at Paris*, in repertory in 1593–4, and written some time after 1589, when Henry III of France died; Henry is a character in the play, which ends with his murder. Only a very reduced text survives, which consists of a series of killings or maimings as Guise and his Catholic followers plot the St Bartholomew's Day massacre of Protestants which took place in Paris in 1572, and in their turn are defeated and slaughtered, a cardinal being strangled on stage 'with violence' (line 1117). This play evokes the immediate context of wars and atrocities which were in the news when Shakespeare began his career as a playwright, though in dealing with events that happened in France, it still concerns a foreign land, where home rules do not apply; and, besides, the French are the enemy in Shakespeare's histories.[10]

SHAKESPEARE'S CHRONICLES OF VIOLENCE: *HENRY VI*, PART I

In choosing to base his early history plays on chronicles of English kings, Shakespeare was working with familiar local settings and Christian values, and was more constrained in the contrivance of spectacle than Marlowe in *Tamburlaine*. But he could also explore the politics of violence and the nature of heroism more acutely.[11] *Henry VI*, Part 1, seems to belong to 1592, and may have been written after Parts 2 and 3 but it has the characteristics of an early Shakespearean spectacular, even if others had a hand in it. It opens strikingly with a funeral procession bearing the 'wooden coffin' (1.1.19) of Henry V in a scene that establishes at once a deep hostility between the Bishop of Winchester, who attributes Henry's victories to 'The church's prayers', and the Duke of Gloucester, who blames Henry's death on the Church:

The church? Where is it? Had not churchmen prayed,
His thread of life had not so soon decayed. (1.1.33–4)

The threat of civil dissension is conveyed as an opposition between religious and secular interpretations of Henry's death. It is also an opposition between two closely related powerful aristocrats, Gloucester and the Bishop of Winchester, both, like Henry VI himself, direct descendants of John of Gaunt. Gloucester, closer to the young Henry VI as his uncle, is appointed Protector of the realm (1.1.38), but Winchester aims to gain such power for himself (1.1.173–7). Historically Winchester, an illegitimate son of Gaunt, was Gloucester's uncle, but from the beginning of the play these two emblematize the deep hostilities among the English nobles that bring about the loss of French possessions and the Wars of the Roses. It is an internecine strife between men who should love like brothers, but instead are barely restrained from re-enacting the Cain and Abel story. As they insult and challenge one another, Winchester needles Gloucester:

Nay, stand thou back – I will not budge a foot.
This be Damascus, be thou cursed Cain,
To slay thy brother Abel, if thou wilt.
                    (1.3.38–40)

The opening of the play thus sets up an inexplicable bitter hostility between the two that is developed into the factions of the white and red roses in the fine invented scene in which Richard (later Richard III) enters quarrelling with Somerset for reasons never explained, and plucks a white rose as the badge of his party. Richard and Somerset were cousins, both descended from Edward III, so that civil dissension in the play is focused in mindless rivalries between close relatives.

Their hostility breaks out into violence on the stage as Winchester's men fight with Gloucester's men in a 'hurly-burly' (1.3.56 SD) and a further 'skirmish' stopped only by the intervention of the Lord Mayor. Later, after rioting in the city, they fight on stage again in the presence of the king, when they enter 'in skirmish, with bloody pates' (3.1.85 SD), and only after two more skirmishes are they eventually pacified, though the hatred between Gloucester and Winchester remains as bitter as ever. The quarrel between Richard, now made Duke of York, and Somerset also is sustained, and breaks out when two of their followers, Vernon and Basset, challenge one another in the king's presence about the colour of the roses they wear. Henry sees this challenge as madness, but his intervention cannot prevent his 'good cousins' York and Somerset from throwing down their gauntlets to fight for 'so slight and frivolous a cause' (4.1.111–15). These outbursts of violence between factions in England relate to the dwindling successes of the English soldiers in France. There the army is led by the old Earl of Salisbury and Talbot, neither of them connected with the quarrel of the roses. The busy action of the war in France is located in three sieges, of Orléans, Rouen, and Bordeaux.

In the first stage battle, the French, besieged in Orléans, are 'beaten back by the English, with great loss' (1.2.21 SD). The French, revived by the arrival of Joan, who demonstrates her prowess by overcoming the Dauphin with her sword, then have their successes. Salisbury is unluckily if sensationally shot in the eye while spying on the French, leaving the field essentially to the clash between Talbot and Joan as leaders, marked in 1.5 by fighting on stage in which first Talbot pursues the Dauphin off the stage, then Joan enters 'driving Englishmen before her'. There is a good deal of action on and at the walls of the city before the English gain the city as the French 'leap over the walls in their shirts' (2.1.38 SD) to escape. The English triumph, however, ends with another funeral procession recalling that of Henry V at the beginning of the play, this time for Salisbury.

In the second siege, Joan tricks her way into Rouen, and takes it from the English, but Talbot and Burgundy recapture the town, 'Lost and recovered in a day again!' (3.2.116). This achievement is again marked by a death, this time of Bedford, the English regent of France, and by the loss of Burgundy and his forces, who are persuaded by Joan to join with the French. The final siege brings Talbot and his army to Bordeaux, where he is attacked outside the walls by the French combined with Burgundy's men, and this time it is Talbot who dies after his son is killed fighting. The match between Joan, who claims in Tamburlaine's language that she is assigned to be 'the English scourge' (1.2.129), and Talbot, perceived by the Countess of Auvergne as 'the scourge of France' (2.3.14), fizzles out for she is not onstage when Talbot's son is hemmed in by three attackers and rescued by his father, or when Talbot dies of his wounds with his son in his arms. In this sequence the action is designed to emphasize the failure of the quarrelling York and Somerset to bring their forces to aid Talbot. Their domestic broils in England lead directly to the defeat of Talbot at Bordeaux, and the loss of English control over France. The Countess had earlier mocked Talbot as a dwarf, and not at all the Herculean figure or 'second Hector' she had expected him to be (2.3.18–19), but in his last fight he is perceived by his son to be heroic as they speak in terms of honour, fame, valour, and chivalry, and old Talbot is gratified to find his son, like the heroes of the *Iliad*, prefers the glory of dying in battle before a 'paltry life' (4.6.45).

Sir William Lucy enters to inquire of the victorious French what has happened to Talbot, pompously listing the titles of 'the great Alcides of the field' (4.7.60), while Joan, who reappears at this point, sees a body that 'Stinking and fly-blown lies here at our feet'. The idea of the heroic Talbot has been unsettled by his references to his son as Icarus, the emblem of the overreacher. Talbot's dying boast that with his son he will 'scape mortality' (4.7.22) is mocked by the bodies onstage that fulfil the promise of the French General in Bordeaux that he would see Talbot 'withered, bloody, pale and dead' (4.2.38). But it is easy to see why Thomas Nashe enthused over the representation of 'brave Talbot', and why his death drew tears from audiences 'who in the Tragedian that represents his person, imagine they behold him fresh bleeding'.[12] He alone on the English side represents a consistent idea of loyalty to England and the king, as well as chivalry, shown not only on the battlefield, but also in his exchanges with the Countess of Auvergne. He is identified with St George as his soldiers cry 'Saint George, a Talbot' on entering Orléans. To him the 'name of knight' is sacred, as he appropriately strips the emblem of the Order of the Garter from the coward Sir John Fastolfe (4.1.40).

If Talbot is compared to classical heroes, Hector and Hercules, he fights as a Christian for God and his country. He ascribes his victories to God (3.4.12), and claims, like the English authors of tracts on war, that 'God is our fortress' (2.1.26). The French equally assume that God is on their side, as when Reignier calls on the citizens of Orléans to 'celebrate the joy that God has given us' (1.6.14). To the French, Talbot is 'a fiend of hell' (2.1.46) and Joan, a 'saint' (1.6.29), while to the English, Joan is a witch (1.5.21) or 'sorceress' (3.2.38). Joan is compared by the Dauphin to an Amazon and to Debora, the prophetess who led the Israelites to victory over Sisera and the Canaanites in Judges 4, so she too has classical and Christian associations. These contrasting perspectives expose the habit each side has of claiming justification for what they do in the name of war. The play is given an upbeat ending when Joan's spirits are for the first time summoned and turn out to be fiends that hang their heads and abandon her. As Joan first entered in thunder, which seemed to mark her as a 'holy prophetess' (1.4.101), so thunder heralds her fall, when she is revealed to be a witch. The play ends with the appearance of Margaret, another powerful female character, who diverts attention to the question of Henry's marriage.

Joan has now become for many interpreters the focus of interest in the play, which is perceived in feminist terms as 'the dramatization of a cultural myth of gender conflict'.[13] Such readings inevitably are affected by the rehabilitation of Joan of Arc, burned as a heretic in 1431 and canonized as a saint in 1920. In the play she is presented ambiguously from her first appearance, and is notable as much for her deviousness as for her prowess in battle. Although initially the French answer to Talbot, she has no part in the sequence of scenes that bring Talbot and his son to their heroic deaths; the structure of the play demands that they be glorified, while she dwindles into a lying strumpet. For the action of the play turns on the contrast and interconnections between the infighting and intrigues among the English nobles, mostly related closely to one another as are Cain and Abel, and the heroic attempts of the professional soldiers, Salisbury, Bedford, and above all Talbot, to defend the English claim to France.

The basic structure of the play is thus a neat one in its insistence on the waste and uselessness of the almost continuous violence of the action. Fighting or skirmishes are called for twenty times in stage-directions, and, in addition, there are marches, the shooting of Salisbury, scaling and leaping over town walls, soldiers entering the house of the Countess of Auvergne, and led in disguise into Rouen by Joan, as well as the entries of York and Somerset with their armies. The pointlessness of the fighting is brought home in the desire of servants, Vernon and Basset, to fight to the death about the colour of the roses they wear. The deaths that punctuate the action not only symbolize the way that the paths of glory lead but to the grave, but also show that the endless violence of factious emulations, challenges, and warfare is ultimately meaningless. The funeral of Henry V begins the play, which goes on to display the deaths of Salisbury, Mortimer, and Talbot. The heroics of Talbot end with his death and defeat, just as the heroics of Joan end with her being sentenced to death as a witch. The violence in this play in the main is aristocratic, and for much of the action Joan is absorbed into the world of the Dauphin; she speaks in blank verse like everyone at court and astonishes Charles with her 'high terms' (1.2.93), as well as with her swordplay. There seems to be an anxious expediency in the way Shakespeare (or his collaborators) scaled her down so as to obliterate her pretensions to heroism at the end, when she rejects her father and tries in devious ways to escape the death sentence.

HENRY VI, PART 2

Henry VI, Part 2 is a very different kind of play; it is more episodic, more wordy, very long and contains a number of huge speeches. The aristocrats swirl around a weak king who fails to control his nobles, continuing the quarrels and intrigues of Part 1. The cast is strengthened by the emergence of two powerful women, Margaret of Anjou, now queen and busy making sure she rules instead of Henry, and Eleanor, Gloucester's wife, who also has ambitions to be queen, and, like Joan, is brought down as a practiser of witchcraft. It may be that Shakespeare's reading in stories of powerful and ruthless women like Violenta in Bandello helped him to create characters like these. In an action that includes a good deal of spectacle, it is 'the extraordinary emphasis on various forms of violence inflicted on human bodies'[14] that remains most notable. But until the Yorkist victory in the battle of St Albans with which the play ends, most of the violence has to do not with generals and soldiers fighting wars, but with kinds of violence that were practised in or familiar to the London of Shakespeare's time, and it involves all levels of society, commoners especially. At first the emulation between Eleanor and Margaret is prominent, marked in the episode where Margaret calls for her fan, and humiliates the proud duchess by boxing her ears, pretending she has mistaken her for a servant. After Eleanor is caught practising witchcraft and sentenced to exile in the Isle of Man, and Margaret successfully conspires to get rid of Gloucester as Protector of the realm, there is little for Margaret to do but endure the disgrace and death of her paramour Suffolk. The nobles are as full of quarrel as ever, with Winchester challenging Gloucester to a duel in 2.1, but their belligerence only serves to provide an opportunity for the emergence to power of York. The most exciting episodes in the action involve the common people. The episode in which Simpcox claims his sight has been restored at the shrine of St Alban follows the scene of Eleanor using witches to raise spirits, switches attention to what commoners get up to, and provides a comic parallel. The witch, Margery Jourdain, is sentenced to be burned at the stake, while Simpcox gets off with a whipping for his less harmful deception.

The element of parody here is continued in the challenge and fight between Horner and his apprentice Peter, who have quarrelled over words alleged by one to have been spoken, and denied by the other. Horner is drunk when he enters for the fight, and Peter terrified, but able all the same to strike down his master in their comic duel with sandbags attached to staffs instead of swords. It remains unclear which of them is right in their challenge about who said what, even though Horner confesses 'treason' as he dies, and the outcome hardly warrants Henry's assertion, 'God in justice hath revealed to us / The truth and innocence of this poor fellow' (2.3.101–2). The violence erupts out of what may have been a misunderstanding on Peter's part, whose command of English is uncertain:

QUEEN: What sayst thou? Did the Duke of York say he was rightful heir to the Crown?

PETER: That my master was? No, forsooth, my master said that he was, and that the king was an usurer.

QUEEN: An usurper thou wouldst say. (1.3.27–31)

This burlesque of aristocratic single combat in the lists, in which drunkenness is taken as validating God's justice, points up both the absurdity and pointlessness of seeking justice through violence.

The commoners are aping their betters, and exposing their high terms to a searching criticism, as is seen in the most powerful dramatic sequence in the play, the scenes of Jack Cade's insurrection, which occupy most of Act 4. Cade has been shown to parody his master York's vocabulary, assertions of royal ancestry, and claims to the throne.[15] In setting himself up as 'king' (4.2.68) his followers both applaud and mock him, but accept his brutal exercise of 'justice', as the Clerk of Chatham is hung for being able to write his name, and Lord Saye executed for speaking French and Latin. Cade's idea of a utopia for commoners, in which seven halfpenny loaves would be sold for a penny and wine would run freely in the conduits instead of water, underlies, but of course does not justify, the wanton violence of his brief reign that culminates in the tormenting of Lord Saye. He makes his exit with his followers carrying the heads of Saye and Matthew Gough mounted on poles as if they were executed as traitors. Cade's arbitrary killings and casual slaughters cast an ironic light on the behaviour of York and the nobles at Henry's court. Their jostlings for power erupt in civil war initiated by the ambitious York immediately after Iden presents Cade's head to the king. Old Clifford and Somerset die in battle onstage, but nothing is concluded beyond York's victory in one battle, in which his son Richard, later Richard III, comes into prominence as the killer of Somerset.

The carnivalesque misrule and anarchy of the Cade scenes are refreshingly comic and enjoyable, especially as Cade, mocking authority, is himself mocked by his followers. Even as he exposes the behaviour of the nobles as essentially trivial, tiresome, and selfish, so his own pretensions are exposed as absurd by the Butcher's commentary to the audience on his address to his followers:

CADE: My father was a Mortimer –

BUTCHER: He was an honest man, and a good bricklayer.

CADE: My mother a Plantagenet –

BUTCHER: I knew her well, she was a midwife. (4.2.38–41)

Figure 4 *Henry VI*, Part 2, Act 4, Scene 7, directed for the Royal Shakespeare Theatre by Adrian Noble in 1988–9. Jack Cade leading his band of rebels who hold up the heads of 'traitors' mounted on poles.

At the same time, the violence he enacts is horrifying. Just before the Cade scenes, Suffolk, trying to flee to France in exile, is captured in a fight at sea, signalled by offstage gunfire. He is handed over to Walter Whitmore, who lost an eye in the fight, and wants revenge, not ransom.

Suffolk, 'muffled up in rags' (4.1.46), throws off his cloak to reveal not only the rich clothes and the emblem of the Order of the Garter, but also an imperious habit of aristocratic speech, as he turns on the Lieutenant, apparently the commander of the ship, and addresses him as 'Obscure and lousy swain' (4.1.50). The Lieutenant is evidently educated and can match Suffolk's classical references, and he has every reason to hate the paramour of Margaret and engineer of the death of Gloucester. So Suffolk is killed, and dies bravely, comparing himself to Cicero, Julius Caesar, and Pompey, all assassinated. Suffolk's death is brutal, his body and head displayed on stage, even if he deserves to die. The capture of Lord Saye by Cade is analogous, and, like Suffolk, Saye quotes Latin and refers to Caesar's commentaries, which is enough for Cade to condemn him. For all his claims to have benefited the people, Lord Saye represents the power of the nobles, and admits that

Great men have reaching hands; oft have I struck
Those that I never saw, and struck them dead.
(4.7.77–8)

In place of such unacknowledged violence, Cade openly takes pleasure in executing Lord Saye, and having his head and that of Gough stuck on poles and brought onstage, where they are made to kiss. This exhibition, based on an incident narrated in the chronicles Shakespeare knew, marks Cade's casual addiction to violence, and he leads off his followers at this point crying 'Kill and knock down!' – kill anyone, destroy everything.

Through all this King Henry embodies an impotent and uncomprehending piety that is taken in by the lies of Simpcox, can see God's justice in the death of Horner, that likes to believe 'Thrice is he armed that hath his quarrel just' (3.2.232), that accepts the loss of all his French possessions as the will of God (3.1.86), and that 'forbears to judge' even the iniquities of Cardinal Beaufort, whose ravings as he dies make his death onstage horrific.[16] All the nobles may appeal to God or Heaven when it suits them, and the Church is represented by the hypocritical and corrupt Cardinal Beaufort. The nobles have a habit, as observed in Suffolk's last scene, of citing Latin tags, quoting from works such as the *Aeneid*, and referring to heroes of the classical world. Margaret likes to think of her affair with Suffolk in terms of the story of Dido and Aeneas. Clifford carries his father's body offstage on his back, 'As did Aeneas old Anchises bear' (5.2.62). As York gains ascendancy late in the play he compares himself to Ajax (5.1.26) and Achilles (5.1.100). The appeals to God and the invocations of classical values are equally emptied of meaning in Henry's court, which is absorbed in quarrels, deviousness, and struggles for power. Cade's disdain for education and open use of violence in his attempt to gain power reflect both upon the high-flown terms used by the nobles when occupied in selfish and sordid conspiracies, and upon their covert machinations in contriving the murder of Gloucester. The ironic interplay between nobles and commoners and the subversive force of the Cade scenes make Part 2 the liveliest of the *Henry VI* plays in performance.

BUTCHERY IN *HENRY VI*, PART 3 AND THE EMERGENCE OF RICHARD III

Alarms, excursions, marches, mark most scenes in Part 3, which is a play of warfare, in which four major battles are staged, 'Wakefield where York was butchered, Towton, where Henry was given his emblematic vision of the horrors of internecine conflict, Barnet where Warwick was slain, and Tewkesbury where the Lancastrians were finally defeated'.[17] The staged violence in the play is often very brutal. The tone is set by the murder of Rutland, 'this innocent child' as his tutor calls him (1.3.8), depicted in the play as a boy and the youngest of York's sons. He says to the ruthless Clifford, 'thou hast no cause', and Clifford's response is to stab him crying, 'Thy father slew my father: therefore die.' This is an excuse not a cause for murder, as is registered in the text of the play in imagery of harmless creatures such as rabbits and woodcocks being trapped, of bears being baited, and of tigers and serpents as emblems of cruelty, imagery which colours the action when Henry is captured by two keepers hunting deer (3.1). One of Cade's leading followers in Part 2 is Dick the Butcher, and the image of butchery underlies the killings in Part 3, imagery which begins with Henry trying to prevent the parliament house being made 'a shambles' (1.1.71), continues in Northumberland's hint that Clifford is no better than a 'slaughterman' in the torture and killing of York (1.4.169), and ends with Henry confronted by Richard who has come to murder him:

So first the harmless sheep doth yield his fleece
And next his throat unto the butcher's knife.

(5.6.8–9)

Henry's reign has brought him nothing but misery, and in the most celebrated scene in the play, he longs to be a shepherd. There, watching a son drag onstage the father he has killed in civil wars, and a father carry on the son he has killed, Henry sees them as 'harmless lambs' at the mercy of wild beasts. He sums up the play in his comment on the violence of the wars:

What stratagems, how fell, how butcherly,
Erroneous, mutinous and unnatural
This deadly quarrel daily doth beget!

(2.5.89–91)

'Butcherly' is an apt term for the main action, halted here momentarily in a tableau that has powerful emotional resonances intimating a general horror at heedless violence.

Margaret is another Violenta with her 'tiger's heart' (1.4.137), the very opposite of what York expects a woman to be:

Women are soft, mild, pitiful, and flexible:
Thou stern, obdurate, flinty, rough, remorseless.

(1.4.141–2)

She accompanies her troops into battle and stabs York in this scene, emblematizing in the first part of the play a world turned upside down, where she acts like the king, and the king behaves like a woman. Then Richard of Gloucester bursts out of the 'ritualized anarchy'[18] of the action as more ruthless and more ambitious than the rest of the factious nobles. In his long soliloquy at the heart of the play, he comments on his own bodily deformities, shrunken arm, unequal legs, disproportion everywhere, 'Like to a chaos' (3.2.161). He seems born out of the political chaos represented in the play, and concentrates in his single person the most uninhibited addiction to violence as a means to power. It is the Crown he lusts for, and in his dreaming, 'How sweet a thing it is to wear a crown' (1.2.29), Shakespeare gives him lines that deliberately echo speeches of Tamburlaine. Richard also compares himself to figures from the epic legend of Troy, to Nestor, Ulysses, and Sinon (who, according to Virgil in the *Aeneid*, persuaded the Trojans to allow the wooden horse into the city). At the battle of Wakefield, York is compared to Hector defending Troy, and later Henry sends Warwick off to muster forces in Coventry with the line, 'Farewell, my Hector, and my Troy's true hope' (4.8.25). Such casual allusions in the *Henry VI* plays might seem to justify a conception of them as 'Shakespeare's epic account of the Wars of the Roses'.[19] But the world of classical epic was one in which violence was a way of life for heroes who had no larger framework to give meaning to their courage and endurance. In the *Henry VI* plays an alternative point of reference is provided by the King, whose 'mind is bent to holiness' (*Henry VI*, Part 2, 1.3.55), as well as by the frequent appeals to God or Heaven in the mouths of other characters.

The invocations of epic heroism and the lip-service paid to Christian values and beliefs in the play merely provide an ironic framework for the *Henry VI* plays in which 'an overall pattern can be discerned of a falling into a world of brute force, in the demise of chivalry in Talbot's death, in the ineffectuality of Christian piety in Henry VI, and the rise of Machiavellian *virtù* in Richard of Gloucester'.[20] All these plays are primarily spectaculars with large casts and much incident and violence, appropriate to the fashion of the times. The plays expose the horrors of civil war, and make drama out of the self-interest of the nobles whose professions of loyalty barely mask their real concern, which is for their own selfish advantage – Clarence and Warwick change sides to no one's surprise. But Shakespeare also relishes the theatrical potential of spectacular violence, as in the incident he invents of Margaret tormenting York with the napkin stained with the blood of his young son Rutland. Perhaps this is why the *Henry VI* plays hardly touch on the religious debates about the nature of war. They are little concerned with the question whether there can be a just war, and 'cannot be said to illustrate either the providential punishment of the house of Lancaster or the divine approval of the house of York'.[21]

In *Tamburlaine* Marlowe played with the notion of his hero as 'the scourge of God', a phrase first heard at 3.3.44 in Part 1, where he is God's agent in punishing Turks and freeing Christians; but in 4.3 the Soldan of Egypt calls him 'The scum of men, the hate and scourge of God', changing the meaning to present him as God's enemy. Tamburlaine likes to portray himself as God's instrument in punishing others, but his overweening claim to be a kind of godhead, 'invested by the hand of Jove' (Part 2, 4.1.151), show why Robert Greene could allude to Marlowe in 1588 as 'daring God out of heaven with that Atheist *Tamburlan*'.[22] Marlowe's subversive characterization of Tamburlaine in relation to God, Mahomet, and Jove has only tenuous links either with the contemporary defence of war as 'a function of divine providence designed to punish sin and crime',[23] or with the perception of corruption and violent crime as another means by which God might scourge the world for sin. In the *Henry VI* plays, Shakespeare is writing about a Christian society, so that any of his characters may appeal to God. In Part 1, for instance, Joan claims the help of 'Christ's mother' (1.2.106) in preserving her chastity so she can be 'the English scourge' (1.2.129), though the English see her as a witch, and she is suddenly exposed as relying on 'fiends' in 5.3. In Parts 2 and 3, King Henry becomes a passive spokesman for Christian values, who is given to communing with God, but is little more than a pawn in the intrigues of his nobles. The corrupt churchman, Cardinal Beaufort, who conspires to murder the good Duke Humphrey, dies raving while the King prays over him, and everyone may pay lip-service to Christian ideals, but it is not until Richard of Gloucester erupts in his long soliloquy in 3.2 of Part 3 that Shakespeare begins to exploit hypocrisy dramatically. His aspirations echo those of Tamburlaine, 'to dream upon the crown' (3.2.168), but his method of achieving his ambitions is quite different. He will suit his 'face to all occasions' (185), as in his response to King Edward's marriage:

No, God forbid that I should wish them severed
Whom God hath joined together ... (4.1.20–1)

The audience is in Richard's confidence here, while Edward takes his words literally. Shakespeare had found a way to create great theatre out of the gap between what we know Richard really means, and what the other participants in the scene assume he is saying.

In *Richard III*, the soliloquies Richard has in each of the first three scenes invite the audience to identify with him and applaud his cleverness in exposing the hypocrisy of others. In his ruthless pursuit of the Crown he becomes, like Tamburlaine, the scourge of God in a double sense. The play is cluttered with the prayers and curses of characters who pay lip-service to religion but who deserve punishment for crimes committed in the past. The long scene that brings the murderers at Richard's behest to kill Clarence is designed to establish these parameters: Clarence hopes his 'deep prayers' (1.4.69) may appease God; the murderers are momentarily troubled by conscience; Clarence reminds them of the biblical commandment against killing, which provokes them to remind him of his part in murdering the Prince of Wales; and after Clarence is stabbed the Second Murderer at once feels remorse, comparing himself to Pilate. Richard is at once a devil, so perceived early on by Anne ('Foul devil, for God's sake hence, and trouble us not', 1.2.50), who nevertheless is seduced by him; and at the same time he is God's scourge to punish the wicked, including his brother Clarence, whose death is pitiful, as he seems in some ways an Abel to Richard's Cain, and yet also exemplifies 'the great and horrible punishments wherewith the Lord in his most righteous judgment hath scourged the world for sin'.[24] The

deaths of Rivers, Grey, Vaughan, Hastings, and, finally, Buckingham, all
might be so interpreted, but as soon as Richard is crowned, he becomes
the scourge of God in another sense, in murdering children, the princes in
the Tower. Simultaneously he begins to be afflicted with guilt ('I am in /
So far in blood that sin will pluck on sin', 4.2.63–4). Richmond arrives
to identify himself with 'God and Saint George' (5.3.271) and slay the
dragon, naming God ten times in his last three speeches. The play is, of
course, set in what Richard calls 'a Christian land' (3.7.115), and is full
of reminders of the civil wars that led to his rise to power; the violence
in the play thus relates to the attempts by Christian apologists to explain
war and murder as instrumental in God's scheme for punishing sin. The
violence in *Henry VI, Part 1* begins when two uncles of Henry challenge
one another, the Bishop of Winchester saying to Gloucester, 'Be thou
cursed Cain, / To slay thy brother Abel if thou wilt' (1.3.39–40), and
all the *Henry VI* plays deal with the internecine conflicts between close
relatives, all descendants of Edward III and his seven sons. The wheel
comes full circle at the end of *Richard III*, when, with the death of the
King, Richmond proclaims peace after a long period when 'England
hath long been mad and scarred herself: / The brother blindly shed the
brother's blood...' (5.5.23–4).

A circuitous route has brought me back to Cain and Abel.
Shakespeare's early history plays begin and end with allusions to their
story. Some of the violence in these plays is reactive, and retaliation or
revenge is a perennial motif in the drama of the period. The most sensational stage violence, however, is not presented in terms of motivation,
but simply as event, as action or display. The opening of *Henry VI*, Part 3
provides a notable example:[25]

EDWARD: Lord Stafford's father, Duke of Buckingham,
    Is either slain or wounded dangerous;
    I cleft his beaver with a downright blow,
    That this is true, father, behold his blood.
MONTAGUE: And, brother, here's the Earl of Wiltshire's blood,
    Whom I encountered as the battles joined.
RICHARD: Speak thou for me and tell them what I did.
YORK: Richard hath best deserved of all my sons. (1.1.10–17)

The sons of York show their father what they have achieved in the battle
of St Albans against the supporters of Henry. Edward displays the bloody
helmet of Buckingham, Montague shows perhaps his sword coloured
with the blood of the Earl of Wiltshire, and Richard (later Richard III)
outdoes the others by revealing the decapitated and bleeding head of

Somerset. Richard kills Somerset at the end of Part 2, leaving his body onstage with the comment, 'So, lie thou there' (5.2.66), so that the gruesome display of his head is a new twist in Part 3, marking the extent to which his violence exceeds that of his brothers. 'Speak thou for me', he says, anticipating his subsequent pleasure in violence for its own sake, and substituting action for words. The *Henry VI* plays develop towards and culminate in the play of *Richard III*, in which Richard's first action is to arrange for the murder of his brother Clarence. In order to achieve the Crown, Richard needs, of course, to get rid of his elder brother, but this motive is not mentioned in the text, which emphasizes rather his enjoyment in his cleverness in stirring hatred, initiating enmities, and provoking Edward to imprison Clarence as a traitor:

Simple plain Clarence, I do love thee so
That I will shortly send thy soul to heaven,
If heaven will take the present at our hands.
                                    (1.1.118–20)

This may be seen as a repetition of the primal scene of violence, the killing of Abel, and it launches the action in this play, in which Richard delights audiences as an early version of the charming serial killer. After experimenting with various kinds of stage violence in the wake of Marlowe's *Tamburlaine*, Shakespeare succeeded in creating a different and more complex kind of overreacher, one who enjoys mocking and subverting the Christian values of his world, until he finds he is trapped in a never-ending sequence of more and more violent killing, and discovers he has a conscience after all.[26]

TORTURE, RAPE, AND CANNIBALISM: *TITUS ANDRONICUS*

It seems that before returning to English history, Shakespeare finally got the Rose spectaculars out of his system by outdoing them in a play set in ancient Rome. He had not only imitated aspects of Tamburlaine in characters like Talbot, Joan, and Richard, but had also mocked him in the figure of Cade; but for all his youthful exuberance in inventing scenes of violence, these had to be plausibly in accordance with English customs and practices. In some ways writing based on English history constrained him, while in other ways he was energized to explore new perspectives in dramatizing civil wars and conflicts involving all strata of society, 'high and low, verse and prose, lords and commons'.[27] The dating of *Titus Andronicus* remains uncertain; it was published in 1594, and could have been first performed in that year,[28] but it belongs with the large-cast spectaculars that were popularized by the success of *Tamburlaine* in the years after 1587. Although there was an emperor Titus who ruled in Rome in the late first century, the play is not based on history, but creates a quasi-historical mythical ancient Rome, one in which all restraints are off, and the dramatist is freed to exploit sensational stage violence in ways that go far beyond what he could do in the *Henry VI* plays. It is as if Shakespeare gives full imaginative scope to the culture of violence he had encountered in ancient epic and in Ovid.

A Captain reports the return of Titus at the beginning of the play from ten years of fighting against 'the barbarous Goths':

> The good Andronicus
> Patron of virtue, Rome's best champion
> Successful in the battles that he fights,
> With honour and with fortune is returned.
>   (1.1.66–69)

His talk of virtue and honour might suggest an ideal Rome where such values are prized. Tamora, indeed appeals to Titus' 'piety', recalling the quasi-religious sense of duty identified with the *pietas* of Aeneas; but Titus blows this away by brutally killing her son; 'O cruel, irreligious piety!' she cries (1.1.133). It does seem that 'Shakespeare first invokes the *Aeneid* as the epic of empire-building, order, and *pietas*, and then allows Ovid's *Metamorphoses* to invade, interpreting the fundamental impulses of Virgil's poem as chaotic, even apocalyptic.'[29] Virtue and honour are drained of meaning in a play that relishes cruelty, and which at once in this opening scene issues a challenge to Tamburlaine, the Scythian shepherd. The sons of Titus take Alarbus away and lop off his limbs, returning perhaps to display them, or perhaps to show bloody swords and hands, and eliciting from Alarbus' brother Chiron the remark, 'Was never Scythia half so barbarous!' (1.1.134). In the most famous scenes of violence in the play Shakespeare seems to be deliberately outdoing the effects other dramatists had created. In *Selimus* (printed 1594), the hands of Aga are cut off at the order of Acomat, who stuffs them in his victim's 'bosom'; a little later Mustaffa 'opens his bosom' and takes these hands out to show them to Bajazet.[30] In another play printed in 1594, *The Battle of Alcazar*, the extant 'plot', or production outline, spells out the properties needed for what the Quarto simply calls 'the bloody banquet' – dead men's heads in dishes and dead men's bones, with a note in the margin: 'Dead men's heads /& bones / banquet/ blood'.

Figure 5 *Titus Andronicus*, Act 3, Scene 1, directed by Trevor Nunn, Royal Shakespeare Theatre, 1972. Titus receives the heads of his two sons, executed by Saturninus, and also the hand he offered in the hope of saving them; he shows the stump of one arm, while his brother Marcus and Lavinia, both her hands cut off and tongue cut out, look on.

Shakespeare pushes the boundaries of such spectacle further. Not only are Lavinia's hands cut off, and her tongue cut out, but Marcus draws attention to the blood that pours from her, 'As from a conduit with three issuing spouts' (2.3.30). She remains a vivid presence onstage through most of the following scene, in which Titus gets Aaron to cut off his hand in the hope of saving the lives of his sons, only for a messenger to return with 'two heads and a hand' (3.1.234). Lavinia is again present in 4.1, when she reveals the names of her attackers by taking a staff in her mouth and guiding it with her stumps. She is also brought back when Titus prepares for his bloody banquet, to hold a bowl in which she collects the blood as Titus cuts the throats of Chiron and Demetrius; and is present, veiled, at the banquet itself, where Titus unveils and kills her. Her silent presence onstage in so many scenes shows Shakespeare making the most of the violence done to her, as she emblematizes the way Rome, as Titus says, has become 'a wilderness of tigers' (3.1.54). In the world the play depicts, violence is inflicted casually, and no one is safe. A Clown appears in 4.3, carrying a basket with pigeons in it; he is commissioned by Titus to take a letter to the Emperor Saturninus. The uncomprehending Clown delivers his pigeons and the letter, wrapped round a knife, in the following scene, and the response of Saturninus on reading the letter is: 'Go, take him away and hang him presently' (4.4.45). The action of Saturninus here in ordering the instant death of the Clown has been seen as 'inexplicable. Unexplained in the sense that no overt reason is given for it'. Just so; the action of Saturninus appears automatic and unmotivated as the Clown, caught up inadvertently in political enmities of which he is ignorant, is casually sent off to execution. If the violence of other characters is often 'selfishly purposeful',[31] they can kill and torture unthinkingly and without feeling, like automatons. The death of the Clown is representative of the action of a play that relishes violence for its own sake.

In the last scenes of the play not only are Chiron and Demetrius butchered, their throats cut, and their blood collected to be served up in a pie, but in addition to this display of cannibalism, Titus kills his own daughter and stabs Tamora, after which Titus and Saturninus are killed onstage. From the initial processional entries of Saturninus and his followers through one door and Bassianus and his followers through another, followed by the arrival of Titus with his sons, his prisoners, men bearing a coffin, and 'others as many as can be', probably through a central opening, the play offers the kind of spectacle that Marlowe, Greene, Peele, and Kyd had made popular. A French tutor in the household of Sir John Harington who saw the play performed there in 1596 reported in a letter home that the spectacle was much more interesting than the narrative ('le monstre a plus valu que le sujet'),[32] and no doubt it was the spectacle that made the play popular enough for it to be issued in three quarto editions in 1594, 1600, and 1611.

After being for long despised or neglected by critics, in recent times the play has had some eloquent defenders,[33] and the interesting film version of it made by Julie Taymor (1999) has won deserved praise. She mixes conventions in the film, and shifts between ancient ruins and modern street or arcade scenes. She has her own style, which brings out the black humour and the horror of the action, and incorporates echoes of other film-makers, turning Saturninus into an effete playboy who is much occupied with orgies in the mode of Fellini's *Satyricon*, and paying homage to Baz Luhrmann's *Romeo and Juliet* and Richard Loncraine's *Richard III*. Amid the vast ruins of a decadent civilization Anthony Hopkins as Titus strides powerfully as a great warrior going mad with shame and grief, while the violent young Chiron and Demetrius appear as modern teenage hoodlums bored with videos and pool, while motor-cycles recreate also something of the world of Mussolini. The film ambitiously seeks to merge ancient and modern, and to comment on the appalling acceptance of, and insensibility to, violence in our own time. The film has drawn praise from critics, and gained a cult following, though neither the play nor the film have a wide appeal. The reason, I think, is encapsulated in Mr Petit's remark in 1596; the subject of the play is there to serve the sensationalism of the spectacle, and the students at Liverpool who linked it to *Pulp Fiction* and called it Shakespeare's Tarantino play have a point: the violence in *Titus Andronicus* is disconnected from any moral centre and so appears gratuitous and designed to shock.

So, in the opening scene, Titus suddenly stabs his own son Mutius for standing in his way and helping Bassianus carry off Lavinia. Here he recalls Tamburlaine, who also kills his own son, but does so in the presence of his army, allies, and conquered kings after a kind of mock trial for sloth and cowardice, so that the scene confirms the way Tamburlaine's conquests have made him more brutal and tyrannical. By contrast, Titus has just arrived in Rome with four survivors of his twenty-five sons, mourning the deaths of those killed in his conquest of the Goths, so his peremptory act of killing one of his remaining sons is shocking. This act appears still more horrific when it turns out to be pointless, since Saturninus at once renounces his desire for Lavinia and takes Tamora as his partner. Titus, the great warrior, having killed his son, then has no one to fight, and can only watch and descend into madness as others intrigue and commit rape and murder in the pursuit of power, until he outdoes them all in violence in preparing his Thyestean banquet. Shakespeare goes beyond Marlowe's Tamburlaine in making Titus kill his own daughter too. In such a world Aaron's protective care for his baby turns out to be shocking too, in one who repents not the evils he has done, but any good deed. In Aaron Shakespeare constructs a new take on the aspiring Tamburlaine figure, a black Moor who aims to 'mount aloft' with his mistress Tamora (1.1.512). In place of Marlowe's single dominant character, Tamburlaine, he creates more than one variant in this play, in Titus, Tamora, and Aaron, just as he does in Talbot and Joan in *Henry VI*, Part 1, and in Richard and Margaret of Anjou in Part 3. In the *Henry VI* plays and in *Titus* Shakespeare also went beyond Marlowe in developing a range of powerful female characters, notably Joan, Margaret, and Tamora, who compete with men on their own terms. These plays all offer interesting pointers to Shakespeare's further development as a dramatist, but in the end they are apprentice plays, with occasional rich imaginative life in the dialogue, that pay homage to Marlowe especially, and relish the passion for sensation and violence that was a feature of the popular theatre in the years following the opening of the Rose in 1587.

NOTES

1. See Peter Spierenburg, *The Spectacle of Suffering* (Cambridge University Press, 1984); also Patrick Collinson, *The Religion of Protestants* (Oxford: Clarendon Press, 1982), who records such punishments in Bury St Edmunds in 1578.
2. According to the *Los Angeles Times*, 13 February 2001, the film grossed $58 million during the weekend that it first showed, making it at that time the third largest opening in Hollywood history.
3. See Eugene M. Waith, *The Herculean Hero* (New York: Columbia University Press, 1962).
4. *Tamburlaine*, ed. J. S. Cunningham (The Revels Plays. Manchester University Press; Baltimore: Johns Hopkins University Press, 1981), 65.
5. Richard Levin, 'The Contemporary Reception of Marlowe's *Tamburlaine*', in J. Leeds Barroll, ed., Medieval & Renaissance Drama in England, 1 (New York: AMS Press, 1984), 51–70, citing 56–7.
6. G. B. Harrison, ed., *Discoveries*, Bodley Head Quartos (London: John Lane; New York: E. P. Dutton, 1923), 33.
7. Joseph Hall, *Virgidemiarum* (1597), cited in Levin, 'Contemporary Reception', 53, and in Andrew Gurr, *Playgoing in Shakespeare's London* (Cambridge University Press, 1987), 211.
8. Levin, 'Contemporary Reception', 57–8.
9. As do Stephen Gosson, *The Trumpet of War* (1598), B8v, and William Gouge, *God's Three Arrrows* (1631), 213; see p. 30 above.
10. Guise and his men chase Protestants onstage crying 'Tue, tue, tue', (340–1), and their shout seems to have been taken over to represent foreigners; so the Spanish villains in *A Larum for London or The Siege of Antwerp* (printed 1602 as played by the Lord Chamberlain's Men) cry 'Tue, tue, tue, tue' (1129) before stabbing two children.
11. In *Shakespeare's Heroical Histories: Henry VI and its Literary Tradition* (Cambridge, Mass.: Harvard University Press, 1971), David Riggs argued that a character like Talbot in *Henry VI*, Part 1 is set apart from ordinary men by fighting 'to exhibit and satisfy his innate nobility of nature' (59–60), a view that seems to me too simplistic. The idea of heroism is qualified by the 'unusual stress on physical horror' that suggests a 'barbarous providence ruling murderous automatons', as J. P. Brockbank put it in 'The Frame of Disorder – *Henry VI*' in J. R. Brown and Bernard Harris, eds., *Early Shakespeare* (London: Arnold, 1961), 73–99, citing 86 and 94.
12. Thomas Nashe, *Piers Penilesse* (1592), in *Works*, ed. Ronald B. McKerrow (London: A. H. Bullen, 1904), 1, 212; cited in Gurr, *Playgoing*, 209.
13. Edward Burns, Introduction to *King Henry VI*, Part 1 (London: Arden Shakespeare, 2000), 37n.
14. Citing Jean Howard's Introduction to the play in *The Norton Shakespeare* (New York: W. W. Norton, 1997), 204.

15. See David Riggs, *Shakespeare's Heroical Histories: Henry VI and its Literary Tradition* (Cambridge, Mass.: Harvard University Press, 1971), 124, and Ronald Knowles, Introduction to *Henry VI*, Part 2 (Arden Shakespeare; London: Thomas Nelson, 1999), 98–9.

16. John Wilders, in *The Lost Garden* (London and Basingstoke: Macmillan; Totowa, N.J.: Rowan and Littlefield, 1978), 63, considers the appeals to providence and God as there for an effect of dramatic irony, and shows that God remains inscrutable; see also Knowles, *Henry VI*, Part 2, 60–1.

17. Michael Hattaway, Introduction to *Henry VI*, Part 3 (Cambridge University Press, 1993), 3.

18. *Ibid.*, 1.

19. *Ibid.*, ix; Riggs in *Shakespeare's Heroical Histories*, 97, sees a 'gradual deterioration of heroic idealism' in the *Henry VI* plays, and James Bulman, *The Heroic Idiom of Shakespearean Tragedy* (Newark, Del.: University of Delaware Press, 1985), writes on heroic conventions in them.

20. Knowles, *Henry VI*, Part 2, 88. See also Phyllis Rackin, *Stages of History: Shakespeare's English Chronicles* (Ithaca and London: Cornell University Press, 1990), for a reading of the chronicle plays in terms of a conflict between 'providential and the Machiavellian notions of historical causation' (46).

21. H. A. Kelly, *Divine Providence in the England of Shakespeare's Histories* (Cambridge, Mass.: Harvard University Press, 1970), 276.

22. Robert Greene, *Perimedes the Blacksmith* (1588), cited in Levin, 'Contemporary Reception', 52.

23. Russell, *Just War*, 292

24. Thomas Beard, *The Theatre of God's Judgments*, A6r.

25. Norman Rabkin has a rather different take on this passage in *Shakespeare and the Problem of Meaning* (University of Chicago Press, 1981), 90–1, and looks for a motive in what he sees as Richard's 'nihilistic and universal hatred' (94). He thinks Macbeth's behaviour, like that of Richard, is 'based on unconscious motives which he is incapable of knowing' (109). One might ask then how anyone can know them.

26. I consider *Richard III* further in the next chapter, in relation to Richard Loncraine's film based on the play.

27. Jonathan Bate, Introduction to his edition of *Titus Andronicus*, Arden Shakespeare (London and New York: Routledge, 1995), 3, 69–79.

28. Heather James, 'Cultural Disintegration in *Titus Andronicus*', in James Redmond, ed., *Violence in Drama*, Themes in Drama, 13 (Cambridge University Press, 1991), 123–40, citing 123. For the influence of Seneca on this play, see Robert S. Miola, *Shakespeare and Classical Tragedy. The Influence of Seneca* (Oxford: Clarendon Press, 1992), 9–25.

29. This play was performed by the Queen's Men, and Scott McMillin and Sally-Beth MacLean believe that Shakespeare may have initially worked for this company when they were competing with Marlowe before 1590; see *The Queen's Men and their Plays* (Cambridge University Press, 1998).

30. Francis Barker, *The Culture of Violence: Tragedy and History* (Manchester University Press, 1993), 168. Barker sees the action of Saturninus here as lacking

'credence according to the positive norms of behaviour the play assumes', but it is hard to find positive norms in a play where almost all the characters are addicted to violence.

31. Cited in Bate, *Titus Andronicus*, 43–4.
32. Bate himself, especially, and see his edition, 33–7.
33. On what he calls the 'splitting' of the Marlovian overreacher, see Bate, *The Genius of Shakespeare* (London and Basingstoke: Picador, 1997), 115–16.

CHAPTER 4

Plays and movies: Richard III *and* Romeo and Juliet

Stage violence evidently appealed for its own sake to audiences when Shakespeare offered them the early histories and *Titus Andronicus*, plays packed with violent incidents, murders, wars, severed heads, rape, and plenty of blood. The Christian context of the *Henry VI* plays and the allusions to the Cain and Abel story hint at a growing concern with troublesome aspects of mindless killings, father against son, son against father, brother killing brother. In his first major tragedies, *Richard III* and *Romeo and Juliet*, Shakespeare develops further an interest in unmotivated or inadequately motivated human violence. *Richard III* begins with Richard casually arranging the murder of his brother for no other reason than that he is 'determined to prove a villain', and *Romeo and Juliet* begins with a street brawl that explodes out of nothing. Such acts might be thought of as essentially empty, that is to say, as having no meaning other than what we attribute to them after the event; but they speak across centuries as representative of the apparently meaningless acts of violence that feature as news items continually at the present time. The past of Shakespeare's early tragedies anticipates in many ways the present, notably in the continuity of the problem of violence, as can be seen in the latest films of *Richard III* and *Romeo and Juliet*, which show how readily the action of both plays can be relocated in modern times. I want to look at these plays in connection with the reworking of them in the films made in 1995 by Richard Loncraine and Baz Luhrmann. Both plays were made into notable films earlier, but as costume dramas. Laurence Olivier's *Richard III* (1955) is framed by the coronations of Edward IV and Henry VII (Richmond), with his own in between. Olivier cut and altered the text to make the film focus on the engaging if paranoiac personality of Richard as he gains and loses the throne. His shadow hovers over everyone, and, humorous and extremely violent by turns, he might be thought of as distantly echoing Hitler, who was in Olivier's consciousness when he played the part of Richard on the stage in 1944.[1] Franco

Zeffirelli's movie of *Romeo and Juliet* (1968) recreated a medieval Verona and filled its streets and especially the marketplace with swirling crowds of gaily dressed youths and noisy action scenes. It was regarded by Jack Jorgens as 'In many ways... a "youth movie" of the 1960s which glorifies the young and caricatures the old, a Renaissance *Graduate*'.[2] In a bleaker world of street violence, serial killers, and international terrorism, both plays demand a different emphasis.[3]

RICHARD III FOR A VIOLENT ERA

Loncraine and Ian McKellen transpose the setting of *Richard III* to a war-torn country that resembles Britain in the 1930s. The movie begins, as credits roll, in a mansion that serves as the headquarters of a king, who is saying goodnight to his son and settling to paperwork. Suddenly a tank bursts through a wall into the room, a rifle-shot splatters the back of the youth's head 'across a painting of an idyllic rural scene,'[4] a guard and adjutant are also killed, and a terrifying figure, in battle-dress and gas-mask, leads a group of commandos emerging, as if from one of Otto Dix's horrific drawings of World War I,[5] from behind the tank. He kicks open doors to find the old king, who is killed by a burst from his Sten gun. This killing brings to an end a period of civil war, but at the same time, the images here of destruction and brutal murder establish the idea of a violent world in which war may break out again. The leader is revealed as Richard when he removes his mask, and we see his staff-car driving through the 'rubble-filled, war-torn streets of the capital' (p. 49), ignored by wandering citizens. It is not known for sure how Henry VI died, but Shakespeare makes Richard stab him to death in *Henry VI*, Part 3 with the boast that he has 'neither pity, love, nor fear' (5.6.68), and McKellen's burst of fire with a Sten gun in his film version is based on this incident. For the first ten minutes or so nothing is said or taken from Shakespeare's play except the names of characters, and the series of images has created a modern setting, suggested a political world involved in internecine strife, and fixed the idea of Richard as a controlling figure, a ruthless soldier who has achieved the victory that has put a new king, Edward, on the throne.

The action proper of the film begins at a victory ball, with music, dancing, and songs courtesy of Christopher Marlowe. Hastings, here Prime Minister, and Buckingham are among the guests. The new king (Edward IV) has an American wife, so it is easy to recall Edward VIII and Mrs Simpson. As Richard, in dress uniform as commander-in-chief, moves through the crowd, he is greeted by the large, imposing figure of Buckingham. Among the guests is Richmond, a 'dashing, young naval officer' (p. 57), who is introduced to the Queen. Brackenbury in the uniform of a Chief Constable with two henchmen in civilian clothes lead Clarence off, ignored by the festive company at large, and noticed only by Edward and Richard. As Clarence goes, Richard stops the music and seizes the microphone used by the female singer. Now at last the text of the play begins, with Richard's famous soliloquy, the opening lines delivered as a toast to King Edward:

Now is the winter of our discontent
Made glorious summer by this son of York...

An Archbishop, who does not appear in the play until Act 3, looks on benignly until, on the line, 'He capers nimbly in a lady's chamber' (1.1.12), Richard moves to an ornate bathroom, continuing his speech, and his concern with his own image is brought home as he soliloquizes before his reflection in a mirror, and includes some lines from *Henry VI*, Part 3, 3.2.182–5, 'Why, I can smile, and murder whiles I smile...' On the lines:

Plots have I laid...
To set my brothers, Clarence and the King
In deadly hate, the one against the other,
(1.1.32, 34–5)

he returns along a walkway where he can see Clarence, handcuffed, being escorted to a launch on the river. The text is heavily cut, as is inevitable in a film made of such a long play, but already Richard's ambition, his lack of scruple, his power as commander with a network of men ready to carry out his orders, as well as his contempt for the royal family, are well established. Richard's moustache and slicked-back hair give him something of a fascist aura, but also suggest an attempt on the part of an ageing man to claim pretensions to youthfulness, while his vitality and physical activity set him off from the effete and somewhat decadent luxury of Edward, his Queen Elizabeth, and their family.

Force of personality rather than charm such as Laurence Olivier exerted make him successful in his wooing of Lady Anne, which takes place in a mortuary in the basement of what might be a World War I military hospital, where hosts of wounded and maimed men are being treated. Leaving the hospital, Richard bounds up a flight of stairs past the wounded and dying, full of vitality and the self-congratulation of 'Was ever woman in this humour wooed?' (1.2.232). An impression of King Edward as a bureaucrat signing papers at his desk, and the Queen as

dedicated to pleasure, drinking champagne in her rooms, is set against
the image of Richard as a man of action, a military officer, one whose
concerns are visually registered in scenes of a parade ground, of horses
in stalls, and of the regimental mascot, a wild boar tended by a corporal
who likes his job. Richard recruits non-commissioned officers, Sergeant
Ratcliffe and Tyrrel (both knights in the play) for personal service, with
Tyrrel as chief murderer. It is Tyrrel and another NCO who carry
Richard's death-warrant to Brackenbury, and murder Clarence as he
sits in a bath reading a newspaper. Here Clarence's nightmare of being
in a kind of hell at the bottom of the sea foreshadows the manner of his
death. The second NCO holds Clarence down as Tyrrel slits his throat
and pushes his head under water, causing an explosion of red in the bath.
The verbal emphasis on blood – bleed – bloody in the play – words that
occur ten times in Anne's cursing of Richard in 1.2 alone – is transformed
into a visual link with Richard in the film, both in the drop of blood seen
on a scalpel when Richard cuts himself deliberately to impress Anne,
and here in the literally bloody killing of Clarence, who is stabbed and
dragged offstage in the play.

The old Queen Margaret, widow of Henry VI, is omitted from the
film version, and absorbed in some measure into Queen Elizabeth and
the Duchess of York, who hosts a great feast, with her guests all in full
evening dress, to denounce Richard. King Edward appears, very ill and
confined to a wheelchair, in a summer-house on the sea-coast, where
he tries to reconcile the factions in the court. News of the death of
Clarence provokes a violent attack of asthma in King Edward, even as
the Duchess of York arrives to lament the deaths of two sons, Clarence
and the King. The scene ends with Buckingham greeting Richard as 'My
Lord Protector', and taking his arm as they go off together, leaving Anne,
now addicted to tranquillizers, on her own, her marriage a disaster. In
these scenes the royal family, Edward, Elizabeth, and their relatives, are
displayed in luxurious surroundings, a ballroom, an elegant breakfast
room, at a state banquet, at a seaside pavilion, and at a country retreat,
while Richard has been living in a barracks. Now that he has become
Lord Protector of the realm, he is seen arriving with Buckingham by
limousine to enter the enormous imposing lobby of his headquarters,
symbolizing his ascent to power, which is also at once displayed in the
splendour of new uniforms. In Shakespeare's play, the death of Edward
at the end of Act 2 is followed by a short scene (2.3) of citizens anxiously
commenting on the fearful state of the realm, and two more scenes
(3.1, 3.2) that bring the young princes to London. In the film, Act 3,

Scene 3, in which Rivers, Grey, and Vaughan are despatched to Pomfret Castle by Ratcliffe for execution, is radically changed, and brought forward to follow Act 2, Scene 2. Grey and Vaughan are omitted from the film, but Elizabeth's brother Rivers, characterized in the film as an effete playboy, is murdered by Tyrrel in an especially brutal way. As he lies naked in bed in an hotel room being pleasured by an air-hostess from the plane that brought him to England, a blade, like a great phallus, is thrust from underneath through his chest (p. 149). Whereas in the play characters like Rivers are taken offstage to be executed, the film sharpens our sense of Richard's utter ruthlessness by such images, and by the sound here of the air-hostess screaming.

In the film Richmond is given considerable prominence long before he appears in the play. He reports the murder of Rivers by Richard to the Queen, and is present when the Prince of Wales is brought by train to be greeted by Richard and Buckingham in morning dress, with the Lord Mayor and the Archbishop. By giving Richmond and Stanley, too, a visual presence in these scenes, Loncraine establishes a growing 'clean' opposition to Richard, who meanwhile destroys the effete and corrupt members and followers of the royal family. The role of Stanley is clarified by giving him a nightmare vision of Richard with the face of a wild boar, its tusks lunging at him as he screams (p. 167). Richard's ruthlessness and addiction to murder are again emphasized visually, when the body of Hastings, executed offstage in the play, is shown jerking at the end of a rope, and when later we see Tyrrel suffocating one of the young princes with a red silk scarf. The film increases the horror of Richard's acts by such physical images, here set off against a peaceful scene on a lawn in the country where four women, Queen Elizabeth, the Duchess of York, Princess Elizabeth, and Lady Anne, are gathered for afternoon tea, all in mourning still, and listening to some of Anne's lines in which she bitterly regrets her marriage to Richard (p. 181; 4.1.65–76).

At the same time business goes on as usual in the city, and Buckingham deals in a Council House with the Mayor and 'a dozen distinguished-looking bankers and civic leaders' (p. 195), while Richard paces in a stylish celebrity dressing-room, attended by a make-up artist and a hairdresser, and again obsessed with his image. Powdered, and his hair 'Brylcreemed', Richard emerges with a prayer-book in his hand to accept the honour. After Richard leaves, the film interpolates a brief encounter between Stanley, Richmond, and the Archbishop, giving the Archbishop lines from Queen Elizabeth's advice to her son the Marquess of Dorset in the play:

If thou wilt outstrip death, go cross the seas,
And live with Richmond, from the reach of Hell.
(4.1.41–2)

Dorset is omitted from the film, and the Archbishop is not present in these scenes in the play, so that once again Richmond is given prominence as the second line becomes 'live, dear Richmond', while the Archbishop, up to this point an ineffectual onlooker, shows that he has at last recognized the true nature of Richard. By bringing on Princess Elizabeth early in the film, and also giving Richmond visual prominence in this way, Loncraine and McKellen display a growing opposition to Richard to replace the denunciations of him in the play by the chorus of suffering women, Margaret, Elizabeth, and the Duchess of York.

It is in the scenes of dealings with the Lord Mayor and civic leaders that Richard, Buckingham, and Catesby appear in elaborate black military uniforms vaguely reminiscent of Oswald Mosley's and Mussolini's black-shirts, uniforms which emblematize the tyranny Richard is imposing. In the play Richard and Buckingham enter 'in rotten armour, marvellous ill-favoured', as if threatened by 'enemies' (3.5.19). The change is significant, enhancing Richard's status as a military leader who draws his power from the army and police he controls. That status is also seen to be in part created by make-up, the media, and display, with Richard's boar-crest prominent, as the episode culminates in Richard's ascent to a podium, where, under arc-lights, a huge crowd in dark shirts salute with raised fists and cheer as Buckingham cries, 'Long live King Richard!' (3.7.239), and chants of 'Amen' are heard. In the play Richard may be played in the manner of Olivier as a consummate actor on his way to the throne, but in the film Loncraine adds another dimension in references to the technology of the 1930s, in making Clarence a photographer, for instance, and in presenting Richard as concerned in several sequences to establish his image, grooming himself as he wants to be seen. He is carefully made-up for the meeting with the mayor, he stages a coronation, and is seen from a distance being crowned by the Archbishop in what looks like a cathedral (though not in the text, a coronation has been included in some stagings of the play, as when Anthony Sher played Richard at the Royal Shakespeare Theatre in 1985). Then, in place of the scene in the play in which he ascends the throne, the film shows the new King and Anne as Queen sitting with courtiers around them in a private cinema as they watch a propaganda film. It is as if Richard's success is more real in image or on film than in substance, and when his chief supporter does not take his hint about getting rid of the princes, Richard's plaintive cry, 'Why, Buckingham, I say I would be King' (4.2.12), takes on a new resonance, since it points to the gap between the sense of domination expressed in the media-created images of royal pomp and his personal insecurity: he is not yet at the top. Immediately before the film cuts to this moment, Richard speaks lines transposed from 4.2.63–5,

> But I am in
> So far in blood that sin will pluck on sin.
> Tear-falling pity dwells not in this eye.

His use of the word 'sin' provides the first hint in the play of Richard's troubled conscience, but in the film the first two lines seem ironic, as if he cannot escape from the habit of a Christian vocabulary, and the third line carries more weight.

The scenes of choric women are abbreviated but women remain prominent as voices of opposition,[6] Elizabeth notably, for whereas in the play it is Richard who stops Elizabeth from leaving, 'Stay, madam, I must talk a word with you' (4.4.199), in the film Elizabeth seeks a confrontation with Richard at his military headquarters in a railway siding where war materials are being loaded and troops are busy. Their dialogue is more fully preserved than that of most scenes in the play, so that Elizabeth is given great prominence here. While her daughter, the Princess Elizabeth, is held like a prisoner outside on the platform, she beards Richard in his carriage, and by her manner makes it apparent that she is revolted by his aim of marrying her daughter. Richmond shortly receives a message that she has agreed that he should marry the Princess, and we see the Archbishop blessing the couple (with some lines borrowed from Richmond's final speech in the play, 5.5.29–33) to complete their marriage ceremony before the final showdown between Richard and Richmond.

Richard is temporarily afflicted with guilt not after seeing ghosts, but after having a nightmare in which the murders of his victims are re-enacted, including that of Buckingham, who has been tortured and garotted by Tyrrel. Richard recovers to fight fearlessly as his troops are bombed into disarray by Stanley, who commands Richard's air force in the film, and now is able to transfer openly his allegiance to Richmond. The line, 'A horse! A horse! My kingdom for a horse!' is given amusing point when Richard's armoured truck is stuck in mud as Richmond's soldiers approach. Richard's final act of cruelty occurs then, as the faithful Tyrrel offers to help him escape, for once fatally misjudging his master's wishes. Richard has no desire to escape, and shoots him in the face at point blank range. There is finally nowhere for Richard to go, and he chooses his own end. He climbs up high on to steel girders in a bombed-out building (actually the shell of Battersea power station) pursued by Richmond. Below all is fire and smoke as Richard accidentally drops his gun and is left at the mercy of Richmond; but in a final stunning image, Richard steps off the girder before Richmond's superfluous bullet strikes him. His body is seen spinning down 'through the hell of smoke and flames' (p. 287), as titles roll and the sound is heard of Al Jolson singing 'I'm sitting on top of the world.'

Richard Loncraine added here the echo of the brutal gangster played by James Cagney, who, at the end of the film *White Heat* (1949), is pursued to the top of gas-tanks by the police, and commits suicide by shooting into the tanks to create a series of massive explosions, huge balls of fire, as he cries, 'Made it, Ma, top of the world'.[7] In this film, Cagney's character, Cody Jarrett, is dependent on his mother, who dotes on him, and it has been argued that Richard is similarly 'obsessed with his mother'.[8] It is true that in his notes to the filmscript McKellen refers to 'the emotional barrenness of Richard's childhood' (p. 144), and comments on his mother's disgust with his physical deformity, hinting that he may have learned from her how to hate (p. 236). But if this idea helped the actor to identify a motivation for Richard, it is barely present in the film, where we are more conscious of Richard's rejection of his mother, marked in his wink to Tyrrel as he pushes his way out after she curses him (p. 239). Cody Jarrett has fits of insanity, notably when he hears that his mother has been shot, and has to be subdued in a straitjacket, whereas Richard only loses his grip momentarily after his nightmare, when Ratcliffe comforts him as he rapidly becomes his old self again (pp. 275–7). At the same time, the connection with a classic Hollywood gangster film is wittily made in the final scene, confirming the visual links established throughout in the 1930s setting with its 'black limousines, jazz, swanky clothes, machine guns', and in the overall shape of the action:

All the elements are there: the troubled relationships with the mother and wife; the bloody elimination of rivals (Clarence, Rivers and the Princes); the meeting where the hero reveals himself (making an example of Hastings); the physical transformation as he reaches the top (adopting a black dress uniform and having his portrait made); the betrayal by, and elimination of, the right-hand man (Buckingham); the fear and isolation; the final moment of defiance.[9]

Shakespeare's play already anticipates such a pattern, and the substantial cuts made in the text for the film, together with the omission of Margaret and of a number of minor characters, help to streamline and clarify this structure in the action.

Loncraine had extensive experience in making TV commercials, which may have suggested the treatment of Richard as narcissistic and obsessed with his image. In his early soliloquies Richard twice refers to a 'looking-glass' (1.1.15, 1.2.260) as he comments on his own deformity, and on his success in winning Anne in spite of his appearance. The film shows Richard as more deeply concerned with the way he looks, studying himself in a mirror, being groomed, almost always smartly dressed, in and out of uniform, and as devoted to watching the film of his own coronation. He is not interested in women except as instruments he can use, and he pays no attention to Anne after their marriage, when she is glimpsed popping pills or injecting herself with drugs before the final image of her sprawled on her bed, dead from an overdose or perhaps murdered at Richard's orders.[10] Richard becomes the only king in the history plays who has no thought at all for the succession to the throne. As king he appears seated in his office at his desk with, behind him, a huge full-length portrait of himself seen from ground level, elevated, and glamorized, standing on a plinth in his new black military uniform. The image is what matters, larger and glossier than life, the sign of his success. So it is appropriate that this Richard orchestrates his own death, stepping off a high girder to disappear into a fiery inferno beneath. This ending, of course, differs from that in the play, in which Richmond kills Richard and proclaims peace and the union of York and Lancaster. The film has Richard at the very end speak lines that in the play precede his oration to his troops before the battle at Bosworth:

> Let's to it pell-mell,
> If not to heaven, then hand in hand to hell.
> (5.3.313–14)

Richard thus invites Richmond to go with him, making us see Richmond standing there as another soldier in uniform who, for all we know, might turn out to be like Richard. Shakespeare could not do otherwise than represent the founder of the Tudor dynasty in a noble and moral light, but the film's very different ending may be seen as true to the spirit of a play that daringly develops Richard as a kind of serial killer who defines and magnifies his image through a series of murders, and calmly chooses his own way to die when he is finally trapped.

Loncraine's film functions on several levels. McKellen's Richard has little of the charm some actors (notably Laurence Olivier) have brought to the part and is portrayed as a nervous, chain-smoking, ambitious killer who mesmerizes his victims by the sheer force of a powerful personality, and who knows exactly when to seize the initiative in order to gain power in a decadent and corrupt world. His vulnerability is suggested not, as in the play, by a troubled conscience, but rather by his need to project an image that he cannot sustain. This is a fitting way to interpret Shakespeare's Richard, who wins our sympathy insofar as, like Marlowe's Tamburlaine, he is a scourge, cleansing the realm of its filth, until the murder of the innocent princes in the Tower brings a revulsion, and proves the first step to his downfall. At the same time, the film locates the action in the political atmosphere of Europe in the 1930s, with Richard as the leader of a black-shirted terrorist force creating a quasi-fascist state, and with reminders of Sir Oswald Mosley's influence in Britain, and of the rise of Mussolini and Hitler. In addition, the film in many ways follows the pattern of the 1930s gangster film, a link that is brought home notably in the final moments. In the play, Richard fights courageously until he is killed in battle by Richmond, who announces 'the bloody dog is dead' (5.5.2), anticipating peace and plenty to come. In the film, Richard has something like an apotheosis, stepping with a grin on his face off the girder into the flames – he has reached the top literally on the high steel joist, and in his career, since there is nothing left for him to do. He thus escapes from the moral closure Shakespeare provided, and we are allowed the gratification of identifying with him still in appreciating the aesthetic appeal of a final act of daring that exemplifies what was great about him. The film cleverly relates aspects of the Richard Shakespeare conceived to twentieth-century phenomena, gangsters, serial killers, the rise and fall of fascist dictators, the power of image-making, and the exploitation of new technologies for political ends, and yet remains a testimony to the enduring power of the play's shocking portrayal of a character who enjoys the practice of violence.

The text of the play is very heavily cut in Loncraine's film, and little remains of the religious language in the play, which frequently sets the lip-service paid by characters like Clarence ('As I am a Christian faithful man', 1.4.4) against what they do; so the two murderers remind him that he is himself guilty of murder (1.4.205–6). This vocabulary comes easily in the text, and at the end Richmond naturally claims the victory in God's name, 'God and your arms be praised' (5.5.1), as if God plays a part in human affairs. Only Richard mocks this assumption, and the film retains, slightly modified, the notable instance when he seeks his mother's blessing (p. 145):

RICHARD: Madam, Mother, I do humbly crave your blessing.
DUCHESS: God bless you – and put meekness in your breast,
    Love, charity, obedience and true duty!
RICHARD: Amen! And make me die a good old man.
    That is the butt-end of a mother's blessing.
    I marvel that her grace did leave it out! (2.2.104–11)

Richard enjoys exposing the hypocrisy of others, as here he knows his mother in fact scorns him, and regards him as her 'shame' (2.2.29). In the film Richmond appeals to God for aid in the battle with Richard, but in the end he is simply a soldier just like his enemy. Appeals to God or to Christian morality are more frequent in the play than in the film, which notably changes the ending, but there is no essential difference. Whatever characters ostensibly believe, they do what is to their advantage, and Richard is so compelling because he cuts through their cant and positively enjoys his violent ascent to the throne. In the film, violence comes naturally to him, and he uses it to his advantage to become king, but at the same time his acts cause him to become increasingly isolated until finally, to maintain his self-image, the image he has cultivated through the media, he ruthlessly and in close-up kills his closest associate and double, Tyrrel, rejecting the chance to escape so that he can stay in control.

ROMEO AND JULIET

The second of these plays, *Romeo and Juliet*, is familiar to everyone as an archetypal story of love between two passionate teenagers. The play also concerns another archetypal situation: that of a feud raging between two similar families and their adherents within a single community, nominally the city of Verona. In the splendid opening scene, servants of the Capulets, armed 'with swords and bucklers', according to the stage-direction, seem to be hoping to encounter 'A dog of the house of Montague', in Sampson's words, so that they can quarrel. When servants of the Montagues appear, Sampson bites his thumb at them in a threatening gesture meant to provoke physical violence, and very quickly swords are out, and a fight begins. When Benvolio tries to intervene to stop them, Tybalt appears, and draws him into the action. A crowd of citizens, angry with both sides, attempts to 'Beat them down' as Old

Capulet enters, calling for his sword, followed by Old Montague, who 'flourishes his blade'. The general disturbance is halted only by the entry of Prince Escalus with his guards. The quarrel of the servants reflects the hostility between the families, as shown at once in the clashes between the younger generation (Benvolio and Tybalt), and the older one. A single threatening gesture provokes a quarrel that escalates rapidly until everyone is involved. No cause is given for the feud other than an 'ancient grudge'. The impression given by the opening is that the servants very much enjoy quarrelling; we are not told what their business is in the streets; they appear to be walking out in hope of finding an occasion to fight. The feud between the Capulets and Montagues has become a way of life, though its meaning and origin are quite forgotten; and everything that happens in the play is shadowed by our awareness of the 'civil brawls' that are so powerfully brought home to us in the opening sequence of action.

In the drama of the late sixteenth century, an addiction to violence, or the choice of violence as a career option by such characters as Tamburlaine or Selimus, typically is associated with outsiders, Muslims, Jews (Barabas), Turks, Moors, savages, representatives of the 'Other', of countries or societies outside the bounds of Christendom. *Romeo and Juliet*, however, is set in a Christian city, as the play constantly reminds us. Friar Laurence, of course, represents what might be called a professional Christianity, and, no doubt costumed appropriately, like his colleague Friar John, serves as a 'ghostly father' (2.3.41) to Romeo, and has the appearance and gestures of a member of a religious order. He greets Romeo with a blessing, 'Benedicite' (2.3.27), offers confession readily, and when troubled calls on 'Holy Saint Francis' and 'Jesu Maria' (2.3.61,65). Other characters use Christian terms and oaths, even Mercutio swearing 'By Jesu' (2.4.30), and none more readily than the Nurse. She shows no scruples in recommending Juliet to marry Paris and commit bigamy, yet, ironically, she habitually uses religious expressions, falling into what are for her clichés of conversation in such phrases as 'God rest all Christian souls' (1.3.18), 'God mark thee to his grace' (1.3.59), 'God in Heaven bless thee' (2.4.192), and 'God save the mark' (3.2.53). Time is measured by the Christian calendar, as Juliet's birthday is on Lammas Eve (1.3.17), and Capulet remembers he last danced at Pentecost twenty-five years ago (1.5.37). Romeo's initial devotion to Rosaline takes Cupid for its god, but he woos Juliet as a pilgrim approaching a saint, seeing her as a 'bright angel' (2.2.26), while to her, even after he has killed Mercutio, he seems paradoxically a 'fiend angelical' (3.2.75). It is appropriate that the last scene of the play takes place in a 'churchyard' (5.3.5, 36) at the funeral monument of the Capulets.

Although the play is set ostensibly in Roman Catholic Italy, it is striking that the servants who establish the idea of the feud between Capulets and Montagues in the opening scene have English names, Gregory and Sampson. They might be in London, and begin with a joke on the idea of carrying coals, referring to the charcoal or sea-coal brought from Tyneside that was needed for the kitchens and hearths of the capital. Other servants are called Susan Grindstone, Anthony, and Potpan; and it seems Will Kemp played the Nurse's man, Peter, since his name is found in a stage-direction in the second Quarto (1599) at 4.5.99, where a little scene with musicians may have been added especially for him as a star clown. He may well have played the unnamed comic servant in 1.2 as well. If the upper-class households of Capulets and Montagues belong to an imagined Verona, the underclass of servants, and also the garrulous Nurse, modelled on the kind of gossip Shakespeare might have encountered often enough, belong to the London of the audience. Shakespeare set his play in old Verona, but updated and localized it for London audiences in this way, so providing a precedent for Baz Luhrmann, who updated the play further and localized it for Hollywood audiences by aligning it with the familiar images of city life in America.

The play is topical in this general sense that in its depiction of street violence it reflects quarrelling such as might have been seen on the streets of London. The play is also remarkable for its portrayal of the spontaneous eruption of such violence for no immediate cause. What the servants initiate in the opening scene is focused in the figure of Tybalt, always itching for a fight and eager to kill the peacemaker Benvolio simply because he is a Montague. At the Capulet feast Tybalt calls for his rapier so that he can kill a masked guest he takes to be a Montague:

Now by the stock and honour of my kin,
To strike him dead I hold it not a sin.
(1.5.58–9)

His hatred and lust to kill require no provocation for him to act, and override the imperatives of his religion, so that he can easily dismiss the notion that murder is a sin. 'Honour', credit or reputation, is merely an excuse for giving way to a primitive urge to violence, as is seen when the fight breaks out between Mercutio and Tybalt in Act 3. Romeo refuses to take up Tybalt's challenge, a refusal seen by Mercutio as 'dishonourable, vile submission' (3.1.72); peace itself is 'dishonourable' by this measure.

After Mercutio is slain, Romeo reacts by taking revenge and killing Tybalt, so becoming trapped in a tragic sequence of events. But Romeo reacts after his kinsman is mortally wounded, while Tybalt and Mercutio, like the servants, do not need a cause, other than the continuance of an ancient feud and an appeal to 'honour', to seek out opportunities for violent action.

In *Romeo and Juliet* Shakespeare depicts the way in which a feud whose cause and significance are long forgotten energizes the urge to violence in the members and entourage of two households. Quarrelling and fighting are more exciting for servants than work, and relieve the boredom for their betters of having nothing to do other than walk the streets, make conversation, tease old women like the Nurse, or become a self-absorbed lover like Romeo. Men go armed and ready for action. The servants wear the livery of their households, and their masters may also be distinguished by dress, and perhaps by accent too, since Tybalt recognizes the masked Romeo as a Montague 'by his voice' (1.5.54). Whatever lip-service is paid to religion, the Montagues and Capulets cannot put an end to their mutual hatred and feuding. By giving the servants English names and accents, so that they might seem to an audience at home on the streets of London rather than Verona, Shakespeare created a play that speaks across the centuries to the recurrent feuding that is all too common in the present day, and that may still be manifested in antipathies and gang wars in modern cities.

Baz Luhrmann reworked *Romeo and Juliet* in the movie he made in 1995, publishing the filmscript in 1996.[11] The film is set in what can be read as contemporary Los Angeles or Miami, a major location being a run-down 'Verona Beach' (echoing such real names as Laguna Beach, as well as the Verona of Shakespeare's play). Much of the film was actually shot in Mexico City, which helped to provide the frequent religious imagery, like the huge statue of Christ seen in relation to the vast mansions that house the Montague and Capulet clans. The activities of the powerful families headed by Gloria and Fulgencio Capulet on the one hand, and Ted and Caroline Montague on the other are newsworthy in their city, so that the opening lines of the chorus are spoken through a television screen by an anchorwoman newscaster under the caption, 'Montague: Capulet. The feud continues.' The wealthy senior members of the two houses drive or are driven about in large limousines, accompanied by bodyguards, reminiscent of gangster movies – we never know how they have come by their riches. When the 'glass towers' of the Capulet and Montague houses are first seen, a squadron of helicopters commanded by Captain Prince of the police whizzes past. A square-jawed Dave Paris is featured on the cover of 'TIMELY' magazine as the 'Bachelor of the Year'. Early on we see Ted and Caroline Montague discussing Romeo in their limousine, and Peter, a servant of the Capulets, who attends the Nurse in the play, now appears as Gloria's chauffeur, announcing the arrival of guests (1.3.100). The scenes relating to the feast and dance at the Capulet mansion shift between a 'grand hall', a ballroom, a bathroom, a powder room, an elevator where Romeo and Juliet kiss, and Juliet's balcony above a swimming pool in a garden attended by a security guard with his dog. The setting of the action can thus be comfortably transformed into a modern city dominated by two families whose power is displayed in the neon signs of their names on their towers.

The young scions of the Capulets and Montagues relate more to the street-gangs of south-central Los Angeles as they carry guns and surge through city streets in fast cars. The opening confrontation between servants of the two houses, and between Benvolio and Tybalt, involves gunplay, takes place in a petrol-station, and ends with a conflagration as Tybalt's cigarette butt ignites a slick of petrol and the station goes up in flames. The riots appear to extend through the city, and their destructiveness is symbolized in the ruined cinema by the beach where Romeo hangs out. These are not, of course, impoverished black youths, but rather as in Shakespeare's play, bored youths from wealthy families with too much money and nothing to do. They reflect the gun culture of present-day America, and make shocking the incongruity of religious emblems in such a culture. On his first appearance Tybalt opens his black jacket to reveal the image of a Madonna and child on his T-shirt, even as he aims his gun at Benvolio and Gregory. As Romeo leaves the Capulet mansion at the end of the dance scene (1.5 in the play, pp. 60–1 in the screenplay), Mercutio joins him, handing him his gun, which he ignores, preoccupied as he is in gazing up at Juliet's window, so that Mercutio is left to take care of it; the camera then shows Juliet in close-up before panning on to the gun of Tybalt, who is watching. 'My only love, sprung from my only hate' (1.5.138) is spoken by Juliet costumed for the masque as an angel with wings, so that her words are exemplified in the visual context of religion and guns.

The appearance of Friar Laurence in 2.3 is prefaced by a vision of 'a monumental church crowned with a towering Madonna' (p. 73), and he is seen at work in a ramshackle greenhouse on the roof of it. In this scene he robes himself as a priest preparing for mass, and we glimpse a children's choir singing hymns. In 2.6 (p. 93) Friar Laurence is seen preaching from a pulpit as he speaks lines beginning 'The sweetest honey / Is loathsome in his own deliciousness', and marries Romeo and Juliet hurriedly after a prayer at the end of the service. After the death of Mercutio, stabbed with a shard of glass by Tybalt, the unarmed Romeo chases after the killer, who drops his gun when hit by a car; the gun lands at Romeo's feet, and he shoots Tybalt even as he is scrambling up the steps towards the huge monumental figure of Christ. Romeo's line 'O, I am fortune's fool!' (p. 111; 3.1.137) is spoken as he stares up at the statue of Christ. The outside and interior of the church are seen again in 4.1 (pp. 132–5), and then the sacristy, where Juliet pulls a gun on the Friar. In the final scenes of the film, Romeo is sought by Captain Prince in a helicopter, and by police in cars, who shoot at him as he forces his way through huge doors into the church. There 'hundreds of lit candles' surround a transparent tent shrouding the sleeping Juliet (p. 155), and when she awakes to find Romeo poisoned, she shoots herself with Romeo's gun. The camera pauses on the statue of the Madonna, then tracks over the church to the front steps as two stretchers are loaded into ambulances in the presence of police cars, 'media vans', and a crowd of onlookers.

The young Montagues and Capulets, accustomed to wealth and leisure, have nothing to do but drive about, and are first seen rioting at a petrol-station. They choose to spend time in the ruins of a demolished cinema at 'the grubby shore of Verona Beach, housing a collection of sex clubs and strip joints, populated with prostitutes, drag queens, clients, and street people' (p. 17), and in the nearby pool-hall. While Gloria and Fulgencio Capulet down champagne and whisky, the young drink beer and try drugs. They are deliberately rejecting the lifestyle of their seniors, which is reflected in the figure of Paris, who is described in 'TIMELY' magazine as having 'Excellent breeding, sums of love and wealth, absolute power and a good name' (p. 23). Mercutio appears in drag to shock everyone at the Capulets' ball and his Queen Mab speech on dreams is cleverly associated with hallucinatory drugs in a box of pills, one of which Romeo takes. The ball becomes for him a series of 'grotesque images of avaricious decadence' (p. 46) as the drug works on him, until he recovers by sticking his head in a basin of water. Romeo, costumed as King Arthur, draws Juliet, dressed as an angel, away from the dancing partner Gloria has thrust on her (Paris decked out, amusingly, as an astronaut), for the tenderness and religious imagery of their initial love scene. They embrace and kiss in an elevator, seeking privacy in the only place where they can be alone together. The grossness and wasteful display of the crowded ballroom scenes as witnessed through Romeo's point of view show why the young prefer to hang out around Verona Beach.

The symbolism of the costumes is too easy, with the angelic Juliet matched by Tybalt appearing as Lucifer, attended by servants dressed as demons; but the appearance of these characters, and especially that of Mercutio cavorting as a drag queen, exposes the absurdity and extravagance of the ball as an expression of the bad taste and misused wealth of the Montagues and Capulets. Their lifestyle is shown as artificial and focused on display compared with that of the underworld of the beach, or with the love that overwhelms Romeo and Juliet. Later, when Romeo has to leave town following the death of Tybalt, he flees, on the advice of Friar Laurence, to Mantua, which turns out to be a wasteland, a desert cluttered with trailer homes, such as may be found in parts of California. The desolation of the scene suggests Romeo's state of mind, as he lies in a trailer listening to music relayed on a Walkman$^{®}$, and so does not hear the knock of the postman who tries but fails to deliver the Friar's message. Balthasar arrives by car along the highway that stretches off into the distance, to tell Romeo that Juliet is dead, and Romeo jumps into the driver's seat as the car is seen speeding off. He is next seen back at Verona Beach, where he obtains poison from the owner of the pool-hall, and is spotted from a police car as he leaves the building. After a brief car-chase, Romeo jumps out and runs to the church, with police in pursuit of him. From the police point of view Romeo is just another criminal from the beach area.

In his film of *Romeo and Juliet* Baz Luhrmann sees the play not simply as a timeless tragic love story, but as concerned with the inescapable violence that recurs in what we think of as civilized society. The antagonism between the followers of the Capulets and Montagues, who are identified by the colours of the livery they wear, has no rational basis, but has become a matter of displaying toughness and insisting on superiority for Gregory and Sampson, the Capulet servants, in the opening scene; Sampson will in sheer bravado 'take the wall of any man or maid of Montague's' (p. 2; 1.1.12). Such aggressive behaviour and demonization of others was common enough in Shakespeare's age, and continues in the present time in, for example, the rivalries between crowds of soccer fans, who also often wear the colours of their team, Manchester United as against Liverpool, Rangers as against Celtic, and may come to blows for no other reason than to assert dominance. More immediately, in relation to Los Angeles, the film makes its viewers think of the notorious violence

of rival street-gangs mainly in the south-central areas of the city. The
Capulets and Montagues are of the same faith, and St Peter's church is
a visual presence in the film, but their quarrel seems to anticipate also
such civil violence as is practised in Northern Ireland in the name of
a religion that is based on love. The two powerful families in the film
are emblematized visually in their houses, huge structures which suggest
corporate business empires in ruthless competition in a modern urban
environment; Ted and Caroline Montague could be an old WASP family,
while Gloria and Fulgencio Capulet, with their black-clothed and sinister
henchman Tybalt, could be thought of in terms of a Mafia link.[12] Wealth
does not bring peace or happiness, as Gloria and Fulgencio take to drink,
while their male followers and heirs spend their time driving at speed,
playing pool, drinking, trying drugs, and quarrelling. The film ends as it
begins, with the image of a TV anchorwoman who speaks the last speech
of the Prince in the play. On the final couplet,

For never was a story of more woe
Than this of Juliet and her Romeo,

she 'changes beat to the next story' as her voice fades out (p. 162). The
news of the death of the lovers will give way to other stories on television,
and many of these will be of the same kind, reporting more outbreaks of
murder and mayhem on the city streets.

  The film retains Shakespeare's language in most of the dialogue
though the play is heavily cut, and adds visual allusions that, so to speak,
update the text. Shakespeare's swords become guns, but in close-up
Benvolio's gun is labelled 'Sword 9mm Series 5', and Capulet reaches
for a 'long sword' (1.1.75) that in the film becomes his rifle, labelled
'Longsword', mounted on his car. This visual representation of words
helps to integrate ancient and modern: Shakespeare's play and the
modern world. It has been argued that the film marks its fidelity to
Shakespeare even as it at the same time points up its distance from
Shakespeare's text,[13] but this is not the way I experience the movie;
these visual devices are there to help make *Romeo and Juliet* accessible
to the pre-teen and teenage culture of America. It is as if the play were
remade for MTV. It is introduced by an anchorwoman for a TV news
channel, the police hover in their noisy helicopters over a cityscape with
cars screaming violently through the streets, and the film is littered with
ubiquitous pop magazines, advertising, and religious images reduced
to 'fashion statements, corporate accessories, features of everyday design and expressions of extreme spiritual devotion; they are so full of

meaning yet so ubiquitous as to be virtually meaningless'.[14] Romeo and Juliet die in a huge cavernous church lit with masses of candles and bluish neon-lit crosses, where she puts his gun to her head to kill herself as the police chief, Captain Prince, bursts through the door. The setting is so overblown as to turn the splendid tomb where the lovers lie into a shrine fitting a pop idol, a sentimental gesture in a society where Christian images are everywhere, but their message ignored in the violence of daily life. The filmscript was published together with the text of the play as 'The contemporary film. The classic play. William Shakespeare's Romeo & Juliet' in 'Hodder's Children's Books' (UK) and 'Dell Books for Young Readers' (USA). In a prefatory note Luhrmann does not appear to have children in mind in promoting the film by saying that everything in the movie was drawn from Shakespeare, 'violence, murder, lust, love, poison, drugs that mimic death, it's all there'. In fact, he gave his young audiences an innocent-seeming and somewhat androgynous hero and a delicate heroine they could identify with as yearning for a private space; they want to be different from the rest in a world where too many adults and parents are dedicated to wealth and greed, and male youths are focused on violence and drugs.[15]

The films of both *Romeo and Juliet* and *Richard III* bring out a continuing significance of the plays as concerned with recurrent and endemic forms of violence. The film of *Richard III* focuses on a figure who enjoys the violence he uses to achieve power in a corrupt society, and who can be reinterpreted in association with the twentieth-century dictator, the fascist politician, the gangster, and the serial killer of modern times. In *Romeo and Juliet* violence breaks out spontaneously, it seems, for although any cause for hostility between the Capulets and Montagues is buried in history and is no longer remembered, the mindset of the young of both houses and their followers guarantees that bloodshed will continue. The lost historical cause in effect becomes an excuse for them to do what they want to do and indulge in the competitive verbal and physical hostilities that give them excitement. The play shows the terrible consequences such violence can have for those who need to escape from it, and offers no prospect that the cycle of violence will be halted. Both plays depict societies that pay lip-service to a Christian religion that has little bearing on how men and women act. The unworldly Archbishop in *Richard III* is largely ornamental, while the extravagant display of visual reminders of Catholic practices in the film of *Romeo and Juliet*[16] provides an ironic counterpoint to the violent behaviour of a self-destructive society. Both plays and films are relevant not only to our times, but arguably to the human condition, as archetypal treatments of the problem of violence as the expression of something inevitable in human society. We can identify with the lovers as victims of the violence that is generated by their society, and with Richard because he cheerfully does away with a series of corrupt figures who are little better than he is, and we can vicariously indulge our own violent instincts through him. The film adds another dimension in portraying him as a personality, a star, established so by the media, who stages his own last performance to match that of James Cagney as Cody Jarrett in *White Heat*, a tribute to the power of Hollywood in sustaining the myths of violence that haunt our society.

These films successfully use Shakespeare's language, but in severely truncating each text and inventing powerful visual images they transform the original play while finding striking modern analogies for the dramatic action. Prior to the making of these films both *Richard III* and *Romeo and Juliet* had been staged with modern settings and costumes, the former with reference to twentieth-century forms of tyranny, the latter with reference to motor-cycle gangs. The films by Baz Luhrmann and Richard Loncraine go much further in showing how incisively these plays connect with the problem of violence in its most troubling twentieth-century manifestations. *Richard III* can be related both to the emergence of the serial killer, so bearing on the contemporary concern with violent crime, and the emergence of ruthless dictators who succeed in imposing their image and their forms of terror on entire peoples. If this play focuses on a charismatic individual, the feud between the Montagues and Capulets in *Romeo and Juliet* can be linked to warring street-gangs in modern cities, and, on a larger scale, to societies and countries where conflicts based on religious, ethnic, or other animosities provoke recurrent violence. So, although the films I have been discussing alter, diminish, and omit aspects of the plays as Shakespeare wrote them, nevertheless they constitute interpretations that succeed in translating into visual terms one of his basic preoccupations, which was with the problem of human violence.

NOTES

1. In an interview in 1966 reported in the *New York Times*, Olivier said of his stage performance, 'There was Hitler across the way, one was playing it definitely as a paranoiac'; this is cited by Constance Brown in her essay on the film in *Film Quarterly*, 20 (1967), 23–32, reprinted in Charles W. Eckert, ed., *Focus on Shakespearean Films* (Englewood Cliffs, N.J., 1972), 130–45, citing 132.

2. Jack J. Jorgens, *Shakespeare on Film* (Bloomington: University of Indiana Press, 1977), 86.

3. The action of the film *West Side Story* (1961), based on *Romeo and Juliet*, pitched rival gangs of white and Puerto Rican immigrant youths against one another in twentieth-century New York. The movie focuses narrowly on two groups of teenagers, and street violence is softened when presented as ballet or in song and dance routines. Baz Luhrmann, however, was by no means the first to perceive the relevance of the Romeo and Juliet story to city life in the modern world.

4. Ian McKellen, *William Shakespeare's Richard III*, a screenplay by Ian McKellen and Richard Loncraine (Woodstock, N.Y.: Overlook Press, 1996), 47. Subsequent page references are to this edition.

5. As noted by James N. Loehlin in ' "Top of the World, Ma": *Richard III* and Cinematic Convention', in Lynda E. Boose and Richard Burt, eds., *Shakespeare, the Movie: Popularizing the Plays on Film, TV, and Video* (London and New York: Routledge, 1997), 67–79, especially 69.

6. In 'Looking at Shakespeare's Women on Film', in Russell Jackson, ed., *The Cambridge Companion to Shakespeare on Film* (Cambridge University Press, 2000), 241–60, Carol Chillington Rutter argues that the film 'locates in women's voices the only source of moral opposition to his [Richard's] nihilistic agency' (citing 248). I think this is an exaggeration, but it draws attention to the importance of women in the film.

7. See Loehlin, ' "Top of the World, Ma" ', 75–7.

8. *Ibid.*, 74.

9. *Ibid.*

10. For a discussion of Richard's ambiguous sexuality in the film, and his inability to provide for a Yorkist succession to the throne, see Steven M. Buhler, 'Camp *Richard III* and the Burdens of (Stage/Film) History', in Mark Thornton Burnett and Ramona Wray, eds., *Shakespeare, Film, Fin de Siècle* (Basingstoke: Macmillan; New York: St Martin's Press, 2000), 40–57.

11. Page references are to *William Shakespeare's Romeo & Juliet*, screenplay by Craig Pearce and Baz Luhrmann (New York: Bantam Doubleday, 1996; London: Hodder Children's Books, 1997).

12. Barbara Hodgdon sees Capulet as representing Mediterranean old world, and Montague as affiliated with 'old money'; she thinks the Capulet boys 'inhabit a New World Latino culture'. See her interesting essay, 'William Shakespeare's *Romeo + Juliet*. Everything's Nice in America?', *Shakespeare Survey*, 52 (1999), 88–98, citing 95.

13. W. B. Worthen, 'Drama, Performativity, and Performance', *PMLA*, 113 (1998), 1093–1107, citing 1104.

14. Philippa Hawker, 'DiCaprio, DiCaprio, Wherefore art thou, DiCaprio?', *Meanjin* (March, 1997), 6–16, citing 14; my attention was drawn to this article by Courtney Lehmann, 'Strictly Shakespeare? Dead Letters, Ghostly Fathers, and the Cultural Pathology of Authorship in Baz Luhrmann's *William Shakespeare's Romeo + Juliet*', *Shakespeare Quarterly*, 52 (2001), 189–221.

15. James N. Loehlin, noting many allusions to earlier movies in Baz Luhrmann's *Romeo and Juliet*, relates it to a string of teenage films produced since the 1950s (including *West Side Story*; see note 3 above), films in which young lovers 'resist the corrupt values of their parents and so fall victim to a violent and uncaring society'. These links are important, and help to explain the appeal of Luhrmann's film to teenagers, who may well have responded to it as a 'love story for a generation that can't imagine a future'. However, Luhrmann's youth gangs are themselves also violent and uncaring, addicted to drugs and guns, their violence breeding yet more violence. See '"These violent delights have violent ends": Baz Luhrmann's Millennial Shakespeare', in *Shakespeare, Film, Fin de Siècle*, 121–36, especially 121–3 and 129.

16. These reminders include the red cross superimposed on a small ampersand in the title of the film, a cross reminding us of the star-crossed lovers, the cross of Jesus, images of which recur in the movie, and the blood so often shed in the action. The cross does not appear in the title of the screenplay as printed. For speculation about the 'politics of appropriation' involved in Luhrmann's title, see Courtney Lehmann, 'Strictly Shakespeare?', 189–97.

CHAPTER 5

Shakespeare on war: King John *to* Henry V

In this chapter I am concerned with Shakespeare's deepening interest in violence in his later history plays, written between about 1596 and 1599. These plays differ from the *Henry VI* plays and *Richard III* in being more concerned with issues than with events, and among these issues the problem of violence is prominent, but dramatized as inextricably bound up with politics, war, and the problems of kingship. Shakespeare seems especially interested in the role of the soldier in peace and in war, in the pursuit of 'honour' as both fame (reputation) and virtue, and, especially in *Henry V*, in the emerging question whether there can be a just war. I leave aside *Richard II*, which differs from the others in its distancing, in the pageantry and ritual that mark its medieval atmosphere, whereas the play-world of the other histories connects directly with the world of the audience, as in the prose tavern and low-life scenes in *Henry IV*. Historically the reign of Henry followed that of Richard, and Henry is shadowed in both parts of *Henry IV* by his sense of guilt for deposing Richard. In other respects, however, *Richard II* seems more remote from *Henry IV* than *King John*, a play which is thematically closer to *Henry IV* and *Henry V* in dealing, not in the end very satisfactorily, with issues of politics and war that become central in these later plays. Furthermore, in the character of the Bastard Faulconbridge Shakespeare, in this play too, provides a direct link with his audience. The date of *King John* is disputed, but it may well have been written in 1596, a little later than *Richard II*,[1] and the play may be taken as a starting point for Shakespeare's developing involvement in these history plays with issues related to violence.

MUDDLED PATRIOTISM IN *KING JOHN*

That 'good blunt fellow' (1.1.71), the Bastard Philip Faulconbridge, serves as a commentator and possibly authorial spokesman in *King John*, a chronicle play that struggles to find coherence in dealing with the sprawling history of an early medieval monarch who reigned from 1199 to 1216. The reign of King John figured prominently in the official homily against 'Disobedience and Wilful Rebellion' appointed to be read in churches from 1571 onwards, and in many other polemical tracts, because of his dispute with the Catholic Church in Rome and the civil wars that affected his last years. The play also is concerned with the legitimacy of John's claim to the throne and the problem of succession, issues that were topical in the 1590s.[2] At this point in his career, however, Shakespeare seems uncertain in his handling of these matters. The issue of succession erupts in the opening scene, in which Shakespeare suggests that John is king by 'strong possession' rather than by right (1.1.40), a right which by implication belongs to his nephew Arthur, son of his elder brother Geoffrey. John's right is then set teasingly in relation to the rights of the two brothers, Robert and Philip Faulconbridge, the younger, Robert, being legitimate, the elder, Philip, illegitimate, the bastard son of Richard I, Coeur de Lion. Their dispute is resolved by giving Philip recognition as a knight and the name of his father, Richard, while Robert keeps the inheritance of his father's lands. But Shakespeare seems less interested in this initial question of legitimacy for itself than as a means to establish the Bastard as a central figure in the play.

When King John resolves the dispute between Robert and Philip, the dialogue marking the ceremony of converting Philip into Sir Richard is given formality by rhyming lines, and after it the Bastard, as the stage-directions continue to call him, is left alone for the first of the informal soliloquies that give him special prominence. In it he mocks his new status by parodying conversation to suit 'the age's tooth', which is to say, the chit-chat expected of a man about town in Shakespeare's and the audience's London:

'O sir', says answer, 'at your best command,
At your employment, at your service, sir'.
'No, sir', says question, 'I, sweet sir, at yours';
And so, ere answer knows what question would,
Saving in dialogue of compliment,
And talking of the Alps and Apennines,
The Pyrenean and the river Po,
It draws toward supper in conclusion so.
                              (1.1.197–204)

The Bastard sketches what he mockingly calls a 'worshipful society' (1.1.205) devoted to observing others, concerned with 'exterior form', and practised in affectation, as in their talk of travel. So he establishes at

once his credentials, vigour, honesty, and lack of self-importance, characteristics that set him apart in a court where he can say what he pleases,
as being at once of the royal blood and of no consequence.

He has promised to follow John and his mother Eleanor to France
to fight for them, and the action switches to Angers for a sequence of
scenes that turn the siege of that city, taken rapidly by John according to
the chronicles, into a protracted affair and an occasion for a good many
formal speeches that put off for a time the inevitable war. Shakespeare
created two unhistorical figures in this sequence, Hubert, a leading citizen
of Angers who becomes a supporter of John and his agent in relation
to Arthur, and the Duke of Austria, who sports a lion-skin and was
responsible for the death of King Richard according to Philip of France
(2.1.5). Hubert is necessary to carry on the machinations involving Arthur
and the matter of John's legitimacy, which lead to Arthur's death in Act 4.
Austria is necessary to provide a foil for the Bastard. The Duke of Austria
who took Richard prisoner in fact died in 1194, some years before the
siege of Angers, and he had nothing to do with the death of Richard. His
lion-skin is a somewhat absurd emblem of his warlike nature, and he is
in France to fight for the right of Arthur, claiming:

The peace of heaven is theirs that lift their swords
In such a just and charitable war. (2.1.35–6)

It is, of course, by no means clear which side is in the right, and the war
is postponed while the two kings, Philip of France and John of England,
make formal speeches demanding the allegiance of the city, and the two
formidable women, Constance, mother of Arthur, and Eleanor, mother
of John, snarl at one another. An indecisive battle between the French
and English leaves both claiming right to the city, at which point Hubert
craftily proposes a solution – create Arthur Duke of Brittany, let Blanche,
John's niece, marry Louis the Dauphin, and so patch up the quarrel, and
the town will open its gates. Louis produces a lover's speech to order, and
the match is arranged, with John giving away most of his lands in France
as a dowry.

The Bastard sees through the diplomatic talk and Hubert's craftiness,
setting blows in opposition to words:

Our ears are cudgelled; not a word of his
But buffets better than a fist of France.
Zounds, I was never so bethumped with words
Since I first called my brother's father dad.
                    (2.1.464–7)

He is for simple solutions, for settling affairs by violence, but here he acknowledges the power of words to work just as well as blows. At the same time, he sees how words may complicate matters, mislead, or conceal hypocrisy, and how the arrangement proposed by Hubert smacks of expediency. The whole sequence thus leads towards the Bastard's famous soliloquy on 'commodity' when he is left onstage at the end. He plays upon this word, which he associates with what we now call the profit-motive, the hope of gaining an advantage, that, like the bias that determines the run in a game of bowls, sways people to give up 'all direction, purpose, course, intent' (2.1.580). It has caused the French to abandon an 'honourable war' (585) fought for conscience and God, and perversely it has caused King John to surrender most of his French possessions. As a 'beggar' himself, the Bastard knows it is easy to abuse the rich, and he is not simply being virtuous, since he hasn't yet been tempted; but what underlies his powerful speech is a Shakespearean wariness about negotiation and policy. All the formalities and ritual exchanges of kings and heralds he sees as screening political solutions made for self-interest, and the possibility of fighting a 'just' or 'honourable' war in good conscience appears much more attractive.

However, this idea is quickly subverted by the intervention of Pandulph, raised in the play from Bishop of Norwich to the rank of Cardinal and, as papal legate, given authority to stir up a different quarrel between the French and English, over John's refusal to accept Stephen Langton as Archbishop of Canterbury. The offence is to the Church, but, having excommunicated John, Pandulph urges Philip of France to put his vow to heaven before his promise to John, and make war as 'the champion of our church' (3.1.181). So on Blanche's wedding day, when her loyalties are torn between her husband and uncle, and between her father and grandmother, war is resumed, and the Bastard at last gets to fight with the Duke of Austria, after provoking him whenever the chance has offered itself. Some skirmishes may have been staged, but the main visual impact of the war is the Bastard's entry when he unceremoniously dumps a property head on the stage with the remark: 'Austria's head lie there' (3.2.3). King John enters with the captured Arthur, and does not seem to notice the severed head, simply calling on the Bastard to get back to the fight. After more skirmishes John returns and sends the Bastard off to England to collect money for him from the monasteries. This dismissal of the Bastard, who oddly goes willingly, and the reduction of him to a tax-collector is curious. His entry in conquest with Austria's head comes roughly at the midpoint of the play's action, and marks his triumph in war on behalf of John. The property head seems there to divert the audience, and no comment is needed to identify it also as an emblem of the brutal violence of warfare.[3] Up to this moment in the action the straightforward bluntness of the Bastard has countered the expediency and sophistry of the political negotiations between the French and the English courts, but when he carries on his grim trophy of a head he exposes the horrific limitations of a preference for war over diplomacy. From this point on his role dwindles almost to vanishing point until the final scenes of the play.

It is Constance, grieving mother of Arthur, who now becomes a foil to the politicians characterized by their chilly indifference to suffering or concern only for 'commodity', for what is politically advantageous. Her genuine passion for her endangered son contrasts with the devious calculations not only of the French, but also of Cardinal Pandulph, who explains to Louis the Dauphin why the death of Arthur would work to his benefit by stirring up revolt in England, and of John, who tries to persuade Hubert to murder him. Constance knows that Arthur must die for John to feel safe on his throne, and Shakespeare makes the most of the threat of torture and violence and the pathos of the boy's expressions of love for his keeper as Hubert makes preparations to blind the boy with hot irons. In 4.1 executioners twice enter with instruments of torture, the second time bringing on, presumably, a brazier of red-hot coals that cool as Arthur distracts Hubert with his talk. Shakespeare exploits the visual impact of the threat of torture, and then, in 4.3, the spectacle of the death of Arthur as he leaps from the 'wall' of his prison and dies onstage. The scenes involving Arthur are drawn out to show the casual violence of the world of the play, as well as to provoke both the anger of the nobles and King John's temporary repentance when they believe Arthur has been murdered. John's main concern is to win over his nobles again and deal with a French invasion; once he thinks Arthur lives, he loses interest in him, and is concerned only with the use to which the news can be put. This sequence is largely Shakespeare's invention, and forms a somewhat unconvincing bridge between events in the early years of John's reign and the rebellion and war that brought it to an end. The Bastard reappears to prevent the nobles from attacking Hubert, whom they believe to be responsible for Arthur's death, and both Constance and Eleanor are reported to have died.

The removal of Arthur and the strong, emotional female characters permits a shift back to conditions that in some ways parallel those of Act 2, in a final act that again shows swift changes in policy effected

for expediency, as when John yields his crown up to Pandulph and acknowledges the authority of the Pope in the hope that the Cardinal
will persuade the Dauphin to abandon his invasion of England. The
Bastard is restored to prominence at the end of Act 4, when, after failing
to calm the anger of the nobles, he is given a prescient soliloquy anticipating the 'imminent decay of wrested pomp', the decay of King John
who, with the death of Arthur, appears to have taken or 'wrested' power
by force. Just as in his speech on commodity at the end of Act 2, the
Bastard again reflects on the world from an independent standpoint; in
the earlier soliloquy he criticizes both the French and English kings and
the agreement (composition) they have cobbled together, 'Mad world,
mad kings, mad composition!' At the end of Act 4, with the nobles going
over to the invading French, and Arthur dead, he cries:

I am amazed, methinks, and lose my way
Among the thorns and dangers of this world.
                    (4.3.140–1)

England, he says, is 'left / To tug and scramble' in civil war, and heaven
frowns on the land. Even so, he remains loyal to John, and when
Pandulph's devious attempts to restrain the French fail, he takes charge
of the king's business and his forces. He welcomes the prospect of battle
with the Dauphin, and makes a rousing patriotic speech anticipating
Henry V and depicting John as a 'gallant monarch' in arms and poised
'like an eagle' to strike invaders of his nest (5.2.148–50). In fact John is
sick, and shortly dies, poisoned by a monk, while the French give up the
fight when they learn their supply ships have been wrecked. When the
English nobles in turn discover that the Dauphin plans to execute them
if he wins the battle, they return to support John. The oath of allegiance
to France, sworn upon the sacrament, and which Salisbury said 'never
shall be broken' (5.2.8), is proved to be worthless, like other promises and
political deals in the play. This emphasis on deviousness, on a dominat-
ing concern with expediency and self-interest (commodity), leaves only
the boy Arthur unscathed.

The Bastard, it has been said, 'is the most prominent character in the
work but arguably less a coherent fictional figure than a series of dis-
continuous theatrical functions'.[4] Hardly a series, I think, but certainly
the Bastard changes shape between the early and later parts of the play.
In the first part of the play, up to his killing of Austria in 3.2, he has
a swashbuckling independence seen in his sardonic comments on the
negotiations between the French and English. His scorn of 'commodity'

makes it impossible to take seriously his final words in the speech, 'Gain, be my lord, for I will worship thee!' (2.1.599). But then he is offstage for about five hundred lines when he is sent to extort money from monasteries for John, thus provoking the monk who poisons the king. He becomes a negotiator like the rest as he tries to pacify the nobles, and at the end he behaves like Kent in *King Lear* in the dog-like loyalty shown in his desire to follow his master, John, in death, and wait on him to heaven (5.7.70–3). In the first part of the play he stands for the prowess of England, and, in the years following the Armada, no doubt found a ready sympathy in audiences. In the later part of the play he is narrowed down to become the loyal servant of a dubious monarch. He becomes momentarily his old self again for the play's final lines, with its rousing patriotic appeal:

This England never did, nor never shall,
Lie at the proud foot of a conqueror
But when it first did help to wound itself.
Now these her princes are come home again,
Come the three corners of the world in arms
And we shall shock them!

The Bastard, 'Brave soldier' (5.6.13), is surely meant to be in armour here, and resume his image as a kind of St George. His words no doubt had a topical resonance in relation to threats of invasion and anxieties about rebellion, and form a neat coda to the play, though they strike a gratuitous note of propaganda, and have little to do with the Bastard of the late scenes.

The Bastard is intriguing as Shakespeare's creation, as a character who is at once the 'most prominent' and somehow out of place. He descends in part from 'brave Talbot' in *Henry VI*, the dedicated patriotic soldier, and he has the satirical impudence of the Vice figure in morality plays. He also possesses the independence of illegitimacy combined with the stature of royal connections. Shakespeare outlines in Faulconbridge a more complex character than Talbot, but the constraints of the main plot do not allow the Bastard to develop, and he is given no female connection, such as Talbot has with the Countess of Auvergne. Furthermore, in a play concerned mainly with the unprincipled manoeuvrings of princes and prelates his prowess as a soldier is largely irrelevant. His one moment of triumph, the overcoming of the Duke of Austria, is ignored by King John, for whom the capture of Arthur is all that matters; and when the French invade at the end the Bastard has no chance to show his courage in the field, for he is hardly involved in the battle scenes (5.3 to 5.5); in any case the French withdraw when 'almost lords' of the field (5.5.8), and the Bastard's army is drowned in the Wash. The Bastard is curiously dissociated from any valuation of his soldiership, which is marginalized in relation to the political scheming that forms the play's main action. However, it could be that the problems Shakespeare encountered in *King John* prompted him to realize more interesting and powerful ways to relate the spheres of politics and of war in his later history plays. The Bastard splits into Hotspur on the one hand and Falstaff on the other.

MODEL WARRIORS AND MODEL RULERS IN *HENRY IV*

Henry IV, Part 1 begins with a king shaken by 'civil butchery' and threats from Wales and Scotland, but the focus in this play is on rebellion, not on political dealing, and culminates in the clash of worthy adversaries, Hotspur and Prince Hal. Their conflict turns on the value of 'honour', a term that carries a range of implications. It is first heard in the mouth of the King when he praises Hotspur, who has won a great victory over the Scots, as 'the theme of honour's tongue' (1.1.80); here the word means good report or fame – everyone will be talking about his prowess in battle. This is the honour Hotspur seeks, gained in facing enemies and fighting, and his hyperbolic ideal, as he imagines great exploits, is to become the Muhammad Ali of warriors, and 'wear/Without corrival all her dignities' (1.3.205). It is an ideal later embodied and questioned by Shakespeare in his creation of Coriolanus. His aspiration is expressed in images at once touching and absurd:

> By heaven, methinks it were an easy leap
> To pluck bright honour from the pale-faced moon,
> Or dive into the bottom of the deep,
> Where fathom-line could never touch the ground,
> And pluck up drowned honour by the locks,
> So he that doth redeem her thence might wear
> Without corrival all her dignities. (1.3.199–205)

The imagery is extravagant, but his ebullient overconfidence in his ability to do the impossible speaks from the heart, and his youthful ambition (Shakespeare makes him an 'infant warrior' at 3.2.113, though historically he was older than Henry IV and twenty-three years older than Hal) to outdo all rivals draws sympathy in the same way that aspirants for gold medals in the Olympics are applauded. Indeed, Hotspur sees war as a kind of game and ends the scene with the hope

O, let the hours be short
Till fields and blows and groans applaud our sport.
(1.3.295–6)

Violence is Hotspur's way of life, and the discordance in the image of battlefields and groans applauding carnage as 'sport' brings home the disregard for life in Hotspur's notion of honour; for him it is sport to kill and maim.

What then of Prince Hal? 'Riot and dishonour stain the brow / Of my young Harry' (1.1.84–5), says the King, so that Hal's riotous or wasteful living and bad report give him a reputation opposite to that of Hotspur. And, of course, it is justified. Hal's idea of 'sport' is to participate in the robbery set up by Gadshill, and expose Falstaff's haste in running away from a fight. The scene shows four rich travellers being bound and robbed, followed by Hal and Poins attacking Falstaff and his companions. This too is a violent sport, if no deaths result. The success of this practical joke on Falstaff is celebrated by a pepped-up Hal in the Eastcheap tavern, the setting of 2.4. This scene begins with the teasing of the drawer Francis. Hal, excited to be on Christian-name terms with barmen, enlists the help of Poins in another practical joke, making a fool of Francis by confusing him with questions he is not given a chance to answer properly, and summoning him at once from two directions. Shakespeare's basic purpose in this episode may have been to show Hal's ability to hobnob with common people, to 'sound the very bass string of humility', but the treatment of Francis hardly shows Hal as 'the king of courtesy', for we watch him humiliate the poor tapster by talking over his head, and dismissing him at last, 'Away, you rogue', to meet the anger of his master the vintner. There is something disturbing about the representation of Hal in this episode, and I think it has to do with a difficulty in Shakespeare's conception.

One common view of Prince Hal places him as holding a balance between Hotspur as 'the excess and Falstaff the defect of military spirit; the former represents exaggerated honour, the latter dishonour'.[5] But for King Henry, Hal is the embodiment of dishonour, and Shakespeare has to dig him out of that pit so that he can eventually be transformed into the top soldier and take all Hotspur's 'proud titles' (5.4.78). In order to do this, he provides Hal with irresponsible companions in Falstaff, Bardolph, and Peto who have no interest in honour at all, so that measured against them Hal will be seen as much better than his father's estimation. But Hal has to be shown as thoroughly enjoying their friendship, and as affectionate especially towards Falstaff, who threatens in his comic splendour to dominate, while at the same time the Prince remains consciously aloof. Hence his soliloquy at the end of 1.2, 'I know you all, and will awhile uphold / The unyoked humour of your idleness'; his words, addressed as much to the audience as to Falstaff and his associates, who are offstage, can seem chilling, especially as they come at the end of a scene in which Falstaff's opening question, 'Now, Hal, what time of day is it lad?', signals an informality and affection in his relationship with a prince that breaks down the barriers of decorum. Shakespeare also wanted to indicate that Hal would 'redeem', or make amends for the time he has been wasting, and keeps reminding the audience, by such episodes as the taunting of Francis, that Hal is at once on the closest terms with, and at the same time consciously superior to, his companions. Hal has to be calculating, and Hotspur is in some ways more attractive because he can speak from the heart, having no need to 'redeem' the military honour he has earned.

Hal devotes himself to Falstaff, who serves both as a substitute father and as a surrogate lover. At the same time Hal has somehow to show the toughness that will prove him supreme in battle. Hal may boast to his father in 3.2 that he will win glory in conquering Hotspur, but he remains 'truant to chivalry' (5.1.94). His transformation into a soldier, leaping into his saddle 'like feathered Mercury' (4.1.106), insofar as it is convincing, is supported by Hal's callousness towards his followers, his readiness to ditch 'plump Jack', his part in driving off Falstaff and the rest after the Rochester robbery, and his humiliation of Francis. But Hal remains a problematic figure because he has to represent two contradictory sets of values. His father is right to see him as embodying dishonour in contrast to Hotspur, and it is a condition from which he can be rescued only by something like a conversion. Falstaff is the fool at the prince's elbow, fulfilling the role of jester by mocking at authority, at the lineage of a house with a dubious claim to the throne, and at 'honour' itself, so exposing the solemnities of the king and his troubles to a healthy and purgative laughter. His orgies have a kind of innocence in them, the innocence of a reveller celebrating the exuberance of the human spirit in contrast to the cheerless burdened court. His misrule generates fun in contrast to the greater misrule in the state, and wasting time with him separates Hal from his father, symbolically releasing him from the taint of usurpation through his mockery of the façade of piety and righteousness Bolingbroke has to maintain as king.

Falstaff has nothing to do with honour, which is a concept he famously rejects: 'Give me life, which if I can save, so' (5.3.60–1). Honour in the play remains identified chiefly with success as a warrior in achieving what Hal calls 'noble deeds' (5.1.92) in combat, and in defending his father in battle he redeems his reputation, his 'lost opinion' (5.4.47). The play's action culminates in the long-anticipated encounter between Hal and Hotspur in the battle at Shrewsbury, and Shakespeare sardonically comments on, to some extent perhaps subverts, the identification of honour with fighting, not only in Falstaff's words, but in his staging of the death of Hotspur. For this takes place while the body of the apparently 'dead' Falstaff lies visible on the stage, killed by the Earl of Douglas. Hal is given a kind of farewell speech over the dead body, 'I could have better spared a better man' (5.4.103), before he exits and Falstaff rises to declare 'the better part of valour is discretion, in the which better part I have saved my life'. It is, of course, basically a comic device to have an actor 'die' and then spring to life again, like Bottom in *A Midsummer Night's Dream*, a device that heightens the audience's consciousness of the action as a stage-play in which all the 'dead' will rise again for applause. Falstaff's question about the 'dead' Hotspur, 'Why may he not rise as well as I?', extends the jokiness, reminding us that the inert Hotspur, too, will return to take a bow. The final encounter between Hotspur and Hal takes place after Falstaff appears to have been killed and before his rising up again, which effectively mocks the idea that 'honour' is worth the loss of 'brittle life'.

There seems no doubt that Shakespeare's sympathies in this play are with the aristocratic values of what Hal calls 'chivalry' (5.1.94), meaning knighthood or martial prowess, the word stemming from the French 'cheval' or horse. The critique of honour is not linked to a critique of violence. Hal's greatest practical joke on Falstaff is to procure him 'a charge of foot' (3.3.187), or infantry, and of the one hundred and fifty ragged 'scarecrows' he presses into service, 'not three' are left alive after the battle. If Falstaff's soliloquy in 4.2 describing his corrupt methods of recruitment would have had a topical appeal at a time when pressing men into military service was something of a scandal, Shakespeare casually wipes them out at Shrewsbury. More attention is given to the horses of Hal and Hotspur than to these foot-soldiers:

I saw young Harry with his beaver on,
His cushes on his thighs, gallantly armed,
Rise from the ground like feathered Mercury,
And vaulted with such ease into his seat
As if an angel dropped down from the clouds

To turn and wind a fiery Pegasus,
And win the world with noble horsemanship.
(4.1.104–10)

Come, let me taste my horse,
Who is to bear me like a thunderbolt
Against the bosom of the Prince of Wales...
(4.1.119–21)

When they eventually clash they are on foot, but the aura of chivalry recalls the trial by combat between Mowbray and Bolingbroke at the beginning of *Richard II*, where Richard hopes to see justice 'design the victor's chivalry'. Noble deeds in battle are certainly made more attractive than the calculating manipulations of politicians such as Henry and Worcester, and such deeds make better theatre, as a comparison of this play with *King John* shows. At the end Douglas, who has 'killed' Blunt onstage and others offstage before being captured, is set free by Hal:

His valours shown upon our crests today
Have taught us how to cherish such high deeds,
Even in the bosom of our adversaries.
(5.5.29–31)

Cherishing 'high deeds' overrides political considerations, and for all Shakespeare's concern with kingship and rebellion, and his splendid portrayal of the rebels and their dissensions, the play fittingly ends with the praise of valour and an endorsement of the violence that can be masked as chivalry.

If in this play Hal takes over from Hotspur as the prince of chivalry, in *Henry IV*, Part 2 he has no part in fighting, and has one scene with Falstaff (2.4) in which he is more observer than participant. Shakespeare makes him keep a low profile, so that he can emerge at the end of Act 4 to shed his 'wildness' (4.5.152) and show that he is ready to take on the Crown as a 'true inheritor', no longer contaminated by the usurpation of which his father is guilty, the 'indirect crooked ways' by which he became king. Part 1 focuses on youth, not only that of the 'infant warrior' Hotspur and his counterpart Hal, but that claimed by Falstaff, who cries as he robs rich merchants, 'they hate us youth... What, ye knaves, young men must live' (2.2.85, 90). Falstaff behaves like an ebullient and irresponsible youth. By contrast, Part 2 is an old person's play, in which the Lord Chief Justice, the Archbishop of York, old Northumberland, Henry IV, Ancient Pistol ('Ancient' in age as well as in rank, equivalent to 'Ensign'), Shallow, Silence, Doll Tearsheet, and the Hostess all belong with Falstaff in their sense of ageing. Falstaff is no longer Hal's constant companion, but is watched by him and Poins who aim to see him 'bestow himself tonight in his true colours' (2.2.163–4). Disguised as drawers, they see him as a 'withered elder' (2.4.258), so directing the audience's view of Falstaff with Doll on his knee:

FALSTAFF: I am old, I am old.
DOLL: I love thee better than I love e'er a scurvy young
    boy of them all. (2.4.271–3)

Shakespeare points up Falstaff's age in his first appearance, when he insults the Lord Chief Justice by harping on his age, earning the retort, 'Is not... every part about you blasted with antiquity?' In place of Hal, Falstaff is provided with a page as a companion, who mocks and exposes his master, serving as a visual reminder of his contrasting age as well as size.

The Falstaff of Part 2 is tetchy and quarrelsome, and no longer shielded by Hal from the law in the person of the Lord Chief Justice. He becomes the focus of violence in the play. He is now a military officer, accompanied by his ensign, Pistol, and Corporal Bardolph, all of whom go about armed. He is surrounded by new companions (Pistol, Doll, the Hostess) who help to emphasize not only his age, but his less attractive qualities. The Hostess accuses him of stabbing her (literally as well as figuratively in the act of sex), and he draws his sword on Fang and Snare, the bailiffs she employs to arrest him in 2.2. He drives Pistol out of the tavern, wounding him in the shoulder, in 2.4. The rebels who put together an army to meet the King's forces at Gaultree seem as disillusioned as King Henry, and there is none of the excited anticipation of battle found in Part 1. The war, in effect, is displaced on to Falstaff, who is summoned from the tavern to raise a company and fight for the king. Whereas in Part 1 he describes his method of recruiting soldiers in an amusing soliloquy, in Part 2 we see him and Bardolph misusing the King's press grossly as a way of making money in a scene that highlights his age in relation to Shallow and Silence, who recall an event of 'fifty-five year ago' (3.2.210). The soliloquy he is given this time reveals his contempt for Shallow and the plan to make more money out of him. No battle is fought in this play, for Prince John notoriously tricks the rebels into dismissing their forces while keeping his own intact, then promptly arrests and executes their leaders. The only fighting occurs somewhat oddly after this scene, when with the stage-direction 'Alarum. Excursions.', or some appearance of skirmishes, Falstaff encounters Sir John Coleville, who surrenders to him without a fight. Falstaff, as we might expect, arrives late at Gaultree for what seems to amount to a mopping-up operation after the rebellion is effectively quashed.

The very idea of war may be contaminated by associating it and valour with Falstaff (who claims to have defeated in Coleville a 'most furious knight and valorous enemy', 4.3.38–9). For the violence associated with him operates mainly outside the law, as we are reminded by the penultimate scene in the play in which Doll and the Hostess are arrested on the charge that 'the man is dead' whom they and Pistol beat. It is in this context that Prince Hal, sanitized by being separated from his old companions, dissociated from corruption, from war, and from the political deceptions practised by his brother Prince John, ascends to the throne, with a vision of ideal civil government under king, parliament, and good counsel:

Now call we our high court of parliament,
And let us choose such limbs of noble counsel
That the great body of our state may go
In equal rank with the best governed nation.
(5.2.134–7)

If there is a problem in the play, it is not in the representation of Falstaff, whose antiquity, corruption, and inclination to violence are consistently emphasized, so that his famous opening gambit, 'I am not only witty in myself but the cause that wit is in other men' (1.2.9–10), comes to seem a way of cheering himself up, since his wit is at once blunted by the good sense of the Lord Chief Justice. The problem is once again in Hal, who, as in Part 1, has to be transformed from a joker dressed as a tapster into a king full of responsibility. I do not think Shakespeare's attitude to violence changed, only that he found it dramatically convenient in Part 1 to elevate the idea of martial prowess and make Hal a model soldier, while in Part 2 it was necessary to associate violence with lawlessness so that Hal could be transformed into a model ruler.

HENRY V AND THE IDEA OF A JUST WAR

It is in *Henry V* that violence becomes a troublesome issue. Olivier's vision of the play as a national epic celebrating heroism in the face of immense odds, appropriate propaganda in World War II, has faded, to be replaced by a sense of Henry as an ambivalent, if not hypocritical, figure, and by a new historicist/cultural materialist emphasis on the ideological implications of what Stephen Greenblatt called 'a poetics of Elizabethan power'.[6] The play has been seen as offering an 'imaginary resolution' of the problem of Ireland, where the Earl of Essex, referred to in the Chorus to Act 5, had been sent in March 1599 by Queen Elizabeth I in the hope of settling affairs there. It may well be that 'if *Henry V* represents the fantasy of a successful Irish campaign, it also offers, from the very perspective of that project, a disquietingly excessive evocation of suffering and violence';[7] but the problem of violence does not depend on the ideological implications of contemporary troubles in Ireland, for it also emerges out of the different ways in which Shakespeare found it necessary to dramatize history in the two parts of *Henry IV*. As a warrior, the 'warlike Harry' (Prologue, 5) of *Henry V* is to assume the bearing of Mars, recalling not Prince Hal so much as Hotspur, that 'Mars in swaddling clothes' (*Henry IV*, Part 1, 3.2.112). Like Hotspur, he appears invincible, and relishes fighting against huge odds, five to one at Agincourt (4.3.22), crying 'The fewer men the greater share of honour':

But if it be a sin to covet honour,
I am the most offending soul alive.
No, faith, my coz, wish not a man from England.
God's peace, I would not lose so great an honour
As one man more, methinks, would share from me,
For the best hope I have. (4.3.28–33)

So Hotspur, the 'king of honour', as Douglas calls him, sees 'a lustre and more great opinion' in being outnumbered by the king's forces at Shrewsbury (*Henry IV*, Part 1, 4.1.10, 77). Like him, Henry V seeks glory, honour as undying fame, which is the burden of his St Crispin's Day speech.[8]

But Henry is also developed from the Prince Hal of *Henry IV*, Part 2, the sober youth who tries on his father's crown with a consciousness of a burden of responsibilities to come, who is kept removed from war, and who casts off civil disorder and corruption in the person of Falstaff. Shakespeare does a remarkable job in merging Hotspur as warrior and devotee of honour with Hal as responsible ruler, but the contradictions between the two cannot be fully reconciled. One means that Shakespeare adopted of bridging, or at least obscuring, the gap was to present Henry as 'the mirror of all Christian kings' (Chorus, Act 2). In previous history plays Church and State were shown in opposition, in the characters of the Archbishop of York in *Henry IV*, the Bishop of Carlisle in *Richard II*, and

Cardinal Pandulph in *King John*, but *Henry V* opens with bishops providing funding for and defending a monarch who can 'reason in divinity' (1.1.38). The bishops are anxious to scupper a bill that would deprive them of lands bequeathed to the Church, and their tactic is to offer a very large sum in cash to finance war with France. Some think we are meant to notice the 'venality' of their behaviour,[9] but dramatically the emphasis is on the mutual support of king and the 'holy church' of which he is a 'true lover' (1.1.23). The Archbishop of Canterbury proceeds to justify Henry's claim to the French throne by his long exposition of the history of the Salic Law, a speech that may seem largely incomprehensible in its genealogical detail to a modern audience, and was made comic in Olivier's film, but which importantly asserts biblical authority, citing the Book of Numbers, to justify Henry's invasion of France 'with right and conscience'.[10] From this point on Henry frequently appeals to God who, he assumes, is on his side. He expects to gain France 'by God's help' (1.2.223), an aid which seems confirmed when the treason of the Earl of Cambridge, Scroop, and Grey is discovered. In his powerful commentary on his erstwhile close friend Scroop, Henry depicts him as succumbing to the temptation of a devil in a repetition of the temptation of Adam: 'For this revolt of thine, methinks, is like / Another fall of man' (2.2.141–2). The traitors are sent off to be executed, the customary punishment by institutionalized violence, but also to 'damnation' (115) for their sins, which 'God justly hath discovered' (151); by implication, Henry's war is made to appear a just one in Christian terms. This episode confirms Henry in placing his forces in 'the hand of God' (2.2.191), and Shakespeare later gives Henry his fine speech intertwining the fame and remembrance he expects the battle of Agincourt to bring with the memory of the martyr St Crispin, on whose feastday it took place. So before the battle Henry can cheerfully cry, 'How thou pleasest, God, dispose the day!' (4.3.132), because he is confident that God will support the English. On learning of the huge French casualties as against the English losses of only twenty-nine in all,[11] Henry no less than four times in twenty lines gives the credit of victory to God, and calls for the canticle 'Te Deum laudamus' from the order for morning prayer, and Psalm 115, 'Non nobis, Domine', to be sung, both of which were to be found in the *Book of Common Prayer*. In the last act Henry sheds his eloquence to become a bluff, prosaic soldier wooing Katherine and bringing about a 'Christian-like accord' (5.2.345) between France and England.

If the victory of the English at Agincourt is made to appear in *Henry V* as something like a miracle wrought by God, the appeal of the play in the late 1590s had much to do also with the carnivalesque elements provided by the comic characters, especially Pistol. The title-page of the Quarto of 1600, based on an acting version of the play, advertises the play as showing Henry's 'battell fought at *Agin Court* in *France*. Togither with *Auncient Pistoll*'. The Quarto omits the choruses before each act, as well as the Irish and Scottish captains, and leaves out three scenes, including Henry's speech at Harfleur ('Once more unto the breach...', 3.1.); but it preserves most of the Archbishop's Salic Law speech, and significantly expands the role of Pistol. In the Quarto 4.3, the scene in which the French herald, Montjoy, comes to offer Henry the chance to avoid battle if he pays a ransom, is followed immediately by what in the Folio is 4.5, in which the French, in disarray, call for a last desperate charge against the English, and only then, by 4.4, the scene in which Pistol accepts the offer of 500 crowns (200 in the Folio) to spare the life of his prisoner, a French soldier. The transposition of these two scenes in the Quarto means that Pistol and his prisoner are onstage when the King enters with his nobles and other French prisoners in what is now conventionally 4.6. In this scene Henry hears the alarm sounded to warn of the renewed French onslaught, and gives the order 'Bid every soldier kill his prisoner', an order carried through offstage.[12] In the Folio, Pistol is not present, but in the Quarto he has the final word, when, after the king's prisoners have been taken offstage, he ostentatiously carries out the threat he had made in 4.4, cuts the throat of Monsieur Le Fer, and has the last word, 'Coup la gorge', echoing the threat he had made against Nym at 2.1.68.

This rearrangement of scenes to climax in a moment of shocking violence on stage could have been done by the acting company rather than by Shakespeare, and it is suggestive of what audiences looked for and enjoyed. As in *Henry IV*, Part 2, violence in action tends to be deflected away from the King and on to Falstaff's associates, Bardolph, Nym, and Pistol. Nym and Pistol each draw their swords three times, and Bardolph twice, on their first quarrelsome appearance in 1.2. The occasion, a matter of eight shillings, is trivial, and the effect comic, since, of course, their bravado disappears when they are required to fight the French in 3.2. By 3.6. Bardolph is condemned to die for stealing a worthless pax, or metal plate bearing a representation of the crucifixion or some other sacred subject, which was used by the priest to convey the kiss of peace to those attending mass. Then in a speech omitted from the Quarto, Falstaff's page, the boy who follows them, makes his final exit reporting that both Bardolph and Nym have been hanged. Pistol's career ends in ignominy when he is beaten and forced to eat a leek by Fluellen, but he survives, promising to steal to England and find a way to live by theft and by bragging of his service in the war. Though a survivor, he is thus much diminished, and his friends are all dead, including the Hostess, who has died of the pox. In their trivializing of violence, using it for robbery and pillage, or in petty quarrels and civil brawls, Pistol and his companions bear away the stigma attached to violence carried out for display or for corrupt purposes, in contrast to the violence of a war fought, as Henry claims, with the sanction of God.

In *King John* and in *Richard II* the succession to the throne is a central issue. The Bastard Faulconbridge stands for a martial heroism that is marginalized in an action concerned with political intrigues, and *Richard II* focuses on the self-destruction of Richard as he gives way to Bolingbroke. In *King John* it is the Duke of Austria, made ridiculous by wearing a lion-skin, and mocked by Faulconbridge, who claims to be in France to fight a just war on behalf of Arthur (2.1.36), and the question whether a war can be just is not pursued. Like some earlier histories, *Henry IV* deals mainly with civil war, and however sympathetically Hotspur or Falstaff, the forces of rebellion or misrule, are shown, order is restored in the end. *Henry V* thus set new dramatic challenges for Shakespeare in an action centrally concerned with an English king invading France and making war there. Whereas in the *Henry VI* plays Shakespeare seemed to relish opportunities for providing exciting spectacles of violence in the context mainly of civil wars and constant change, now in *Henry V* he could hardly avoid dealing with the problematics of Henry's war against France. Linking Henry continually with God, and claiming divine support for Henry as a 'Christian king' (1.2.242) helps to justify his actions. It now may seem odd that he claims to be invading France in God's name, and puts the blame on to the Dauphin for the deaths that will result:

But this all lies within the will of God,
To whom I do appeal, and in whose name
Tell you the Dauphin I am coming on
To venge me as I may, and to put forth
My rightful hand in a well-hallowed cause.
(1.2.290–4)

How can vengeance be linked with the 'will of God' and 'well-hallowed'? The answer can be found in the justifications for war that appeared in an age when England was continually engaged in or threatened by wars, and the lame or superannuated soldier was a common figure in the London streets.[13] In a typical tract, *The Trumpet of War* (1598), Stephen

Gosson appeals to the Old Testament, citing Exodus 15 on the over-throw of Pharaoh and his host: 'The Lord is a man of war.' He argues that war is justified by necessity: 'It may be just and necessary in two ways, the one is in defence of the innocent, the other is in revenge of injuries',[14] injuries that include hurt to the fame and honour of a prince. So Henry speaks of seeking revenge in God's name and demands that the French 'take mercy' on those who will suffer because of the war (2.4.103).

Yet twice in his speeches at Harfleur (once in the Quarto, which omits 3.1) Henry is given lines that vividly imagine the horror and butchery of war:

The fleshed soldier, rough and hard of heart,
In liberty of bloody hand shall range
With conscience wide as hell, mowing like grass
Your fresh fair virgins and your flowering infants.
What is it then to me if impious war,
Arrayed in flames like to the prince of fiends,
Do with his smirched complexion all fell feats
Enlinked to waste and desolation? (3.3.11–18)

Is this simply rhetoric designed to convince the Governor of the town that he will be 'guilty in defence' (43)? The lines now suggest a deeper, even perhaps a personal sense of the horror and futility of war, but this may to some extent reflect a modern sensitivity. For Shakespeare and his age war was explained as one way in which God scourged the sins of men; so Thomas Beard and others linked war with plagues, floods, and famine as signs of God's anger with corruption and sinfulness on earth. The evils of war were explained as 'the fruits of sin, the wages of sin, and the cause of sin',[15] thus allowing for a never-ending cycle of violence, as validated by such biblical texts as Leviticus 26.25, 'And I will bring a sword upon you, that shall avenge the quarrel of my covenant: and when ye are gathered together within your cities, I will send the pestilence among you; and ye shall be delivered into the hand of the enemy.' Such arguments also allowed any enemy to be demonized as unjust and sinful; so Stephen Gosson condemned Spain, presumably seduced by the devil,[16] for fighting unjust wars, while defending those conducted by Elizabeth as 'very charitable and just'. Henry's Harfleur speeches perhaps show no more than Shakespeare's familiarity with and exploitation of contemporary arguments that justified wars undertaken by England (punishment for sin), while condemning wars undertaken by enemies as unjust (the fruits of sin). Hence Henry's war against the

French is fought in the name of God, while if the French fight they will be 'guilty in defence' and engaged in an 'impious war'.

In his debate with the common soldiers, Williams and Bates, in Act 4, Henry asserts that his cause is 'just', and when Williams raises the question what 'if the cause be not good?', the king counters by expressing a common view when he says, 'War is his [God's] beadle, war is his vengeance; so that men are punished for before breach of the King's laws in the King's quarrel' (4.1.167–9). The anxiety of Williams that few men can die well in battle recalls Henry's Harfleur speech in 3.3, in which he invokes an image of soldiers running amok, of 'The blind and bloody soldier with foul hand' defiling women and murdering infants. At these points in the play the idea of war itself as impious is developed, and the gruesome vision of horrors, of naked infants 'spitted upon pikes' and so on, provides a sensational backdrop to the action of the play, something to engage the imagination of the audience. Speeches such as Henry's at Harfleur, like the order to kill his French prisoners, help to support arguments that the play displays contradictions and instabilities that subvert what is ostensibly a national epic of martial heroism. World War II brought home the horrors of modern warfare, so it is not surprising that many productions of the play in recent decades have emphasized violence in the play in order to question a simple acceptance of a heroic myth about Henry.[17] So, for example, when the treason of his former friends is revealed in 2.2, Henry has been made to attack Scroop physically and knock him to the floor. The bodies of the boys killed by French renegades, as reported by Fluellen in 4.7, may be brought onstage and displayed. The Boy who accompanies Bardolph and Pistol and who is presumably killed with the other boys has been carried on by Fluellen or, in Kenneth Branagh's film version (1989), in Henry's arms. The execution of Bardolph has often been staged, though this, too, is simply reported in the text (by the Boy in 4.4) as having taken place on the orders of Exeter. Branagh's film imitated Adrian Noble's 1984 production at the Royal Shakespeare Theatre in showing Bardolph executed, by garrotting, or by hanging (Branagh's film) in the presence of Henry.[18] In the most subtle effort to interpret *Henry V* as subverting its heroic values, Stephen Greenblatt argues that:

The play deftly registers every nuance of royal hypocrisy, ruthlessness, and bad faith – testing, in effect, the proposition that successful rule depends not upon sacredness but upon demonic violence – but it does so in the context of a celebration, a collective panegyric to 'This star of England', the charismatic leader who purges the commonwealth of its incorrigibles and forges the national state.[19]

This is an understandably jaundiced late twentieth-century reading of a play for an age that equates politics with hypocrisy and bad faith, and is anxious about the containment of subversive elements. But it is not Shakespeare's vision that Henry's rule depends on 'demonic violence'. Modern productions of *Henry V* may stage extensive violence, but the text does not, and Henry is shown in action as charismatic leader, not killing people. As in *Henry IV*, Part 2, violence is deflected away from the king and on to others, notably Pistol and Bardolph, and Fluellen, whose respect for the 'law of arms' establishes an idea of proper military conduct in the play. In this context Henry becomes angry for the first time in France (4.7.54), and takes reprisal upon the French who kill boys and steal: 'the king most worthily hath caused every soldier to cut his prisoner's throat. O, 'tis a gallant king!' (4.7.8–10). In this context, too, Fluellen beats and humiliates Pistol, the braggart who represents the opposite of the good soldier.

Greenblatt's argument seems built on some general anxiety about the nature of 'successful rule', but the play is not testing any proposition, nor is it confirming 'the Machiavellian hypothesis that princely power originates in force and fraud'.[20] All forms of power and modes of social control have always depended on the use or threat of force and it is absurd to think of the execution of traitors or the arrest by constables of the Hostess and Doll in *Henry IV*, Part 2 as 'demonic violence'. Shakespeare mythologizes Agincourt as a miraculous English victory, and, just as our own countries do in relation to enemies in the present day, demonizes the Other, in this case the French, whose fault it is ('you yourselves are cause', 3.3.19) if soldiers are given licence to 'imitate the action of the tiger' (3.1.6). Such demonizing is commonplace in English tracts on war that condemned the wars conducted by enemies such as Spain, finding their hostilities 'in the Indies, in Portingale, in Granada, in the low countries, in France, and against us to be uncharitable and unjust',[21] while God as 'a man of war' supported the English, smiting the Spanish, or French in Shakespeare's play, as he smote the Pharaoh and the Amalekites (Exodus 15, 17). Unruliness and subversion indeed have always harassed the agents of power, and it may be that originally the emergence of princely power was 'produced' by human urges to break fences and transgress rather than the other way round. In *Henry V* Shakespeare makes such unruliness funny, but also despicable, as tainted by a wanton violence manifested in quarrelling, boasting, and stealing, in contrast to a heroic concept of Henry's English war, valorized as divinely sanctioned rather than demonic.

Henry, it has been said, is shown from the start as anxious about 'the question of responsibility, always trying to shift the burden – to Canterbury, for inciting him to war; to the Dauphin, for sending him the tennis-balls; to the French king, for resisting his claim; to the citizens of Harfleur, for presuming to defend their town'.[22] I prefer to see him as a spokesman for Shakespeare who seeks to address both sides of the issue, not to assign blame, so leading to the scenes where Henry debates the question with Williams and Bates before launching into his soliloquy on ceremony. For the matter of the individual soldier's responsibility versus that of the king in war is not dealt with in tracts on war. In the view of Bates, 'obedience to the king' wipes out any crime committed by him as a soldier, but what, asks Williams, if the king's cause 'be not good', and how can men die well in battle? Henry's response, to generalize from tracts that war is God's punishment for men's wickedness, evades the question, and the scene shifts into Henry's soliloquy, which is a kind of complaint about the burden of responsibility that gives a king sleepless nights. The king cannot have the heart's ease that 'private men enjoy' (4.1.233), a reflection perhaps on the harsh necessity that compels Henry to sanction the execution of old friends such as Scroop and Bardolph. The soliloquy ends referring to the watch the king keeps to 'maintain the peace', a line that is odd in relation to the watch that he and his soldiers have been keeping to win the war. It is possible that Shakespeare had in mind another argument found in tracts about war, which, as a kind of 'public execution of justice', could be defended as aiming to bring about peace and order;[23] but I think the soliloquy expresses Shakespeare's own reflections on political responsibilities at the time he was writing the play. It is marginally relevant to the action, and was omitted from the Quarto, which suggests it may have been cut in performance.

The Quarto preserves what follows almost immediately, the dramatically important moment when Henry kneels and prays for God's support in the battle that is about to begin. His main concern is to beg that God will overlook the sin he did not commit in the deposition of Richard II, but for which he still feels guilt, 'Since that my penitence comes after all, / Imploring pardon' (4.1.300–1). For Stephen Greenblatt 'these expiatory rituals...are worthless' and merely expose Henry's 'bad conscience'; for Alexander Leggatt, the scene shows that 'Kingship can never again be the sacred office it was for Richard', and that 'the ceremonies of kingship... are worthless'.[24] Both these explanations label what Henry is doing as worthless, but miss the theatrical point of this moment when Henry drops the mask of authority and speaks for himself in a prayer that brings an intimate revelation of feelings of guilt in relation to his father's usurpation of the throne. For the battle of Agincourt is dramatically God's answer to this prayer, an astonishing victory in which the English lose only twenty-nine men. God's pardon is shown in this, which is why Henry insists, 'O God, thy arm was here' and 'God fought for us' (4.8.105, 119), and calls for the singing of a familiar psalm that begins, 'Not unto us, O Lord, not unto us, but unto thy name give the praise.' Henry is God's agent, fighting a war validated by God's support, and designed to bring about the peace acclaimed in the final act: 'Peace to this meeting, wherefore we are met' (5.2.1). So I think Shakespeare's treatment of violence in this play would not have dismayed those in his audience who liked to believe England had a just cause in the wars then taking place. At the same time, the anxieties of Henry, as revealed in his images of the horror of 'impious war' and in his questioning of the king's responsibilities, complicate his character and suggest that Shakespeare was troubled by issues that remained unresolved for him.

NOTES

1. The Oxford and Norton one-volume editions of Shakespeare's works (1986, 1997) date the play to 1596, after *Richard II*. In his thorough examination of the dating of *King John* in his separate edition of the play for the Oxford Shakespeare series (Oxford University Press, 1989), 2–15, A. R. Braunmuller settles for the mid-1590s, leaving indeterminate its relation to *Richard II*.
2. See *King John*, ed. A. R. Braunmuller, 16–17, 57–60.
3. Compare the entrance of Richard holding the bleeding head of the Duke of Somerset in *Henry VI*, Part 3, 1.1.16, discussed above, pp. 52–3.
4. Walter Cohen, in Stephen Greenblatt, ed., *The Norton Shakespeare* (New York and London: W. W. Norton, 1997), 1019.
5. *Henry IV*, Part 1 (The Oxford Shakespeare. Oxford University Press, 1987), ed. David Bevington, Introduction, 42.
6. Greenblatt, *Shakespearean Negotiations* (Berkeley and Los Angeles: University of California Press, 1988), 64.
7. Jonathan Dollimore and Alan Sinfield, 'History and Ideology: the Instance of *Henry V*', in John Drakakis, ed., *Alternative Shakespeares* (London and New York: Methuen, 1985), 206–27, citing 225–6.
8. The Quarto text reduces Henry's three references to honour in this speech to one.
9. Katharine Eisaman Maus in *The Norton Shakespeare*, 1449.
10. It is notable that the Quarto, an acting version that omits all the Choruses, keeps all but twenty-two of the Archbishop's very long speech of sixty-three lines.

11. Holinshed gives this figure, but with the qualification 'as some do report', and goes on to say that writers 'of greater credit' affirm that five or six hundred English were killed.

12. In the Folio the scene ends with Henry's order, 'Then every soldier kill his prisoners! / Give the word through', the last line implying again that the killing is imagined as taking place offstage. Gary Taylor thinks the prisoners should be killed onstage, so as to stress 'Henry's cold-blooded murder of defenceless French prisoners' (*Henry V*, ed. Gary Taylor, Oxford University Press, 1984, 33), but the text indicates otherwise, though the Quarto offers something of a *coup de théâtre* as well as a *coupe de gorge* in showing Pistol's violent action. In carrying out Henry's order, Pistol loses the ransom he had expected, as Gary Taylor points out.

13. See Nick de Somogyi, *Shakespeare's Theatre of War* (Aldershot: Aldgate Publishing, 1998), chapter 1.

14. Stephen Gosson, *The Trumpet of War* (1598), B6v.

15. A. Leighton, *Speculum Belli sacri*, 1.

16. Richard Bernard, for instance, in *The Bible-Battells or the Sacred Art Military* (1629), 53, remarks that the devil seduces nations to make war, though a 'just war' against an 'infesting enemy' is to be preferred before an unjust peace.

17. Critical commentaries, too, have questioned the myth of the heroic Henry, most notably Joel B. Altman in '"Vile Participation": The Amplification of Violence in the Theater of *Henry V*', *Shakespeare Quarterly*, 42 (1991), 1–32, reprinted in Stephen Orgel and Sean Keilen, eds., *Shakespeare and History* (New York and London: Garland Publishing, 1999), 401–32. See also Alexander Leggatt, *Shakespeare's Political Drama* (London and New York: Routledge, 1988), 121–4, and Norman Rabkin's essay 'Either / Or: Responding to *Henry V*' in *The Problem of Meaning* (1981), 33–62, in which he argues that the play provokes two incompatible readings of the king as 'exemplary monarch' and as 'master manipulator'. Other questionings of the play are discussed by T. W. Craik in his Introduction to the Arden edition (London and New York: Routledge, 1995), 71–5.

18. See Craik, Introduction, 88–92.

19. Greenblatt, *Shakespearean Negotiations*, 56.

20. *Ibid.*, 65.

21. Gosson, *Trumpet of War*, C6r.

22. Leggatt, *Shakespeare's Political Drama*, 133.

23. William Gouge, *God's Three Arrows: Plague, Famine, Sword* (1631), 214.

24. Greenblatt, *Shakespearean Negotiations*, 62; Leggatt, *Shakespeare's Political Drama*, 135.

CHAPTER 6

Violence, Renaissance tragedy, and Hamlet

Hamlet is a pivotal play in many ways, not least in Shakespeare's treatment of violence. It has always been seen from one point of view as a masterpiece in a series of revenge tragedies, amongst which *The Spanish Tragedy* (?1588; printed 1592) and *The Revenger's Tragedy* (1607) are the other most notable plays. However, in these plays, as in *Titus Andronicus*, the action moves towards the completion of revenge in a powerful display of violence, whereas consideration of *Hamlet* has been troubled by the hero's delay in carrying out the Ghost's demand, 'Revenge his foul and most unnatural murder' (1.5.25). The Ghost's imperative has commonly been seen as imposing on Hamlet a duty to rush to his revenge, so that his hesitation has provoked much critical debate. But this inaction is, I think, what makes *Hamlet* a distinctive and unique play that is, in the end, not about revenge so much as about the human impulse to violence. Hamlet broods and talks but cannot act to carry out a plan of retaliation. The turning point in the action of the play comes with the sudden burst of violence in his killing of Polonius. The death of Claudius occurs as one of the 'casual slaughters' Horatio reports at the end, not as a deliberate act of revenge. I see *Hamlet* as an incisive exploration of aspects of violence, a key work in Shakespeare's continuing engagement with this issue. I shall begin with a reminder of the classical and Christian frames of reference that are so important in this play, and go on to consider its relation to the revenge genre before commenting more directly on the action and Hamlet's dilemma.

CLASSICAL VIOLENCE AND CHRISTIAN CONSCIENCE

The development of tragedy in the English theatres during the late sixteenth century owed nothing directly to the ancient Greek dramatists, though something to Seneca. Tragedy in the main grew out of the native tradition of the morality play in a 'continuous adaptation of the discursive and moralizing drama of the late Middle Ages into the polydimensional story-drama of the mature theatre'.[1] By the late sixteenth century stories were often borrowed from Italian *novelle* and histories, reprinted, translated or anthologized in the 1560s and 1570s. Machiavelli's *The Prince* was not translated into English until 1640, but his name became identified with the ruthless use of power to achieve a ruler's ends by any means, in part no doubt through the critique of this work published in French by Innocent Gentillet in 1576 and translated into English in 1602. Geoffrey Fenton also translated from Francesco Guicciardini's account of Italy between 1492 and 1534 in his *History of the Wars of Italy* (1579), detailing many stories of murder and vendetta in the power struggles of Italian city states. Such works helped to foster a double image of Italy as, on the one hand, a centre of culture, wealth, and magnificence, and on the other hand, as 'the Academy of man-slaughter, the sporting place of murder, the Apothecary shop of poison for all Nations'.[2]

Classical tragedy had some impact on the development of English drama through the plays of Seneca, gathered in translation in 1581 in an edition not reprinted until 1927. The extent of his influence has been much debated, and it is hard to judge because it is manifested in scattered allusions, tags, and quotations, and because he also had considerable importance as a Stoic thinker through his prose writings. The plays are closet dramas, exchanges of long, declamatory emotional tirades: 'Typically, the hero of Senecan tragedy undergoes an explosion of passion (*furor*) which elicits on the one hand grief and lamentation, and on the other consolation in the wisdom of stoic philosophy.'[3] Even *Titus Andronicus*, the most Senecan of Shakespeare's plays, owes more to Ovid than to Seneca.[4] The play by Seneca that arguably had most impact, *Thyestes*, which deals with the revenge of Atreus on his brother Thyestes for adultery with his wife and theft of a ram with a golden fleece, certainly offers a horrific image of the banquet at which Thyestes is given roasted or stewed pieces of his own children to eat. Atreus says

A meane in mischiefe ought to be when gylt thou dost commit
Not when thou quytst: for yet even this too little seems to me.[5]

In saying there should be no mean or limit to violence in requiting an injury, he anticipates Claudius' (possibly sardonic) advice to Laertes, 'Revenge should have no bounds', in what is commonly regarded as the major revenge play (*Hamlet*, 4.7.128). In Italy revenge for some offences was sanctioned by law, especially where the seduction of a wife or the betrayal by her of a husband were at issue; infidelity might be brutally punished by torture and murder where aristocratic honour was involved. Private revenge was outlawed in England, but it might nevertheless be practised, and James I found it necessary to issue edicts against duelling. Some cases involving revenge became notorious, such as the poisoning of Sir Thomas Overbury in 1613 by the Countess of Essex in response to his attempt to warn the Earl of Rochester against her. In his well-known essay on revenge, Francis Bacon denounces private revenges as putting the law out of office, but allows finally that public revenges are often successful.

Private revenge is likely to become more common when the law is inefficient or corrupted. In their enthusiasm for the death penalty many Americans at the present time seem to wish to equate legal penalties with retribution, and exact 'life for life' (Exodus 21.23). The authority of the Old Testament is compounded with that of Aristotle, who recommended retaliation against one's enemies as just.[6] It is not always easy to distinguish retribution from justice, as in punishment by execution, when a murderer is himself 'murdered' by lethal injection. Politicians and others reveal their own confusion in public utterances such as the comment by a member of Congress in response to the execution of an army officer in the Middle East: 'It is time the United States, without regard to what anybody else thinks, goes to the root of evil in the Middle East. We need revenge, we need justice.'[7] Justice, of course, depends on what others think, on a generally agreed basis of law, and is not concerned with evil but with criminal offences. The speaker was including a reference to evil in his remark perhaps in order to intensify his sense of outrage, though 'money is the root of all evil' (1 Timothy 6.10) hardly seems relevant. His statement in effect expresses his desire for retribution, but reveals muddled thinking in invoking the Bible and the concept of justice in order to support an urge to retaliate.

Revenge has remained an important theme in much English drama since the emergence of professional theatres in the sixteenth century. The idea of retribution fostered by the rules for punishment listed in Exodus ('Eye for eye, tooth for tooth ...') is countered by the recommendation in Paul's Epistle to the Romans 12.19, 'avenge not yourselves, but rather give place unto wrath: for it is written, Vengeance is mine; I will repay, saith the Lord'. However, both passages can be taken as supporting the idea of retribution, 'that God's own mode of punishment is vengeful'.[8] The law generally establishes a gap between retribution and justice, though the two may overlap, as in the use of the death penalty; and revenge may seem the only way to achieve justice in cases where the law cannot be

effective. English Renaissance drama differs from that of Seneca in having access to a Christian frame of reference. In his translation of *Thyestes*
Jasper Heywood was careful to refer to the gods, and to translate the
crimes of Atreus as 'mischief'. The modern translation by E. F. Watling
instead uses the word 'sin', so giving a strange Christian colouring to
the text of *Thyestes*.⁹ In their relations with the gods, the Greeks and
Romans seem to have been preoccupied with the idea of sacrilege, of
giving offence by failing to carry out rites or sacrifices properly, or by
disobeying the somewhat arbitrary rules that the gods imposed. Hence
their preoccupation with external forces such as Fortune and Fate; they
do not appear to have internalized a sense of sin, such as runs through
the English Bible, obsessively so in the Pauline letters: 'as by one man sin
entered into the world, and death by sin; and so death passed upon all
men, for that all have sinned' (Romans 5.12). The idea that all humans
sin is mitigated by the concept of the conscience that enables us to feel
remorse for our sins, and by the belief in the freely given grace of God:
'For all have sinned, and come short of the glory of God; being justified freely by his grace through the redemption that is in Christ Jesus'
(Romans 3, 23–4).

Christianity begins in the execution of Christ, who 'appeared to put
away sin by the sacrifice of himself' (Hebrews 9.26), and whose blood was
shed 'for many for the remission of sins'. This was the sacrifice to end all
sacrifices, and to mediate possible redemption for all humans. It was to
be renewed vicariously in the eucharistic rites based on the Last Supper,
rehearsing a cannibalistic devouring of the body and blood of Christ
in imitation of the Last Supper (Matthew 26.26–8, etc.). The violence
of blood sacrifice haunts the imagination of artists through the Middle
Ages and the early modern period, in their depictions of the crucified
figure of Christ, of the torments he endured, and of the tortures inflicted
on later saints who were brutally put to death. The New Testament also
gave currency to the idea of Hell (Gehenna) as a place below in which
those who committed evil would be punished by fire (Matthew 5.22),
and this gave scope to the imaginations of artists and writers to invent
horrific images of the tortures of the damned in hell, and to imagine
Heaven as a place of peace high above this world (Matthew 3.16, etc.).
Heywood added a final scene to Seneca's play, in which Thyestes calls
for the 'torments all of hell' to fall on his own head, and assimilates
classical images of the underworld into a Christian concept of Hell.¹⁰
Such translations of Seneca may have helped to foster the easy commerce
between classical and Christian imagery in English Renaissance drama.
Heywood, for instance, wrote a verse preface to *Thyestes* in which the

shade of Seneca appears to him in a dream, carrying the book of his tragedies as garnished by Melpomene in her palace on Parnassus, and somewhat oddly advising him to send his translation to his dedicatee, Sir John Mason, and to pray for him:

This Christmas time thou mayst do well a piece thereof to end,
And many thanks in volume small, as thee becomes, to send.
And tell him how for his estate thou dost thy prayers make,
And him in daily vows of thine to God above betake.

(lines 183–6)

Educated men were trained in Latin at school and would be introduced through collections of 'sentences' or maxims to writers such as Horace and Ovid.[11] At the same time, they came to know the Bible and *Book of Common Prayer* by attendance at church, and so acquired a double frame of reference. Shakespeare, for instance, was able to exploit classical and Christian allusions and imagery in his plays with no sense of discord or anachronism, as, for instance, in *The Comedy of Errors*, which is based on Plautus, and ends at an abbey in Ephesus in a consciousness of St Paul's epistle to the Ephesians, or in *King Lear*, which is set in a pre-Christian age, but has many references to or citations from the Bible, and names Edgar as 'godson' to a king who calls on Apollo yet claims to be 'more sinned against than sinning'.

The violence of the classical world was mediated largely through the idea of the Trojan War in Homer and Virgil, through the tales of Ovid, and through the revenge plays of Seneca. The violence of the Christian world was mediated largely through Italian history and romance, and through the Bible. There were no published English versions of the Bible before the sixteenth century, and the two most widely used translations in Shakespeare's lifetime were the Geneva (1560) and the Bishop's Bible (1568), so that for most people reading the Bible was a relatively new experience. The conflicting attitudes to revenge in the Old and New Testaments have been noticed. Of greater importance for this study is the primal act of violence as perhaps exemplified initially in the huge punishment inflicted on Adam and Eve for disobedience prompted by the subtle serpent, created by God to tempt them, namely expulsion from Eden, toil, and death, as if God could not bear that the beings created in his own image should become 'as one of us, to know good and evil' (Genesis 3.22). Another such scene of violence is depicted in the story of Cain and Abel (Genesis 4.8), a story of two brothers which is related to the killing of old Hamlet by his brother Claudius.[12]

Again, in the Book of Job, God seems to succumb to the temptations of
Satan by inflicting hideous suffering on Job, all his children and servants
reported destroyed and his body covered with loathsome boils. Job has
to endure the longwinded advice of comforters who reproach him without understanding, before God's voice is heard out of a whirlwind asking a
whole series of examination questions that Job sensibly avoids answering,
recognizing perhaps their rhetorical nature as expressing God's power.
Humbling himself before God, 'Behold, I am vile . . . I abhor myself, and
repent in dust and ashes' (Job 40.4; 42.6), Job recovers God's blessing, all
his brothers and sisters come to him, he has sons and daughters again,
and twice as much wealth as before. Why does God submit Cain and
Job to these terrible tests? In his account of Senecan tragedy, Gordon
Braden observes of the behaviour of Nero that 'A ruler whose power goes
beyond all opposition and faction has to create opponents and factions
in order to experience that power.'[13] From one point of view God may be
demonstrating his power in provoking disobedience in Adam and Eve, or
possibly in tempting Cain with the thought of power, 'unto thee shall be
his [Abel's] desire, and thou shalt rule over him', and in allowing Satan
to torment Job. From another point of view, Adam and Eve and Cain act
freely in rejecting God's commands, and sin, while Job, who refuses to
think, with his comforters, that God is punishing him, and who accepts
a mystery beyond his understanding, is rewarded. It is notable that when
God speaks finally to Job, he does so in a series of questions and examples
(Behemoth and Leviathan) that boast of his power and mystique.[14]

God's requirements appear arbitrary, and within a few generations
after Adam, 'The earth also was corrupt before God, and the earth was
filled with violence' (Genesis 6.11). After the destruction of all except
Noah, God had to test those he most blessed, as in tempting Abraham
to sacrifice his son Isaac (Genesis 22); and the multiplication of tribes
and nations led to greater corruption and violence: 'Woe unto the world
because of offences! For it must needs be that offences come; but woe
to that man by whom the offence cometh!' (Matthew 18.7). Humans
are created so that they must offend, and internalize their awareness
of offences as sin or wickedness. In the story of the woman taken in
adultery, the scribes and Pharisees want her stoned and Jesus says, 'He
that is without sin among you, let him first cast a stone at her' (John 8.7).
His listeners, 'being convicted by their own conscience' leave one by
one. The words 'conscious' and 'consciousness' do not occur in the 1611
Bible, where 'conscience' includes the idea of consciousness of evil and
good as the only consciousness that matters.

Sin, good and evil, Heaven and Hell, and conscience are concepts that provide one frame of reference for Renaissance tragedy, the one probably most familiar to the audience. The Bible also suggested the idea of patience in suffering (Romans 12.12, for example) and love, but it is worth noting that the English miracle plays that preceded the development of professional theatre in London displayed scenes of torture in which 'the Apostles were graphically stoned, stabbed, blinded, crucified, and flayed. Other holy men and women had their breasts torn off, and their bodies scourged, shot with arrows, baked, grilled, and burned... No torment was too extreme or too gory for Representation.'[15] Another frame of reference is provided by the emphasis on passion, especially anger and lust, retaliation, and revenge, to be found in Seneca's plays and in Italian *novelle*, together with the political ruthlessness Machiavelli was thought to embody. The overlapping of these two frames of reference contributes hugely to the peculiar richness of English Renaissance tragedy. The most fundamental challenge for the dramatist remained the same for both ancient Greek and Renaissance dramatists, namely, how to comprehend and make dramatic sense of the basic human impulse to violence.

HAMLET AND REVENGE TRAGEDY

In his wide-ranging account of revenge tragedy, John Kerrigan argues that the reciprocity of revenge 'creates violent equality, correcting A's oppression of B by striking back and levelling the odds. The ironies of vengeful equivalence have always been potentially more interesting than the injuries which generate them.'[16] This statement I think untrue. While revenge is a strong motif in some tragedies, it is not a central issue in many of the greatest works, such as *Oedipus the King* and *King Lear*, and what I call the primal scene of violence, especially the act that appears spontaneous or not adequately motivated, is of greater interest in challenging us to face up to our human proneness to violence for its own sake. Indeed, it can be argued that revenge is not really the central issue in *Hamlet*, which has commonly been regarded as the greatest of revenge tragedies. In the twentieth century critics, from A. C. Bradley in his essays in *Shakespearean Tragedy* (1904) to the editors of the three critical editions of the play that appeared in the 1980s, have all had much to say about Hamlet's 'task' or 'duty' to carry out his revenge. Hamlet could be seen as having to deal with 'the predicament, quite simply, of a man mourning for his father, whose murder he is called on to avenge'.[17] The phrase 'quite simply' would seem to exclude any other possibility, and a central concern for many interpreters has been the question why Hamlet delays or avoids taking revenge upon Claudius. Various explanations have been offered. He has, for instance, been seen as pathologically disabled by his speculative intellect in a world of action and by melancholy (Bradley); or handicapped by weakness of character (Dover Wilson); tainted by a 'fatal aestheticism' (Nevo), or inhibited by the inescapable condition of man (Mack); and more often than not he has been regarded as a failure in his 'evasion of the task imposed upon him'.[18] All such accounts of the play have taken for granted that the play's central concern is the need for Hamlet to carry out the Ghost's demand for revenge, and his inability to act is related to the condition of 'Hamletism' that seemed for many to embody the disillusion, cynicism or despair that marked a century in which two world wars were fought, and the new media technologies of film and television made all too familiar the horrors of Nazi gas-chambers, of the Vietnam War, of atomic bombs, and of the resurgence of genocide. In fact, as John Kerrigan observes, Hamlet does not respond to the Ghost by promising to revenge: 'Hamlet never promises to revenge, only to remember'[19] – to remember the Ghost, and to memorize his 'commandment'.

Revenge is not the dominant concern in *Hamlet*, as can be seen in comparing it with a play that is in some measure a spin-off from it, namely *The Revenger's Tragedy*. This play begins with Vindice, whose name means revenge, bursting with anger as he holds the skull of the woman once betrothed to him, and contemplates the Duke of some unnamed vicious Italianate court and his family as they pass in procession over the stage. From the opening moment the action is thus determined by Vindice's cry:

Vengeance, thou murder's quit-rent, and whereby
Thou show'st thyself tenant to Tragedy,
O, keep thy day, hour, minute, I beseech,
For those thou hast determined! (1.1.39–42)

The play looks ahead to vengeance being 'paid' as 'quit-rent', or requital, not only for the rape and murder of Gloriana by the Duke, but for the rape of Antonio's wife, a 'religious lady' (1.1.111), by the Duchess's youngest son, and her Lucretia-like suicide. Most of the male characters in the play are caught up in a desire for revenge of some kind as the only redress for crimes, since the law, as administered by the Duke, is corrupt. The first act ends with a group swearing on their swords to revenge the death of Antonio's wife if 'Judgment speak all in gold' (1.4.61). Vindice claims a high moral ground in his missionary zeal to 'blast this villainous dukedom vexed with sin' (5.2.6), but his long obsession with obtaining revenge contaminates him, so that he is shown taking increasing pleasure in torture and murder. He becomes morally indistinguishable from other revengers in the masque of four revengers followed by 'the other masque of intended murderers' in Act 5, where all look alike and could substitute for one another. The play closes on a Christian moral pattern in which all the guilty, including Vindice and his brother Hippolito, meet with retribution finally, so that Antonio is left in charge at the end, and can cry 'Just is the law above!' But the action throughout is also self-consciously theatrical, as Vindice contrives plots, and stages his own scenarios and plays within the play.

In so doing, Vindice often includes the audience in his denunciations of luxury, wealth, ambition, and lust, so that the unnamed court in the play may reflect the licentiousness and corruption perceived by some spectators as present at the court of James I and in Jacobean London. As the opening scene looks ahead to the completion of patterns of revenge, so the action presses forward, stressing the present tense. 'Now' is the most frequently occurring adverb in the play, giving a sense of urgency as well as a sense of immediate relevance to the world of the audience:[20]

Now 'tis full sea abed over the world;
There's juggling of all sides. Some that were maids
E'en at sunset are now perhaps I' the tollbook.
This woman in immodest thin apparel
Lets in her friend by water; here's a dame,
Cunning, nails leather hinges to a door
To avoid proclamation; now cuckolds are
A-coining, apace, apace, apace . . . (2.2.136–43)

The play thus speaks home to a London audience through images such as that of the woman letting in her friend by water (the Thames?), and by various forms of direct address. The Italianate setting permits the audience to associate the depiction of intrigue, lust, and murder with a foreign country, but at the same time to enjoy the *frisson* of recognizing satirical relevances to their own city and court. As in *Hamlet*, the protagonist is something of a misogynist, for whom women may represent an ideal of virtue, as embodied in his sister, Castiza (signifying Chastity), but more commonly are seen as a source of corruption, of the wealth and sex that fascinated people then as now: 'were't not for gold and women, there would be no damnation' (2.1.257).

However, in this play the skull is displayed as a *memento mori* in the opening scene, and becomes an instrument of vengeance when Vindice presents it, masked and dressed up, to the Duke as a 'country lady', and the Duke is poisoned as he kisses it. In *Hamlet*, by contrast, the skull seen only in Act 5 is that of Yorick, and it serves as a reminder of the past, of Hamlet's childhood. In *The Revenger's Tragedy* most of the characters are engaged in a feverish pursuit of pleasure, sex, and power:

> Banquets abroad by torchlight, music, sports,
> Bare-headed vassals that had ne'er the fortune
> To keep their own hats on, but let horns wear 'em;
> 'Nine coaches waiting, – hurry, hurry, hurry!'
> (2.1.203–6)

When Vindice broods on his world as he contemplates the skull of Gloriana again in Act 3 he questions this pursuit of luxury and pleasure, seeing the court as absurdist and the people in it as mad:

> Surely we are all mad people, and they
> Whom we think are, are not. (3.5.80–1)

He includes himself in his general perception of the world of the play, but he speaks as the one rational character who stands aloof and is capable of reflecting on the conduct of others, and who is therefore able to manipulate them and control events. It is thus Vindice who generates most of the 'horrid laughter' that Nicholas Brooke argued is essential to Jacobean tragedy as it developed from late morality plays and violent farce.[21] In the post-*Hamlet* plays Brooke deals with, beginning with *The Revenger's Tragedy*, laughter in response to the satiric perspective of characters such as Vindice is a necessary escape-valve for audiences confronted with atrocities that would otherwise evoke mere horror, as in the torture and poisoning of the Duke, who dies spouting blood in Act 3. The cycle of revenge that begins in the opening scene might never be completed, and only ends when Vindice overreaches by boasting of his wit. Antonio sends him off to execution remarking, 'You that would murder him would murder me', or, by implication, anyone.

In Shakespeare's play, the situation is reversed, as Hamlet himself feels estranged to the point of madness in a court that is going about its orderly business as usual. These differences relate to a more fundamental dissimilarity between the plays, for in response to the Ghost's demand that Hamlet revenge his father's death, he is anxious only to remember and make notes. As remarked earlier, his neglect of revenge has troubled many interpreters of the play, who tend to see Hamlet as 'a man with a

deed to do who for the most part conspicuously fails to do it'.[22] Hence has
arisen a long tradition of seeing Hamlet as irresolute, paralysed in will,
unhealthy, morbid, neurotic, a dreamer who appears a very disturbing
figure in the context of western ideologies that value men of decision
and action, who are ready to do their duty. It is hardly surprising that
since the nineteenth century many actresses have been attracted to the
role, and that Hamlet has been perceived as 'sensitive, intellectual, and
feminine'.[23]

  This perception relates to another difference between Hamlet and
Vindice. Vindice as manipulator effectively controls his world from the
opening scene when he watches the Duke and his court pass over the
stage, identifying them for the audience, and showing he knows their
'characters' or moral qualities. *Hamlet* begins with the question, 'Who's
there?' It is a question that establishes a mood of uncertainty that troubles
Hamlet. When we see the prince in the second scene, outside the circle of
the court and watching them, he does not know how he stands in relation
to Claudius, Gertrude, and the rest, and in his uncertainty about their
identities, he cannot be sure of his own. Claudius, Gertrude, Ophelia,
Polonius, Rosencrantz, and Guildenstern may not be what they seem,
and Hamlet is troubled also by a questionable Ghost, which may be
a devil. Everything is clear-cut for Vindice, whereas Hamlet does not
know what to believe. Vindice watches over a court that is unaware of
his intrigues, whereas Hamlet, 'the observed of all observers', is under
constant surveillance by Claudius or his agents. The play suggests various
reasons why Hamlet does not rush to act out revenge, and every age
tends to focus on the aspects of his multifaceted character that mirror its
problems.

HAMLET, THE GHOST, AND THE 'NAME OF ACTION'

The idea, common in the late nineteenth- and twentieth-century interpretation, that Hamlet fails to carry out an appointed task or duty is based
on his encounter with the Ghost of his father in Act 1, and our understanding of this encounter relates to the presentation of the Ghost in the
first scene. The startling opening of the play presents anxious sentries on
watch, so anxious that Barnardo, coming on duty, challenges Francisco,
who should be the challenger. A 'strict and most observant watch' (1.1.74)
is being kept in anticipation of an invasion by an army led by Fortinbras
to recover for Norway lands taken by old Hamlet. Barnardo, Marcellus,
and Horatio continue to maintain a look-out primarily for this reason,

and Barnardo explains the appearance of the Ghost of old Hamlet as related to the former King who 'was and is the question of these wars' (1.1.114). This speech of Barnardo's is found in the 1604–5 Quarto of the play, not in the Folio text, and could have been cut later to hasten the entry of the Ghost, whose stage appearance proved far more exciting than discussion about war. When *Hamlet* was first performed, however, the image of wartime would have had vivid resonances for a London audience at a time of invasion scares, the threat of uprisings in Ireland, and the extended saga of the siege of Ostend that lasted from 1601 to 1604.[24]

The Ghost duly appears as a 'warlike form', in 'the very armour he had on / When he the ambitious Norway combated' (1.1.63–4), according to Horatio, who speaks as if he had witnessed the battle with his own eyes. Not until near the end of the play does it emerge that the old King fought old Fortinbras thirty years previously, on the very day Hamlet was born (5.1.142), so that Horatio, his fellow student, and presumably about the same age as Hamlet, cannot have seen old Hamlet at that time. This inconsistency is not noticed in performance, or often in reading, and seems designed to support an image of old Hamlet as a warrior king. Shakespeare had recently worked on *Julius Caesar*, which could have influenced his use of classical names in *Hamlet*, such as Horatio, Marcellus, Claudius, and Laertes, and also his references to Caesar and various classical deities, but this classical contextualizing goes deeper. In the Quarto, Horatio recalls in this scene the apparitions that preceded the fall of Julius Caesar in 'the most high and palmy state of Rome', thereby associating old Hamlet directly with ancient Rome. These lines were omitted from the Folio, possibly cut in performance because they do not advance the action, or alternatively because they mislead by suggesting the Ghost is merely a portent of disasters to come. But the passage shows how Shakespeare's mind was working to create a complex idea of the Ghost as not only a sort of epic figure, at once associated with ancient history, with old battles fought against Norway, and with heroic values, but also someone known to Horatio, and connected to a present time of war when it seems that history may repeat itself in an invasion of Denmark by young Fortinbras. Old Hamlet's world was one of violent warfare, as he is remembered for smiting the Norwegians and the 'sledded Polacks', as well as for killing old Fortinbras in single combat; now, in a different age, Denmark is preparing for another war, with young Fortinbras.

The first audience to see *Hamlet* staged was, I suspect, startled by the Ghost's appearance in armour – the only ghost in early modern English drama to be so costumed.[25] I assume that the Ghost appears just as Horatio describes him in 1.2, armed 'at point exactly, cap-à-pie', or, as he later says, 'from head to foot', and wearing a helmet with the 'beaver up'. 'Cap-à-pie' was a technical term for a full suit of armour of a kind that went out of use by the early sixteenth century, as fighting became more a matter of guns than hand-to-hand combat. Such full body armour was obsolete by 1600, except for jousting in tournaments. Visually, with his complete armour and his 'martial stalk', the Ghost seems to emerge from a distant age when fighting was the normal way to conduct affairs, even as he is also old Hamlet to the life, so that Horatio reports to Hamlet, 'I think I saw him yesternight' (1.2.189), his beard grizzled 'as I have seen it in his life' (1.2.241). The armour of the Ghost marks not only his association with an older way of life dedicated to violence, but also his cultural distance from Hamlet, the student who has returned to a Denmark ruled by diplomacy rather than arms. By this time, Hamlet has already, in his 'O that this too too sullied flesh would melt' soliloquy, compared his father with Hyperion the sun-god and with Hercules (1.2.140, 153), so enhancing his association with the classical world. This comparison also shows how Hamlet idealizes his father as a warrior-hero, and distances him further by mythologizing him as a classical deity. There is thus a curious built-in contradiction in the physical presence of the Ghost who interviews Hamlet late in Act 1, and in effect becomes the living man again, gesturing, passionate, bearded, armed, and carrying his marshal's truncheon, an actor visibly turning into Hamlet's father when he begins to speak. He carries the authority not only of a 'supernatural being, King and father',[26] but also of the martial heroes of the classical world. But Hamlet has responded to the appearance of the Ghost with his cry:

Angels and ministers of grace defend us!
Be thou a spirit of health or goblin damned,
Bring with thee airs from heaven or blasts from hell,
Be thy intents wicked or charitable,
Thou comest in such a questionable shape
That I will speak to thee. (1.4.39–44)

All those forms of authority are thus put in question in relation to a Christian pattern of values, and the Ghost is 'questionable' not only as inviting question, but also as doubtful, of uncertain origin.[27] The Ghost's first words suggest he has come from Purgatory (where his 'foul crimes' are to be 'burnt and purged away'), but Hamlet refers only to Heaven and Hell, so that his frame of reference seems to be Protestant. The authority of the Ghost is in any case immediately qualified,[28] for when he addresses Hamlet directly, he speaks in the voice of a Senecan revenger, invoking classical values again in calling on Hamlet to 'Revenge his foul and most unnatural murder':

HAMLET: Murder?
GHOST: Murder most foul, as in the best it is,
But this most foul, strange and unnatural.
HAMLET: Haste me to know't, that I, with wings
As swift as meditation or the thoughts of love
May sweep to my revenge. (1.5.25–30)

Hamlet's immediate reaction to the Ghost's words is often taken as signifying an acceptance of a duty to revenge: 'He now also has his directive, a commission that is also a mission. His reaction to the Ghost is like a religious conversion.'[29] Hamlet's immediate response, however, is spoken in the context of the Ghost's Christian qualification of his Senecan call for revenge, since in condemning murder as 'most foul' at the best, he at once exhorts Hamlet to kill his murderer and at the same time denounces the idea of revenge killing. Moreover, the Ghost shows little haste in enlightening Hamlet, but goes on at considerable length.

As the Ghost continues with his extended account of Gertrude transferring her affections to Claudius, and of Claudius poisoning him, his emphasis is on the sinful nature of these events and on the horrible effects of the poison on his body. The heroic image of the warrior in armour is disconcertingly transformed as his speech continues into that of an ageing monarch obsessed with his body and accustomed to taking an afternoon nap in the orchard. The Ghost is troubled with a moral disgust on the one hand, and a physical revulsion on the other, and the two meet in his sermonizing about Gertrude's behaviour:

So lust, though to a radiant angel linked,
Will sate itself in a celestial bed
And prey on garbage. (1.5.55–7)

The moral and physical disgust associated with lust and garbage is seen also in the Ghost's horror both at the appearance of his body, covered by the poison with a 'loathsome crust', and at being denied the sacraments at his death. The Ghost becomes flesh in his anxiety about what happened to his body, and in his outrage at the idea that the 'royal bed of Denmark' should become 'A couch for luxury and damned incest' (1.5.83). The Ghost's moral outrage, expressed in Christian terms, echoes that expressed by Hamlet in his first soliloquy in 1.2,

who, like his father, thinks of the marriage of Claudius and Gertrude as
incestuous (1.2.157); the Ghost adds adultery as a further charge (1.5.42).
Both also have a kind of voyeuristic horror in imagining what goes on
in the 'incestuous sheets' of the 'royal bed'.

In the Ghost's long narrative the idea of revenge becomes diluted, and
almost lost, especially as he ends by telling Hamlet to leave his mother to
her conscience and to heaven. His final imperative is 'Remember me',
and this is what catches Hamlet's attention:

> Remember thee?
> Ay, thou poor ghost, whiles memory holds a seat
> In this distracted globe. Remember thee?
> Yea, from the table of my memory
> I'll wipe away all trivial fond records,
> All saws of books, all forms, all pressures past
> That youth and observation copied there,
> And thy commandment all alone shall live
> Within the book and volume of my brain,
> Unmixed with baser matter. (1.5.97–106)

Hamlet indeed dwells above all on remembering the Ghost and on
wiping away all other records he has kept in the notebook of his memory.
But what exactly is he to remember, and what is the 'commandment'
he wants to register there? The Ghost's imperatives have shifted from
'Revenge' (25) through 'bear it not' (81) and 'Taint not thy mind' (85)
to 'Remember me' (91). The word 'commandment' incorporates 'command', appropriate to a figure appearing as a great warrior and wielding
a marshal's truncheon, and this is how Hamlet recalls this moment later
in 3.4, when he expects the Ghost, appearing for the third time, to chide
him for neglecting to carry out his 'dread command'. In 1.5, however,
'commandment' had a much more immediate sense for Shakespeare and
his audience, one derived from its use in the Bible, specifically in relation
to the ten commandments (Exodus 20.3–17) given by God to Moses,
which were by law inscribed or hung on the walls of parish churches
in England. Prominent among them is the injunction, 'Thou shalt not
kill', so that the term in itself contains the contradictory impulses that
characterize both the Ghost and Hamlet, namely a quasi-Senecan
desire for revenge, and a Christian inhibition against taking life.

In his study of *Pagan Virtue*,[30] John Casey argues that 'we inherit a
confused system of values; that when we think most rigorously and
realistically we are "pagans" in ethics, but that our Christian inheritance
only allows a fitful sincerity about this' (pp. 225–6). He observes that our

society admires qualities derived from the ancient Greeks and Romans, what he calls the 'irascible' virtues, 'pride and shame, a sense of the noble, a certain valuing of pride, courage and ambition' (p. 212), as against compassion, meekness, pity, and love that we associate with Christ. He thinks Shakespeare was confused, and instances *King Lear* to argue that the play 'uncomfortably combines, without reconciling, "pagan" and Christian elements' (p. 225). It seems to me rather that Shakespeare was fully aware of the differences between these inherited sets of values and in *Hamlet* used them to establish the character and dilemma of his protagonist. Hamlet sees his father in ideal terms, associating him with classical deities, Hyperion, Jupiter, Mercury, or with heroes such as Hercules. Old Hamlet is established for us in the opening scene by Horatio as a warrior who put Denmark at risk in challenging old Fortinbras to single combat and killing him, and Hamlet's remarks about his father confirm this image of a hero from the past, possessing 'An eye like Mars to threaten and command' (3.4.57). Hamlet the father represents martial honour, and is associated with the irascible virtues; he is distanced into something of a mythical figure – doubly distanced as a quasi-mythical figure in the history of Denmark, and by association with the classical world.

Hamlet is presented as a student, whose training in the classics is reflected in his language, in his image of his father, and in other ways, as when he invites the players to rehearse a speech describing the death of Priam based on the *Aeneid*. For Hamlet his father is measured against the heroes of the Trojan War. In challenging old Fortinbras, old Hamlet behaved like the heroes of the *Iliad*, making courage a prime virtue, and courting death in war: 'in heroic societies life is the standard of value. If someone kills you, my friend or brother, I owe you their death and when I have paid my debt to you their friend or brother owes them my death.'[31] In that simpler world of masculine values, revenge could be seen as a virtuous act. It may be with this in mind, so to speak, that Hamlet asks the player for a speech loosely based on the story of Troy as told to Dido by Aeneas in Virgil's *Aeneid*, Book II, a speech that narrates the revenge taken for the death of his father Achilles by Pyrrhus, whose 'roused vengeance' drives him to butcher the old king, 'mincing' his limbs in full view of Queen Hecuba. In this speech Pyrrhus is depicted visually as painted ('o'ersized') with blood ('coagulate gore'), physically transformed by his indiscriminate butchery of 'fathers, mothers, daughters, sons', as he pursues an obsessive quest for revenge.[32] The atrocity is registered in the image of him 'mincing' with his sword the limbs of defenceless old Priam, an image that hardly allows the faintest flicker of 'horrid laughter'. The speech is doubly distanced from the main action as derived from Virgil and supposedly extracted from an unknown academic play. So Shakespeare can expose us to the horror of revenge without a need for an escape-valve, and so by this example show why Hamlet is unable to rush to carry out revenge on Claudius. The speech brings out the full nastiness of what Pyrrhus does, ensuring that, in spite of the classical imagery, and the appeals to Fortune, as though it is Priam's bad luck to suffer thus, we are also made aware of the 'hellish' nature of the black and bloody murderer.

Hearing this speech prompts Hamlet to launch into his soliloquy, 'O what a rogue and peasant slave am I', a tirade against himself for not having spoken out or taken action against Claudius, culminating in the cry 'O, vengeance!', found only in the Folio text and thought by some to be an actor's addition. This cry marks a turning point in the soliloquy, for now Hamlet begins to reflect rather than curse; and though 'prompted' to revenge, as for the moment he claims, 'by heaven and hell' (2.2.586), he goes on to question whether the Ghost may be 'a devil' tempting him to damnation. So he veers from an heroic stance applauding the idea of revenge to a Christian anxiety about the nature of the Ghost, and ends by deciding to try to 'catch the conscience of the king', using the New Testament term that specifically relates to a consciousness of sin; it is as if Hamlet links Claudius to those sinners who condemned the woman taken in adultery and were 'convicted by their own conscience' (John 8.9). Hamlet's shift from Thyestean revenge to Christian conscience parallels the Ghost's swerve from his demand for revenge to his anxiety that Hamlet should leave Gertrude to her conscience. The Ghost does not represent the simple heroic warrior Hamlet would like him to be, but a more complex figure who defines virtue not in terms of an heroic code but in relation to lust.

In the *Iliad* women are taken by the victors in battle as spoils of war, but the Christian morality that the Ghost preaches is focused on sexual relations, and he is especially outraged by thoughts of incest and adultery, as if he has in mind Christ's sermon on the mount, 'whosoever looketh on a woman to lust after her hath committed adultery with her already in his heart' (Matthew 5.28). The Ghost's concern here in 1.5 with 'luxury and damned incest' in turn echoes Hamlet's thought in his first soliloquy, where he, too, is already tainted in mind by his disgust with sullied flesh, and with his mother's marriage to Claudius. Indeed, he begins by rejecting suicide because 'the Everlasting' has 'fixed his canon' 'gainst self-slaughter' (1.2.132), recalling again the sixth of the ten commandments, 'Thou shalt not kill' (Exodus 20.13). When Hamlet modulates in his 'O, what a rogue and peasant slave am I' soliloquy from cursing and shouting for vengeance into an anxiety that the Ghost may be a devil, he again seems trapped in the conflict between the heroic ethos exemplified for him by the image he has of his father, and the Christian values the Ghost and he also share, and which are assumed as a common frame of reference by the other characters.

Hamlet takes the performance of 'The Mousetrap' as causing Claudius, 'frighted with false fire', to reveal his guilt when he suddenly calls for lights and leaves the stage. It is equally likely, as Guildenstern reports, that Claudius is angered, as well he might be, by Hamlet's identification of the murderer in the play as 'nephew to the king' (3.2.246) – pointing to himself as potential murderer of his uncle. However that may be, Hamlet seems prepared to act in 'the witching time of night' as he goes to 'speak daggers' to his mother and encounters Claudius at prayer. Inevitably, it seems, Hamlet is inhibited from carrying out revenge now that he has the perfect opportunity. It is, of course, ironic that his chance comes when Claudius is kneeling and has just confessed to God and to the audience his 'offence' in repeating the primal 'brother's murder' committed by Cain. In his soliloquy here Claudius drops the royal plural to reveal directly to the audience that he is deeply troubled, has a conscience, and would like to repent; it is his most sympathetic moment in the play, and Shakespeare has contrived a situation in which for Hamlet to stab the King in the back would seem appalling, both in Christian terms, and in terms of the heroic warrior code. Hamlet stands with drawn sword, the King at his mercy, but cannot carry out an act that would associate him with the image of Pyrrhus killing Priam. Claudius appears to Hamlet to be an image of silent contrition, and there is no reason to accept the view expressed by Hazlitt and endorsed by many later critics that Hamlet here finds 'an excuse for his own want of resolution' by deferring his revenge.[33] Even though Hamlet has worked himself into a passion as he prepares to go to speak with his mother ('Now could I drink hot blood', 3.2.392), he characteristically pauses and substitutes talk for action. In his savage night-time mood when 'hell itself breathes out / Contagion to this world' his words recall the horrible vision of 'hellish Pyrrhus', 'horridly tricked / With blood of fathers' (2.2.457–65); even so, he cannot do the deed, and his desire to guarantee the damnation of Claudius serves to highlight the appalling nature of the murder Hamlet contemplates. Insofar as he is stymied by the thought that his uncle might go to heaven rather than to hell if he is killed while praying, the effect of the scene again is to make us see revenge as repellent. Hamlet will never find 'a more horrid hent' (3.3.88) or opportunity because when he thinks about revenge he cannot carry it out. The encounter with Claudius may be seen as a particular instance of the problem Hamlet grapples with in his 'To be or not to be' soliloquy. In that speech he contemplates both action, taking arms against a sea of troubles, and inaction, death, even suicide. In the end he chooses for the time being to endure the 'ills' he has and take no action, and blames his inertia on 'conscience', meaning both moral inhibition against wrongdoing, and the burden of consciousness.[34]

HAMLET'S 'BLOODY DEED'

What happens when Hamlet comes into the presence of his mother in 3.4 is therefore crucial in the action of the play. He forces her to sit down, physically handling her in a way that makes her cry out, for fear that he may murder her, and in response to her shout, 'Help, ho!' a voice is heard from behind an arras, 'What ho! Help!' Hamlet does not identify the voice, but draws his sword and stabs through the curtain. It is the first time he has not paused to reflect, and his act appears spontaneous. When Gertrude asks what he has done, he replies, 'Nay, I know not. Is it the King?' The phrase 'Nay, I know not' marks the unthinking nature of his deed as an unpremeditated act of violence. Hamlet diverts attention from it as if he is unable to face what he has done, and his reaction to the discovery that he has killed Polonius appears callous. Ignoring his own deed, he concentrates all his attention on his voyeuristic imaging of his mother's sexual relations with Claudius in a greasy pigsty of a bed, as he tries to force her to share his disgust with her marriage in order to persuade her to forgo:

> the rank sweat of an enseamèd bed,
Stewed in corruption, honeying and making love
Over the nasty sty. (3.4.92–4)

She has risen to see what Hamlet has done, as he presumably draws the arras and reveals the body. Bidding a quick farewell to Polonius as a 'wretched, rash, intruding fool', he turns back to her, once again making her sit down and listen to him. What has he done? It is not premeditated murder, or a *crime passionnel*, since his passion is directed against his mother in the scene, and he does not at once know whom he has stabbed. It is not an accident, though there is an accidental aspect to the deed in that stabbing blindly through an arras might merely wound rather than kill. Hamlet hopes he may have killed the King, but really has no idea who is hiding there. One might argue that he transfers his anger with his mother momentarily to the figure behind the arras, or that his frustration in passing up the chance to kill Claudius at prayer causes this sudden act of violence, but there is no adequate explanation of why Hamlet behaves as he does. His killing of Polonius is best thought of as a lashing out, a spontaneous act that may in some way release pent-up feelings and frustrations associated with his uncle, his mother, Ophelia, and the general state of affairs in Denmark, but it remains in the end inexplicable. It is a primal act of violence.[35]

It is extraordinary that Hamlet continues for about 150 lines to excoriate his mother in his anxiety to persuade her not to sleep with her present husband, Claudius; it is as if he must avoid a full recognition of his own act in killing Polonius. He calls on her to repent, to confess herself to heaven, and asks her pardon for presenting himself as representing virtue in criticizing her vice: 'Forgive me this my virtue... Virtue itself of vice must pardon beg.' His 'virtue' is focused in his horror at her sexual behaviour, and, as if to pull him back from his obsession with sex, the Ghost returns, seen only by Hamlet, to whet his 'blunted purpose', and remind him of more important matters. In the first Quarto the stage-direction calls for the Ghost to enter 'in his night gown', not in the armour he wore in Act I, and it seems that the actors who played this shortened version costumed the Ghost to suit the Queen's private apartment or closet. It may make better sense if he is seen (or merely heard clanking, as a projection of Hamlet's imagination) in armour, as again an emblematic warrior figure calling on Hamlet to remember: 'Do not forget' (3.4.110) – that is, unless irony is intended in the gap between a night-gowned figure and Hamlet's instant recall of the Ghost's 'commandment' (1.5.102), now reduced to a simple military 'dread command' (3.4.109). Since the Queen does not see the Ghost here, the audience may think it is an hallucination perceived only by Hamlet, confirming his eccentric behaviour in the scene, which Gertrude regards as madness, and so reports to Claudius in the next scene (4.1.7). Hamlet's speech is rational except for its obsessive concern with sex, which is morally disturbing to him in a way that the killing of Polonius is not. Polonius is dismissed as a 'wretched, rash, intruding fool', and then forgotten for 120 lines, after which Hamlet reconstructs what he has done by appointing himself as heaven's agent of punishment:

> For this same lord,
> I do repent. But heaven hath pleased it so
> To punish me with this and this with me,
> That I must be their scourge and minister.
>
> (3.4.174-7)

Here he casually pushes responsibility away from himself, and shows no remorse, treating the corpse with a mocking detachment as he makes his exit, lugging 'the guts into the neighbour room'. Has the body of Polonius, bloodied from the sword-thrust, been visible on stage throughout the scene? If so, it would serve as a reminder of the disparity between Hamlet's fixation on sex and his lack of concern about a man he has killed.

Hamlet has accused his mother of making 'sweet religion' into a 'rhapsody of words', or meaningless medley, which is, ironically, what he now does himself by claiming to be the instrument of providence. Gertrude tells Claudius that he weeps for what he has done (4.1.27), but the Hamlet we see again in the following scenes appears quite unconcerned about it, as he puts on an antic disposition in mockingly talking, first to Rosencrantz and Guildenstern, and then to the King about what he has done with the body of Polonius. It is as if he has accustomed himself to the idea of killing and death, and he openly promises that Claudius will soon follow Polonius on his way to heaven or hell (4.3.34-5). At this point Hamlet is sent off to England, and is offstage for about 500 lines, while the action focuses on Ophelia and Laertes. When we see him again, in the graveyard scene, he is brooding over skulls on the levelling that death brings, and the scene marks his acceptance of the idea of his own death. Hamlet's byplay with the skulls also provides a significant contrast to his encounter with the Ghost in Act 1; there a figure apparently from a life beyond the grave appears in order to be remembered and to demand that Claudius be punished. Hamlet cannot carry out the Ghost's demand until he bypasses his conscience in the spontaneous stabbing of Polonius, after which he seems resigned to the idea of death as the end, as oblivion, in his grotesque image of Alexander the Great's body reduced to a stopper for a beer-barrel.[36] The skulls suggest an image of finality, the body lasting nine years in the ground, the skull of Yorick twenty-three years, in stark contrast to the 'eternal blazon', or depiction of a life beyond mortal experience, of which the Ghost speaks at 1.5.21. The skulls question the possibility of such a world. But then comes the great shock to him of discovering that Ophelia is dead, and he realizes that the grave-diggers have been preparing for the burial of her body. This is the only death that moves him, not to a recognition that he might be to blame for her suicide, but rather to anger at the ostentatious grieving of Laertes: 'the bravery of his grief did put me / Into a towering passion' (5.2.79–80).

After killing Polonius, reconciling himself to death as possible oblivion, and discovering that Ophelia is dead, Hamlet revises his attitude to revenge and murder. He has no compunction about sending Rosencrantz and Guildenstern to their deaths in England ('They are not near my conscience', 5.2.58, Folio only), and now accepts (also in lines found only in F) the idea of killing Claudius, 'is 't not perfect conscience,/To quit him with this arm?' (5.2.67–8).[37] This passage is revealing, especially in the use of the word 'conscience' in a sense that conflicts with biblical usage, as in 1 Timothy 1.5: 'the end of the commandment is charity out of a pure heart, and of a good conscience, and of faith unfeigned' – Hamlet cannot kill with a *good* conscience. The general mood of Hamlet after he kills Polonius is one of a sardonic acceptance of the idea of death. At the same time, he distances himself from what he has done by reinventing providence and claiming he is its agent, so that whatever he now does will leave his conscience untroubled. By openly showing his hostility to Claudius, he has ensured that sooner or later they will clash as 'mighty opposites' (5.2.62), and knowing death awaits him, he pushes away any sense of responsibility by referring himself to providence. If there were 'special providence' in the fall of a sparrow, so there would have been in the death of old Hamlet. It is convenient and comforting for Hamlet to claim, 'there's a divinity that shapes our ends' (5.2.10), but he seems really to be cheering himself up and finding a way to rationalize his resignation and the realization that he is unavoidably heading for a final showdown. This resignation is marked in his acceptance of the idea of his own death, the most prominent meaning of 'The readiness is all',[38] and all this time there is no hint of seeking revenge. Hamlet's condition is summed up in his final words to Horatio at 5.2.223: 'Let be', leave things as they are, there's nothing more to be said.[39] So he plays out the fencing match, and it is only after he has his own death-wound that he turns the poisoned weapon on Claudius, not in a plotted revenge, but in a spontaneous act of retaliation.

In neglecting revenge, Hamlet is not 'stifled by remembrance'[40] so much by his inheritance of conflicting classical and Christian values. The heroic code he associates with his father urges him to action, while the Christian code that is given lip-service in Claudius' Denmark condemns revenge and inhibits him from murder most foul. Rulers, however bad, may be God's 'ministers' in punishing the evil that subjects do according to St Paul, and act as revengers 'to execute wrath upon him that doeth evil' (Romans 13.4); the people are required to accept this, 'for conscience sake'. It is a role ('scourge and minister') that Hamlet claims for himself after killing Polonius. From this point on he justifies his increasing acceptance of violence by claiming he is an agent of providence, whereas earlier he had seen himself as subject to 'The slings and arrows of outrageous fortune', contrasting himself with Horatio, the embodiment of Senecan stoicism. As long as he contemplates the idea of revenge, Hamlet cannot sustain resolution, finding 'conscience does make cowards of us all' (3.1.83), and it is his exploration of this issue that makes the 'To be or not to be' soliloquy so central in the play. Only in his last soliloquy, omitted from the Folio text, does he find in Fortinbras an inspiring warrior image resembling that of his father, marching off to fight a war merely for honour, who might prevent Hamlet from 'thinking too precisely on the event' (4.4.41). But this soliloquy is present only in Q2, not in the Folio or Q1, and was, I believe, probably omitted in performance for several reasons. It duplicates Hamlet's self-denunciation in his earlier soliloquy, 'O what a rogue and peasant slave am I' (2.2.550) without advancing the action. With the killing of Polonius and the open hostility Hamlet has shown to the King, the momentum of that action has already shifted towards a final showdown with Claudius. Another self-questioning soliloquy is unnecessary.[41] This soliloquy also echoes the much earlier one, with Fortinbras replacing Pyrrhus as an incitement to Hamlet: 'O, from this time forth / My thoughts be bloody or be nothing worth' (4.4.65–6). But in Act 4 Hamlet is under guard, and at once is taken off to England, bloody thoughts left behind; he returns chastened and unlike his old self several scenes later. The soliloquy, I think, was written to flesh out the figure of Fortinbras, but proved distracting because it presents him through the words of Hamlet trying to rouse himself to action when there is no action in prospect.

Fortinbras resembles old Hamlet as a warrior prince, but he is not, as Horatio supposed in the opening scene, aiming to attack Denmark to recover lands old Hamlet fought to win, but setting off for Poland to fight for a worthless patch of ground in the name of honour. Thus, insofar as *Hamlet* is a revenge tragedy, Laertes is the revenger figure, who, in Senecan fashion, is willing, unlike Hamlet, to burst in at the head of a rabble crying 'Laertes shall be king' (4.5.106), matching Hamlet in having the support of the people (4.7.18). Where Hamlet reflects, seeks proof, hesitates to act, Laertes attacks unhesitatingly without bothering to find out what actually happened. He is analogous to Pyrrhus, driven by passion. Unlike Hamlet, he is eager to reject 'conscience' and 'dare damnation' (4.5.132–3) to get his revenge for the death of his father, and prepared to cut Hamlet's throat in the church (4.7.126). He returns from France equipped with a deadly poison he can apply to a rapier (4.7.140), and proceeds to plot with Claudius a scenario that will ensure the death of Hamlet. Laertes, of course, finds out that his father has been killed only in 4.5, so that the subplot of his revenge is worked out swiftly, but in most respects Laertes from this point becomes a revenger like Vindice or Atreus, and in his difference from Hamlet reveals something about the limitations of the revenge play. Revenge is a frequent motif in drama, but there are, in truth, few major revenge plays, since the basic plot offers limited possibilities of diversity. Revenge is always reactive, secondary, a response to some previous deed, and the most powerful tragedies develop from or culminate in some originating or primal act of violence.

Hamlet remains central in European and American culture as a work that continually challenges interpretation. Although it is commonly regarded as the major revenge play of its period, a concern with the idea of revenge rarely figures in the way Hamlet has been perceived:

The Romantics freed Hamlet the character from the play into an independent existence as a figure embodying nobility, or at least good intentions, but disabled from action by a sense of inadequacy, or a diseased consciousness capable of seeing the world as possessed by things rank and gross in nature, and hence a failure. Hamletism gained currency as a term to describe not only individuals, but the failings of intellectuals, political parties, or nations, and so *Hamlet* was restored to the public arena to characterize the condition of Germany, or Europe, or the world, or the decline of aristocracy in the face of democracy. As the idea of Hamletism prospered, so it came to affect the way the play was seen, and the most widely accepted critical readings of it have for a long time presented us with a version of Shakespeare's play reinfected, so to speak, with the virus of Hamletism, and seen in its totality as a vision of failure in modern men or even in Man himself. [42]

Hamlet has often been extrapolated from the play as someone who reflects, hesitates, is inhibited from acting, or as one who is oppressed by a corrupt world in which action is useless. Such versions of the Prince ignore much that is in the play, but in focusing on action or inaction they are responding in some sense to a central issue in the play, which is not the matter of revenge, but rather the control or release of instinctual drives to violence. If the lines beginning 'How all occasions' are omitted,

Hamlet's last major soliloquy is 'To be or not to be', a question that has immediately to do not with suicide, but with action:

Whether 'tis nobler in the mind to suffer
The slings and arrows of outrageous fortune,
Or to take arms against a sea of troubles,
And by opposing end them. (3.1.57–60)

To 'take arms', like his father, would mean to kill, which was accepted as part of an heroic code, but is rejected by Christian commandments. Hamlet is trapped in the contradictions between the two codes, which make him a subtle explorer of the problem of violence. There is no solution; having passed up a chance to revenge himself on Claudius and worked himself into a passionate state on his way to confront his mother, he spontaneously stabs through the arras to kill Polonius. This deed marks a rite of passage for him. His initial act of violence is also an act of self-definition, releasing impulses he had kept under control. Claudius sees himself as repeating Cain's killing of his brother Abel, but in losing control and committing murder Hamlet also is descended from Cain who, as he says, 'did the first murder' (5.1.77). Having once killed, he finds it easy to continue, reconstructing himself as an agent of providence in punishing others, as in sending Rosencrantz and Guildenstern to their deaths. It is ironic that he is carried off 'like a soldier' at the end, at the order of Fortinbras, who is a reincarnation of old Hamlet in his dedication to war. The violence generated by the Ghost's 'Remember me' brings death to Polonius, Ophelia, Rosencrantz, Guildenstern, Laertes, Claudius, Gertrude, and Hamlet. In the play's final irony Hamlet is anxious about the memory he will leave, a 'wounded name' or reputation, unless Horatio reports truly his story and his 'cause' (5.2.344); but Fortinbras, a type of the warrior Hamlet idealized in his father, sends Hamlet's body off with 'The soldier's music and the rite of war', ensuring that his memory is already being absorbed into the myth of the fighter as hero, into the culture of violence associated with old Hamlet and the new regime. The play remains to tell all of Hamlet's story that we know, which is much more than a tale of war, violence, and revenge; it is a story that probes deeply into the basic problem of human aggression.

NOTES

1. G. K. Hunter, 'Seneca and the Elizabethans: a Case-Study in Influence', *Shakespeare Survey*, 20 (1967), 17–26, citing 24; Hunter downplays the impact of Seneca, but see Robert S. Miola, *Shakespeare's Classical Tragedy* (1992).

2. Thomas Nashe, *Piers Penilesse His Supplication to the Devil* (1592), in *Works*, ed. R. B. McKerrow, 5 vols. (London: A. H. Bullen, 1904), 1, 186.

3. Jonathan Bate, *Titus Andronicus*, The Arden Shakespeare (London: Routledge, 1995), Introduction, 30.

4. See Eugene M. Waith, 'The Metamorphosis of Violence in *Titus Andronicus*', *Shakespeare Survey*, 10 (1957), 40–8, and Jonathan Bate, *Shakespeare and Ovid* (Oxford: Clarendon Press, 1993), 101–17.

5. Seneca, *His Tenne Tragedies* (1581) (Amsterdam: Theatrum Orbis Terrarum Ltd; New York: Da Capo Press, 1969), 38.

6. The relation between retribution and justice is analysed by John Kerrigan in his fine study of *Revenge Tragedy: Aeschylus to Armageddon* (Oxford: Clarendon Press, 1996), especially 21–5.

7. George Gekas, Republican Congressman, as reported in the *Los Angeles Times*, 1 August 1989.

8. Kerrigan, *Revenge Tragedy*, 23.

9. Seneca, *Four Tragedies and Octavia*, transl. E. F. Watling (Harmondsworth: Penguin Books, 1966), 91.

10. *Thyestes*, ed. Joost Daalder, The New Mermaids (London: Ernest Benn, 1982), 81. Kerrigan, *Revenge Tragedy*, 111–12, comments on this scene, and points out that Heywood joined the Society of Jesus shortly after completing his translation.

11. Bate, *Shakespeare and Ovid*, 19–22.

12. See Catherine Belsey, 'Sibling Rivalry. Hamlet and the First Murderer', in Belsey, *Shakespeare: the Loss of Eden* (Basingstoke: Macmillan, 1999), 129–74.

13. *Renaissance Tragedy and the Senecan Tradition* (New Haven, Conn.: Yale University Press, 1985), 15.

14. Kerrigan, *Revenge Tragedy*, 274–7, comments perceptively on the predicament of Job.

15. John Spalding Gatton, ' "There Must be Blood": Mutilation and Martyrdom on the Medieval Stage', *Violence in Drama*, Themes in Drama, 13 (Cambridge University Press, 1991), 79–91, citing 79. See also Jody Enders, *The Medieval Theater of Cruelty* (Ithaca: Cornell University Press), 1998.

16. Kerrigan, *Revenge Tragedy*, 249.

17. Harold Jenkins, Introduction to *Hamlet*, New Arden edition, Series 2 (London: Methuen, 1982), 126.

18. A. C. Bradley, *Shakespearean Tragedy* (London: Macmillan, 1904); John Dover Wilson, *What Happens in Hamlet* (Cambridge University Press, 1935); Maynard Mack, 'The World of Hamlet', *Yale Review*, New Series 47 (1951–2), 502–23; Ruth Nevo, *Tragic Form in Shakespeare* (Princeton University Press, 1972), 162; Martin Dodsworth, *Hamlet Closely Observed* (London: Athlone Press, 1985), 297.

19. Kerrigan, *Revenge Tragedy*, 126.

20. Scott McMillin, 'Acting and Violence in *The Revenger's Tragedy* and its Departures from *Hamlet*', *Studies in English Literature*, 24 (1984), 275–91, especially 282–3.

21. Nicholas Brooke, *Horrid Laughter in Jacobean Tragedy* (London: Open Books, 1979); see above, p. 8.

22. Harold Jenkins, Introduction to *Hamlet*, 139–40. The association of Hamlet with failure has a long history; see R. A. Foakes, *Hamlet versus Lear: Cultural Politics and Shakespeare's Art* (Cambridge University Press, 1993), 32–6.

23. Marilyn French, *Shakespeare's Division of Experience* (New York: Summit Books, 1981), 58.

24. See Nick de Somogyi, *Shakespeare's Theatre of War* (Aldershot: Ashgate, 1998), ch. 6, 222–52; he claims that 'Barnardo and Francisco's nervous guard takes place against a backdrop of national mobilization of the sort renewed in London in the summers of 1599 and 1601' (228).

25. According to Eleanor Prosser, *Hamlet and Revenge* (Stanford University Press, 1967), 120, 255.

26. G. R. Hibbard, Introduction to *Hamlet* (Oxford University Press, 1985), 185.

27. The first use of the word in this sense recorded in the *Oxford English Dictionary* dates from 1607, but Shakespeare surely had both meanings in mind here.

28. Stephen Greenblatt has made much of what he sees as theological resonances in the Ghost's association with purgatory, but I think he ignores the theatrical effect Shakespeare seems to be seeking. He has nothing to say about the Ghost's appearance in armour, and takes Hamlet's cry 'Hic et ubique?' (1.5.164) when the Ghost moves around in the 'cellarage' to be a telling allusion to 'traditional Catholic ritual'. If the phrase is cited from a Catholic prayer, then the reference may be satirical, for the area below the stage was conventionally known as Hell, corresponding to the 'Heavens' depicted on the canopy above. The Ghost is a more questionable and ambivalent figure than Greenblatt allows. See *Hamlet in Purgatory* (Princeton University Press, 2001), 234–7; see also Roland Mushat Frye, *The Renaissance Hamlet* (Princeton, 1984), 14–24; Avi Ehrlich, *Hamlet's Absent Father* (Princeton University Press, 1977), 38–9; and Jenkins, 457–9.

29. Philip Edwards, Introduction to *Hamlet* (Cambridge University Press, 1985), 39, 45.

30. John Casey, *Pagan Virtue. An Essay in Ethics* (Oxford: Clarendon Press, 1990)

31. Alasdair MacIntyre, *After Virtue: a Study in Moral Theory* (London: Duckworth; Notre Dame, Ind.: Notre Dame University Press, 1981), 115.

32. This image curiously recalls the Ghost's disgust at the 'loathsome crust' that Claudius' poison spread over his body (1.5.72), a connection that is also suggestive in explaining why Hamlet resists revenge however much the 'motive and the cue for passion' may stir him.

33. William Hazlitt, *Characters of Shakespeare's Plays* (1817), in *Complete Works*, ed. P. P. Howe (21 vols., London: J. M. Dent and Sons, 1980), IV, 234.

34. There has been much debate among critics, between those who claim the word here means consciousness and those who argue that it has a religious meaning; see *Hamlet*, ed. Jenkins, 492–3. I think both senses are very much in play here.

35. Andrew Gurr argued that the killing of Polonius is a turning point in the play; see *Hamlet and the Distracted Globe* (Edinburgh: Scottish Academic Press, for the University of Sussex Press, 1978), 76–9; see also Alexander Welsh, *Hamlet in his Modern Guises* (Princeton University Press, 2001), 62.

36. See above, p. 22. The deep anxiety of poets and dramatists in Shakespeare's age about the possibility that death might be merely annihilation is the concern of Robert N. Watson in his *The Rest is Silence* (1994), and is discussed by Michael Neill in *Issues of Death* (1999). Hence the importance of remembrance for Hamlet, and the distress of Laertes at finding his father buried with 'No trophy, sword, nor hatchment o'er his bones' (4.6.211), or nothing to commemorate him.

37. The Quarto text breaks off at 'is 't not perfect conscience', leaving the question incomplete.

38. Jenkins cites Matthew 24.44, 'Therefore be ye also ready: for in such an hour as ye think not the Son of man cometh', but the passage shows Hamlet simply as prepared for an early death, not as concerned about salvation; see also J. V. Cunningham, *Woe or Wonder: the Emotional Effect of Shakespearean Tragedy* (1951; repr., Denver: Alan Swallow, 1960), 8–13.

39. In his edition Jenkins takes 'Let be' as meaning 'Enough, forbear', and says editors are wrong to take the phrase as expressing resignation, but both meanings may be present; see *OED*, 'be'4, and Matthew 27.49 (1611 version).

40. Kerrigan, *Revenge Tragedy*, 186; he calls Hamlet's final assault on Claudius 'spontaneous retaliation, not long-nurtured vengeance'.

41. See Foakes, *Hamlet versus Lear*, 92–4.

42. *Ibid.*, 44.

CHAPTER 7

The central tragedies and violence

Hamlet's inner struggle ends when he breaks free from the moral restraints his Christian inheritance imposes on him and kills Polonius in a
spontaneous act of violence. In a few plays Shakespeare almost succeeds
in imagining a dramatic world constructed in a language without
Christian religious associations, but he could never quite avoid the vocabulary of the Bible. It was the most powerful cultural influence in Britain
during his time in the new translations of Tyndale and Coverdale that led
to the Geneva Bible of 1560 and the Bishops' Bible of 1568. Shakespeare's
intimate knowledge of these is evident throughout his plays and poems.
It is astonishing that he comes so near to creating a pagan world in his
Roman plays and in *King Lear*, but even in these a Christian thought
or image bursts through the surface from time to time: 'Our army lies,
ready to give up the ghost' (*Julius Caesar*, 5.1.89; compare Mark 15.37);
'Is it sin / To rush into the secret house of death?' (*Antony and Cleopatra*,
4.15.84–5; compare Romans 6.7); 'O dear father, / It is thy business that
I go about' (*King Lear*, 4.4.23–4; compare Luke 2.49). It was natural for
him to think in terms of the polarity of good and evil, heaven and hell,
and to use the familiar language of the Bible and the *Book of Common
Prayer*. At the same time, the enormous impact of Homer, Virgil, Ovid,
and Seneca offered a different frame of reference and posited heroic
ideals of manliness that accepted as a way of life the violence that was
rejected in the New Testament, but continued at all times to be practised
in the Europe of Shakespeare's time. The dramatic possibilities arising
from the disparities between classical and Christian values were explored
further by Shakespeare in his treatment of violence in the tragedies that
followed *Hamlet*.

Iago and the aesthetics of murder

The action of *Othello* is, so to speak, conditioned by the violence of war,
the 'Cyprus wars, / Which even now stands in act' (1.1.148–9). Othello

himself claims to know little of the world other than fighting; the 'dearest action' of his arms has been in the 'tented field' (1.3.86). His conversion through love and marriage to peaceful ways is something extraordinary, as Laurence Olivier showed when he made his first entry smelling a rose and preventing a fight with his order, 'Keep up your bright swords, for the dew will rust them' (1.2.59). Iago, the agent of much of the play's violence, is, by contrast, a soldier who cannot adapt to peace. He has fought in Rhodes and Cyprus, and now finds himself like a ship unable to sail for lack of a breeze, 'be-leed and calmed / By debitor and creditor' (1.1.29–30). 'Debitor and creditor' continues his slur on Cassio as a 'counter-caster', suggesting he is a mere book-keeper, and the whole phrase implies that Iago thrives on action, on the 'trade of war' in which he has killed men (1.2.1). If he is 'be-leed' himself, he can provoke others, as when he succeeds in putting Cassio 'in some action' (2.3.56) that will give offence. Cyprus is now at peace, the Turkish fleet storm-tossed and destroyed, but still a watch must be kept, and everyone goes armed. Iago all too quickly provokes Cassio into drinking too much and drawing his sword against Roderigo; but what gives this scene its vivid sense of casual violence is the way the brawl expands, as Cassio fights with and wounds Montano. For Iago this provides a substitute for 'action glorious' in battle as 'Pleasure and action make the hours seem short' (2.3.367). He has a careless attitude to life, as expressed in his song in this scene: 'A soldier's a man, / O, man's life's but a span' (2.3.66–7), a reference to Psalm 39.6, 'Behold, thou hast made my days as it were a span long' (*Book of Common Prayer*), a span being a 'handbreadth' (King James Bible) or very short space. So Iago works on Roderigo to convince him that to kill Cassio would be a matter of 'courage and valour' (4.2.216), or, as Roderigo is persuaded, ''Tis but a man gone' (5.1.10). Violence comes naturally to Iago.

If this is one perspective on Iago, Shakespeare also looked back to Aaron and Richard III in creating him, all of them characters who may be seen as related to 'stage Machiavels; the Devil and Vice of pre-Shakespearian drama; the clever slave of classical comedy'.[1] But Iago exceeds these figures, as he exceeds the worst 'villain' Emilia can imagine in turning Othello against Desdemona:

EMILIA: I will be hanged if some eternal villain,
    Some busy and insinuating rogue,
    Some cogging, cozening slave, to get some office,
    Have not devised this slander, I'll be hanged else!
IAGO: Fie, there is no such man, it is impossible.
                        (4.2.132–6)

Emilia's description comes near enough to Iago to suggest the possibility that she suspects him, but it falls short of what the audience sees; Iago is more complex and more interesting. Emilia points to one of the possible motives for Iago's actions, to get Cassio's office, but Iago notoriously hints at various motives, all plausible, none persuasive, so that in spite of much debate about them, interpreters have never been able to put aside Coleridge's famous comment on his soliloquy at the end of Act 1, 'the motive-hunting of motiveless Malignity'.[2] In his edition of the play, E. A. J. Honigmann seeks to show that various conscious motives Iago mentions, resentment at Cassio's appointment, hatred of Othello, desire to have Cassio's office, as well as some possible unconscious ones, such as envy of social privilege, and artistic pleasure in manipulating others, are recalled at various points in the play.[3] Add to these potential motives the others Iago suggests in his early soliloquies, namely suspicion that Othello has had sexual relations with Emilia ('I know not if 't be true', 1.3.386), and his own lust for Desdemona (2.1.289), and the list grows long. But noting further possible motives and more speculation about unconscious impulses does not make them more convincing, but rather has the opposite effect, which I suspect was what Coleridge had in mind.

In a late notebook, Coleridge developed his concept of Iago: arguing that all his various assigned motives are 'alike the mere functions of his own intellectual superiority & a vicious habit of assigning the precedence or primacy to the intellectual instead of the moral'.[4] One might go further and say that Iago cleverly perceives various motives that could plausibly help to explain his actions, and enjoys exhibiting them as a kind of intellectual game, but really does not need them. Attention to the illusion of his motivation has led to various interpretations of the character, and S. E. Hyman provided a kind of critical genealogy of five different takes on Iago: first as traditional stage villain derived from the Vice of the morality play; secondly, as satanic; thirdly, as artist; fourthly, as latent homosexual; and lastly as Machiavel.[5] No one of these does justice to the character Shakespeare created, nor do all together; Iago exceeds the sum of them, as well as the other roles Honigmann observes, of malcontent, voyeur, and humorist. Coleridge points to a kind of intellectual detachment in Shakespeare's representation of Iago, an ability to engage with and disengage from others in the play that is established through his controlling perspective in the first two acts, in which he has more to say than any other character, including four soliloquies directly addressing the audience, as well as a substantial speech delivered as an aside. He is onstage through most of the scenes in the early part of the play, as manipulator of Roderigo, as observer of Othello, whose wife Desdemona he brings to the council scene (1.3), as teaser of Desdemona, and as deviser of the cashiering of Cassio. We are invited to identify with Iago in these scenes, and to appreciate the devastating skill with which he gets his way. Indeed, if he betrays a weakness here, it may be marked in his invention of various motives, as if he has some deep need to find excuses for what he does.

At the beginning of the play Iago already hates Othello (1.1.5–6), and although the first reason he gives to Roderigo is that Cassio has been promoted to an office he coveted, it is hardly credible as a basis for hatred, especially if he is seen from the start as a sort of master-sergeant, lower-class, and 'In a world of masters and servants, one of the servants'.[6] Iago himself acknowledges that 'We cannot all be masters' (1.1.42). Cassio has a superior class standing as an officer, a standing confirmed and enhanced when he is appointed Governor of Cyprus in Othello's place in Act 5. Iago is baldly labelled 'a villain' in the 'Names of the Actors' listed at the end of the Folio text, and he may be considered an embodiment of human destructiveness,[7] characterized here, as I suggested earlier, as a becalmed soldier who is addicted to violent action. Shakespeare naturally suggests a Christian frame of reference for a play concerned with Venice in recent times, and containing perhaps a reminder to audiences at the Globe of the defeat of the Turks at the battle of Lepanto in 1571. Iago's casual use of Christian terms is evident in the way, for instance, in which he says to Roderigo of Othello, 'Though I do hate him as I do hell-pains' (1.1.152), or in the oaths (found in the Quarto of 1622, but omitted from the Folio) that help to establish Iago's character in the opening scene, ''Sblood' (= God's blood), and 'Zounds' (= by Christ's wounds). Here Iago, as often, may be thought of as using religious terms deliberately to influence Brabantio and Roderigo, and his freedom with oaths justifies Brabantio's response to the concealed figure who baits him about his daughter, 'What profane wretch art thou?' (1.1.113).

In putting pressure on Roderigo to follow Desdemona to Cyprus, Iago preaches a kind of mock sermon to him, in which he notoriously rejects the very concepts of morality and of love in favour of the idea that human beings fashion themselves, subject only to their own reason and sensuality, so that love he identifies with lust, and he simply abolishes the notion of virtue and vice: 'Virtue? A fig! 'tis in ourselves that we are thus or thus' (1.3.321). In effect he rejects the Christian placing of humanity between heaven and hell, even if he seems naturally to rely on the moral vocabulary of the time in calling on 'Hell and Night' to aid him at the end of this scene. He also exploits this vocabulary elsewhere, as, for example, in misleading Montano to think that drunkenness is the 'vice' that counterbalances Cassio's 'virtue' (2.3.116–17). The first part of the play indeed establishes Iago as emotionally independent of others, including even his wife Emilia, whom he treats almost with contempt as if 'his own marriage has gone dead'.[8] He is a clever con man, manipulating others as his puppets, a dramatist casting others in his contrived scenarios, an artist who allows each of us, as an 'involved, but secure, observer',[9] to enjoy the aesthetic experience of his entrapment of Othello. A. C. Bradley was right to emphasize this aspect of Iago's character: 'he is an artist. His action is a plot, the intricate plot of drama, and in the conception of it he experiences the tension and the joy of artistic creation.'[10] Iago, however, is not, as Bradley seems to imply, a master plotter, but rather a deviser of schemes thought out on the spur of the moment, as marked in his soliloquies, for instance when he cries 'How? How? Let's see.' (1.3.392), or thinks of arranging for Cassio to be seen with Desdemona by Othello:

> Ay, that's the way!
> Dull not device by coldness and delay!
> (2.3.375–6)

In such ways Iago is portrayed as an opportunist who has no long-term plan but makes use of the chances that fall in his way, such as Cassio's weakness for drink, and the handkerchief Emilia finds and gives him. He does not, however, perceive the longer-term consequences of his devices.

One of the central and deepest ironies in the play relates to Iago's casual association of himself with the devil and hell in spite of his rejection of any authority but himself. In his soliloquy at the end of Act 2, he enjoys the paradox that in advising Cassio to plead with Desdemona for his reinstatement as Lieutenant, he is recommending a course of action that leads 'Directly to his good', and at the same time to his destruction. He sees what he is doing as a sort of contradiction in terms, a theology of hell:

> Divinity of Hell!
> When devils will the blackest sins put on
> They do suggest at first with heavenly shows
> As I do now. (2.3.339–42)

At the same time as he sees his actions in terms of hell, he dissociates himself from 'devils' as 'They' in contrast to himself as 'I'. He speaks as if he can 'put on' sins like clothes or as a pretence, and discard them at will, and he thinks he can use devilish means to his own ends, yet remain superior and independent.

As Iago draws Othello into 'the net / That shall enmesh them all' (2.3.350–1), he plants suspicions by talking generally of cuckolds, jealousy, guilt, and the kinds of 'pranks' Venetians are known for, all as proceeding from his 'love and duty' (3.3.197). Only then does he directly involve Desdemona by reminding Othello that 'She did deceive her father' (3.3.209), a thought that affects Othello as if it opened up a new and horrible perspective on Desdemona and his marriage. Othello's response, 'I am bound to thee for ever', is seemingly a way of thanking Iago for his protestations of love, but resonates with the deeper sense of an indissoluble and lasting bond uniting the two characters. The word 'ever' pushes the relationship beyond any conception Iago has had; he has rejected any concern with eternity and dismissed religion with his ''tis in ourselves that we are thus or thus', but in enmeshing Othello he also, without meaning to do so, enmeshes himself. In his success at making Othello torture himself with jealous suspicion, Iago has his moment of gloating: as the downcast Othello approaches, he seems to take over something of the latter's majestic vocabulary:

> Not poppy nor mandragora,
> Nor all the drowsy syrups of the world,
> Shall ever medicine thee to that sweet sleep
> Which thou owedst yesterday. (3.3.333–6)

But if there will be no forgetfulness for Othello, neither will there be for Iago, and the word 'ever' returns to haunt both of them. For now that Iago has set him on the rack, Othello demands that he provide proof, not merely verbal insinuations that may be 'slander' (3.3.371). Iago is driven to invent the lecherous dream he attributes to Cassio, and finally claims to have seen Cassio using the handkerchief given to Desdemona by Othello. Iago achieves his aim, of convincing Othello that Desdemona is adulterous, but only at the cost of trapping himself as well in the 'violent pace' of the general's 'bloody thoughts'. When Othello kneels to offer his terrible vow of revenge on Cassio and Desdemona, Iago cannot draw back, but has to join him in kneeling and swearing to carry out 'What bloody business ever' he may command. Othello has exchanged Desdemona's love for Iago's, and Iago finds he has created a bond from which he cannot escape. If he at last gets the promotion he wanted ('Now art thou my lieutenant'), he shows in his exit line how he is himself caught in the net he devised: 'I am your own for ever.'

His final word here, 'ever', carries Iago beyond the quick gratifications of cheating Roderigo and getting Cassio cashiered, for there is no backing off from eternity. He is forced to go on convincing Othello that Desdemona is false, and does so by making him misinterpret Cassio's description of Bianca's doting love in 4.1. There is no alternative, except to admit that he has slandered Desdemona, and invite the wrath of Othello. So Iago finds himself not only committed to whatever Othello proposes, as in agreeing to murder Cassio (3.3.476), but taking control again in recommending Othello to strangle Desdemona in 'the bed she hath contaminated'(4.1.205). Othello reacts to his growing belief in Desdemona's adultery as a confused Christian who is conscious of invoking the powers of hell in seeking vengeance, and yet wants to 'Damn her, lewd minx: O damn her, damn her!' (3.3.478). Looking at the dead Desdemona at the end he imagines himself cast into hell at the last judgement ('at compt'):

> when we shall meet at compt
> This look of thine will hurl my soul from heaven
> And fiends will snatch at it. (5.2.273–5)

For him Iago is a 'demi-devil', and the punishment of 'this hellish villain' is left to Cassio finally, so that Iago is judged in Christian terms by others; but though he may use such terms himself when it is to his advantage, for instance, in presenting himself to Othello as honest and virtuous ('O grace! O heaven forgive me!', 3.3.376), he cannot be defined simply in terms of good and evil. His last words, 'What you know, you know', suggest that there is something we do not know, but also that we have all the necessary evidence about him. And what that evidence shows is a character who, for all his attractive cleverness, torments others and kills without compunction, who enjoys deceiving, tricking, and humiliating others, and who can stab his friend and his wife without hesitation.

There are no adequate motives for what he does, and if he is 'ensnared' in the trap he sets for Othello, it is in body, not in soul, since Iago does not recognize a life eternal, even if the irony of his commitment to 'ever' would bind him to Othello in hell – this may be how others in the play and Christians in the audience choose to see him, but Iago's violence appears part of him, a given, not a moral choice. Here Shakespeare develops a new kind of figure, whose urge to destroy others brings little or no gain for himself, and in the end results in self-destruction; a figure whose ostensible motives provide no adequate accounting for his actions, and who thrives on resentment and hostility to others. Othello typifies the hero whose values shift uncertainly between a pagan heroic ideal, derived

from a warrior ethos here associated with his mysterious past and African
origins, and a Christian sense of morality associated with his allegiance to
Venice. Iago adopts whatever stance best serves his immediate purposes,
but has no larger commitment than to himself. Violence is his mode
of self-expression, and by building up the action of the play initially
through the perspective of Iago's point of view, Shakespeare anticipates
a modernist perception of the possibility of murder conceived not as a
means to an end, but as an end in itself, and allows us to respond to Iago
primarily in aesthetic rather than moral terms.[11]

LEAR'S CLIMATE OF VIOLENCE

Dr Johnson's outrage at the death of Cordelia as 'contrary to the natural
ideas of justice, to the hope of the reader'[12] has been echoed by many,
especially by those who see her as almost saintly, a figure emblematic
of compassion. The 1608 Quarto of *King Lear* provides evidence for this
version of the character in the description of her in 4.3, a scene omitted
from the later Folio text (1623). In this scene a gentleman reports her
reaction to the casting out of Lear by Goneril and Regan in terms that
transform her from the obstinate daughter of the opening scene into a
Christianized image of pity: 'There she shook / The holy water from
her heavenly eyes' (4.3.30–1). In both texts of this generally pagan play
she is associated with Christ when she returns in 4.4, anxious to find and
help her father, and in a paraphrase of Luke 2.49, 'I must go about my
father's business', she cries, 'O dear father, / It is thy business that I go
about' (4.4.23–4). In the Folio, however, which I take to be Shakespeare's
revised version of the play,[13] Cordelia becomes a more complex figure. In
the Quarto she is accompanied by a doctor, as if she is solely concerned
to restore her father to health. The Folio requires her to enter 'with
drum and colours' at the head of an army, as if her purpose is to rescue
Lear, emphasizing her 'preparation' for war (22) and determination to
reinstate her 'aged father's right' to rule as king. The staging in the
Folio provides a dual perspective on Cordelia. Her determination in
leading her soldiers may be seen as consistent with her obstinacy in the
opening scene, while her concern for her 'dear father' now also displays
a quite different aspect of her character. Visually she is Queen of France,
armed perhaps, and leading an invading force into England on behalf
of Lear, as her 'colours' show, presumably those of France, and different
from those of the 'British powers' (21) she is opposing. It is one of the
terrible consequences of Lear's violence in the division of his kingdom

and treatment of his daughters that in order to aid him Cordelia must return to England as an enemy of the state, so that some political grounds could be argued for her death when she is captured.

It is Edmund who orders her killing, and he also has what may be seen as plausible reasons for putting his writ on her life. Edmund may be considered as a shrunken Iago, who bounces on stage with vitality and, in a play short on soliloquies, has three in his first scene, establishing a bond between him and the audience through his ebullience and energy, as well as his rebellious stance in a hierarchical society that snubs him as a bastard. His father, Gloucester, who has a role in the senior power structure of a patriarchal tyranny, humiliates him in the opening scene by publicly branding him with the stigma of 'whoreson', so that Edmund's contempt for custom, law, and legitimacy expressed in his first soliloquy in 1.2 has been seen as 'revolutionary scepticism' that rejects the 'obsession with power, property and inheritance' of an authoritarian society.[14] It soon becomes apparent, however, that there is no such depth to Edmund, whose manipulation of Edgar (his Roderigo) is directed towards gaining status and property: 'Let me, if not by birth, have lands by wit' (1.2.181). After he succeeds in getting his father to banish and promise to disinherit Edgar, Edmund next finds a way to rid himself of his father. He apparently steals the letter Gloucester received from supporters of Lear and locked in his closet (3.3.11), and hands it to Cornwall (3.5.10) knowing that it will brand his father as a traitor. This way Edmund stands to gain his father's title and property: 'That which my father loses, no less than all' (3.3.24). It is only when he allows both Goneril and Regan to think he accepts the favours they offer him that he realizes he is trapped, and will have to get rid of one of them and of Albany if he is to be free. He may even glimpse some further possibility of gaining power, though he says nothing specifically about this, and it seems almost as an afterthought that he determines to subvert Albany's intended mercy to Lear and Cordelia:

> As for the mercy
> Which he intends to Lear and to Cordelia,
> The battle done and they within our power,
> Shall never see his pardon; for my state
> Stands on me to defend, not to debate.
>   (5.1.66–70)

Edmund's selfish scheming hitherto has been designed to gain land and status, but ordering the murder of Lear and Cordelia goes far beyond such an aim, and would bring him no immediate advantage.

I think an audience at the play is not likely even to notice that possible reasons might be argued to explain the death of Cordelia as justified politically or motivated by Edmund's ambition. For we see her first as a victim, cast off by her father, in effect, to exile in marriage to the King of France, and later as devoted nurse of Lear when he is reduced to 'infantile need',[15] and requires mothering. We never see Cordelia as a married woman, since the King of France vanishes after the opening scene. Indeed, when she and her father are taken prisoner by Edmund's forces in 5.3, Lear imagines their future together as if they will be everything to one another in prison, and embraces her as if they were married:

> Have I caught thee?
> He that parts us shall bring a brand from heaven,
> And fire us hence like foxes. (5.3.21–3)

The idea is that it would need a firebrand from heaven to smoke them, like foxes, out of their hole, or, in other words, that no human agency may separate them. The lines may also carry an echo of the promise made in the marriage service, 'to love and to cherish, till death us do part'. In dismissing her in the opening scene Lear says he had hoped to set his rest 'On her kind nursery', and this hope is ironically fulfilled when, saying little, she appears as an embodiment of loving care in the final scene, combining aspects of a nurse, mother, daughter, and wife. Her death by hanging, as if she were a common criminal, at the whim of Edmund, is thus especially repellent, and affects us as a gratuitous and meaningless act of unnecessary violence.

How does her death emerge from and relate to the action of the play? The patriarchal society depicted in *King Lear* is not associated with any particular time, but if it has a connection with that of the ancient 'historical' Lear of around BC 800 who figures in Holinshed's *Chronicles*, its addiction to violence links it with that primitive age. It is in any case important to notice that the violence we first see is practised by Lear and his followers, and is vividly registered in the opening scene. In his rage Lear threatens to kill Kent, apparently drawing his sword (1.1.162–3), and in the Folio text has to be restrained by Albany and Cornwall (or possibly Cordelia; the speech prefix 'COR.' could refer to either). He goes on to banish Cordelia with terrible verbal violence 'for ever' as a stranger, a foreigner (which she will become as Queen of France) no more to him than a cannibal. Lear's habit is to lash out when angered. In 1.3 Oswald reports to Goneril that he struck her 'gentleman', and in the next scene Lear assaults Oswald, and rewards Kent for tripping and beating him.

Both Goneril and Regan complain about the riotous behaviour of Lear's hundred knights, though the impact these knights have in the play depends on the way a director presents them. Some directors, perhaps wishing to make Goneril and Regan appear plainly wicked, have merely brought on a few extras to drink, laugh, and hang about. Some, however, have followed Peter Brook in making them aggressive, as in his 1962 production and 1970 film of the play, in which they wreck the hall in Goneril's palace where we are to imagine them gathered for dinner in 1.4. Brook favoured the 1623 Folio text, in which the contemptuous language used by Goneril in speaking to Oswald in 1.3 ('Idle old man… Old fools are babes again', etc.) was cut, so that this scene emphasized the violence of Lear and his knights. Two other speeches were added for Goneril in the Folio at 1.4.315–27, and a third for Regan in 2.2, stressing further the danger presented by Lear's hundred knights and their 'riots' (2.2.335). From Goneril's point of view, it makes sense to demand that Lear 'disquantity' his train to fifty, for Lear's 'insolent retinue' of a hundred knights creates a rival authority in her household:

> that on every dream,
> Each buzz, each fancy, each complaint, dislike,
> He may enguard his dotage with their powers
> And hold our lives in mercy. (1.4.317–20)

The Folio text gives more weight to the violence of Lear and his knights, and makes the complaints of his daughters more plausible. The most actively riotous of Lear's followers is Kent, who is put in the stocks for abusing and beating Oswald in a reworking of Cassio's pursuit of Roderigo; just as Cassio loses his head and uses his sword to wound Montano, so Kent draws his sword to fight with Edmund (2.2.45). Kent resembles Lear in giving vent to anger by striking out, and when asked to explain his attack on Oswald can only say, 'His countenance likes me not' (2.2.91). Lear has taken for granted the use of violence in exercising authority as king, and has encouraged his followers, the knights, and especially Kent to do likewise on his behalf. Whatever we may think of Goneril, Regan, and their agent Oswald in the first two acts, it is Lear himself who provides a role model for them.

It proves a hard lesson for Lear to learn, that when he gave away his authority to his daughters he also empowered them to use violence, against his follower Kent first, and then against himself, as they humiliate him and drive him towards madness. Lear's addiction to violence licenses Goneril and Regan, as soon as they have power, to behave as he did when king. But the blinding of Gloucester in Act 3 marks a significant shift; the violence of Lear and Kent was sparked by anger, and we may allow that a blow struck in passion can be partially excused, that, as Kent says, citing a proverb, 'anger hath a privilege' (2.2.71). Cornwall claims this privilege when he says 'our power / Shall do a courtesy to our wrath' (3.7.25–6) in dealing with Gloucester; however, he does not strike out in anger, but rather prepares in cold blood to torment his helpless victim, first ordering servants to bind him to a chair, while Regan plucks his beard. The preparations for torture are staged to make the scene more horrific, before Cornwall gouges out one eye, and then a minute or two later, after a servant has given him his death-wound, destroys the other. Not only has Edmund stolen and passed on to Cornwall the letter Gloucester has received from France, but Oswald has reported the sending of Lear to Dover, so that Cornwall and Regan have nothing to learn by questioning the old man. Regan says as much, 'we know the truth' (3.7.43), so that their grilling of Gloucester and brutal blinding of him appear merely gratuitous and are made the more outrageous in that they are guests in his house. In performance the blinding was for long either omitted or concealed from the audience by having Gloucester face the rear of the stage, but since Peter Brook's production of 1962, in which Cornwall gouged out an eye with one of his spurs, it has often been done in full view. There is no evidence as to how the scene was played in Shakespeare's time, other than the stage-directions that require one servant to draw his sword on Cornwall, and Regan to snatch a sword from another servant and stab the first from behind. The violence of this scene marks a qualitative shift in the play and quite overshadows anything done previously by Lear or Kent or the knights, and the death of Cornwall at the hands of his servant provides some relief from the sense of wanton savagery in the treatment of Gloucester.

This action, the first in which blood is shed, is the prelude to more violence, to the killing of Oswald by Edgar, the deaths of Goneril and Regan, the battle between the English and French forces, the fight between Edgar and Edmund, and the hanging of Cordelia. I think as readers or audience we accept the premise of a violent world, and recognize it as relating to our own, whatever the ostensible setting of the play. The violence of Lear and Kent may dismay, but does not appal because it springs from anger. I commented earlier (p. 13) on one production in which Edgar was presented as obsessed with a need to revenge what was done to his father, so that he blinded Oswald with his staff, and at the end of a 'savage duel' with Edmund, tried to gouge out his eyes.[16] Such a

Figure 6 *King Lear*, Act 4, Scene 6, directed by Adrian Noble, Royal Shakespeare Theatre, 1982. Edgar killing Oswald in the presence of his father Gloucester, whose eyes have been gouged out by Regan and Cornwall.

treatment of Edgar, I think, goes against the thrust of the play, which is to show him as acting only in self-defence when Oswald threatens to kill him (4.6.233–4). The fight with Edmund is staged as a ritual encounter in response to Edgar's challenge, at a time when civil war and a French invading force have done away with any other forms of justice. We are bound to see it in some sense as symbolic of good overcoming evil, even if it is at the same time disturbing as a fight between brothers, recalling the story of Cain and Abel, but with the difference that the Abel-figure is the victor, achieving his self-definition, the recovery of his status, through violence.

In establishing a climate in which 'his countenance likes me not' is sufficient excuse for a beating, the initial violence of Lear and Kent prepares the way in some measure for more terrible acts of violence that in turn lead to the breakdown of order and internecine strife of the last scenes, in which Cordelia arrives from France as an invader, and is taken prisoner with Lear as traitors in their own land. The personal chaos that afflicted Othello is broadened here into a national chaos that afflicts everyone in *King Lear*. The blinding of Gloucester and the hanging of Cordelia horrify because these acts, carried out against a defenceless old man and a girl, are seen as gratuitous, done merely for the satisfaction or pleasure of the perpetrators. At the same time, these deeds grow out of the dynamics of the play, and, though they shock, they do not surprise, because they represent an extension of that licence to violence that Lear has established by his own conduct and that of his followers. Lear teaches his daughters and their husbands by example how violence may be used to maintain power. The action at the end is carefully orchestrated. The two elder sisters cannot control their mutual passion for Edmund, and turn on one another. Goneril poisons Regan before her own death is announced by the entry of a Gentleman wielding a 'bloody knife' (5.3.222). Momentarily an audience might gasp to think the knife signals the death of Cordelia, but in fact it comes 'from the heart' of Goneril, perhaps stabbed in a last fierce burst of energy by the dying Regan. They die by mutual violence, and Albany calls for their bodies to be brought on stage at 5.3.229 even as he orders the dying Edmund to be carried out.

The stage-direction, found in the Quarto and Folio texts, calling for the bodies of Goneril and Regan to be displayed, is unusual; typically a body so conveyed would be male, and carried in state, to be mourned or buried.[17] Shakespeare designs the action to ensure that the bodies of all three of Lear's daughters are seen on stage when finally the old King carries on the dead or dying Cordelia. The effect is to reinforce a sense that the violence initiated by Lear has proliferated to bring about not only civil war and war with France, but the destruction of his entire family. The bringing on of the bodies Albany greets as a 'judgment of the heavens' (5.3.230), but the visual presence of the dead bodies of Goneril and Regan as Lear brings on the dead or dying Cordelia seems rather to show that in some ultimate sense the judgement is on Lear himself, who is finally responsible for the deaths of his daughters. Where *Othello* focuses on an individual who pursues murder for its own sake, *King Lear* presents a larger and more profound image of an authoritarian society ruled by a tyrannical monarch who assumes the right to use violence when he is angered, and who, by handing power to his elder daughters, licenses them to use their new-found power in horrific ways. The play makes us acutely aware of the horror of gratuitous violence, and offers no consolatory prospect that humans might act differently.

MACBETH, CORIOLANUS, AND MANLINESS

When the fog clears from the brief opening scene of the Weird Sisters in *Macbeth*, King Duncan and his attendants enter to the sound of a call to arms, as if near a battlefield, to meet a 'bleeding Captain'. The visual image of red blood, real or imagined, recurs throughout the play as the ineradicable stain of violence. The Captain reports the defeat of the rebel Macdonwald in 1.2 in terms relating to butchery. In the battle Macbeth:

With his brandished steel,
Which smoked with bloody execution,
Like valour's minion carved out his passage,
Till he faced the slave;
Which ne'er shook hands, nor bade farewell to him,
Till he unseamed him from the nave to the chops,
And fixed his head upon our battlements. (1.2.17–23)

The resonances of this extraordinary passage include the suggestion of carving meat, and splitting or ripping open (figuratively from the seam of a garment) Macdonwald's body from the belly (navel) to the 'chops' (Folio text), which meant not only jaws or 'chaps'[18] but cutlets or pieces of meat. The lines suggest that Macbeth's 'steel' struck fire, while 'smoked' also suggests the steam rising from gushing blood. Macbeth is both the darling of 'valour', the bravest of men, and a cruel monster, killing his enemies like animals, the product of a culture of violence. Shakespeare deliberately altered his source here, for according to Holinshed, Macdonwald committed suicide; at the same time, he develops in striking images the references in Holinshed to Macbeth's 'cruel nature'.

This is all we know about Macbeth initially, that he is a warrior who seems to delight in killing, as if 'to bathe in reeking wounds / Or memorise another Golgotha' (1.2.40–1) according to the Captain's report. Golgotha was the 'place of a skull', of the dead, where soldiers took Christ to be crucified (Matthew 27.27–35). The implications of this reference are not easy to tease out: are Macbeth and Banquo perceived as turning the battlefield into another place of skulls in killing indiscriminately all who come in their way? Are they to be seen as like the soldiers who crucified Jesus, who seems curiously aligned with the enemy here? In what way do their actions 'memorize' or make memorable another Calvary, unless by converting the battlefield into a graveyard? The lines suggest that Macbeth is justly described as 'Bellona's bridegroom' by Ross (1.2.55), referring to the Roman goddess of war. His one concern has been fearlessly

to create 'Strange images of death', as Ross remarks later (1.3.97). Here
in the early scenes Macbeth is represented in ways that might justify
Malcolm later calling him a 'butcher' (5.9.35), a fighter so habituated
to carnage that he is not troubled by the horror of the killings he has
carried out.

When he learns from Ross that he has become Thane of Glamis and
been made Thane of Cawdor as the Witches prophesied, he turns aside
to brood on the news, and shows that he has already contemplated the
possibility of becoming king, for he sees it as a prologue to the 'swelling
act / Of the imperial theme' (1.3.128–9), where 'swelling act' suggests
both the growing crowd attendant on those who become king and the
acting out or performance of obtaining the throne. Murdering the King,
however, which is the idea that surfaces in this aside, is not so easy – in spite
of his familiarity with strange images of death – imagining the 'horrid
image' (135) of murdering Duncan unsettles him and almost disables
him from acting, as for a time 'function is smothered in surmise'. Lady
Macbeth seems driven by a simple ambition in urging him to the deed
as if 'Only look up clear' (1.5.70) is all that it requires. By contrast, the
series of great speeches in which Macbeth frets about the assassination
lose their way in an obscurity that expresses emotional turmoil rather
than an understanding of the issues. So, for example, the last lines of
his soliloquy in 1.7 reverberate with meanings and echoes that require
extensive commentary to tease out, and which an audience is not likely
to grasp:

And pity, like a naked new-born babe
Striding the blast, or heaven's cherubin horsed
Upon the sightless couriers of the air,
Shall blow the horrid deed in every eye,
That tears shall drown the wind. I have no spur
To prick the sides of my intent, but only
Vaulting ambition, which o'erleaps itself
And falls on th' other. (1.7.21–8)

The sudden shifts from 'babe' to cherubs 'horsed' on winds, to blind
'couriers', to seeing eyes, to tears, and then to the spurs of another kind
of horse do not allow any easy understanding of these lines in reading
them, much less than when heard in a theatre. What they do dramatically
is establish that Macbeth does not fully understand himself, or what he
is saying; his words convey the anguish of a tortured mind and a sense
of bewilderment.

These lines and his other soliloquies show that Macbeth does not really comprehend the reasons why he is drawn, in spite of his full consciousness of the 'deep damnation of his taking off' (1.7.20), to murder Duncan. If the spur were merely ambition for the Crown, he could overcome it; he has, in any case, the prophecy of the Weird Sisters that he will be king. Macbeth's broodings on the deed before the murder culminate in his vision of the air-drawn dagger covered in blood which guides him towards Duncan's chamber, and symbolizes the compulsion that drives him. Macbeth is represented as a warrior who is accustomed to making 'images of death' on the battlefield, but now he is driven to face the challenge of a different kind of killing, and it is that inner drive that overcomes his moral revulsion at murdering his king, a kinsman, and a guest in his own house. Indeed, killing Duncan is the ultimate murder, for in a play that celebrates a warrior culture, and begins and ends in battle, he is an anomaly, saintly, meek, and virtuous. Lady Macbeth does not understand Macbeth either, and may marvel at his words (3.2.54), but she goads him with a challenge that reinforces his compulsive drive:

> Art thou afeared
> To be the same in thine own act and valour
> As thou art in desire? (1.7.39–41)

She taunts him with the hint of cowardice, of a want of courage and manliness, daring him to be 'so much more the man' and kill the King. Her 'desire' is for the crown, but his is larger, since it includes the urge to test himself to the limit. As he realizes the horror of murdering the King and its moral consequences he wins our sympathy, but as he overcomes that horror he also excites a measure of admiration for his ability to meet such a challenge, and for the sheer daring of it.

Lady Macbeth invokes the heroic values that establish his role as a warrior, and implies that if he cannot do this deed he would have to 'live a coward' (1.7.43) in his own self-esteem. This is the term that rattles Macbeth, since it undermines his notion of what it is to be a man:

> I dare do all that may become a man,
> Who dares do more is none. (1.7.46–7)

Lady Macbeth plays on the idea of manliness as daring, the courage to go beyond limits, to meet any challenge, and also to carry out what he has sworn to do – though nowhere in the text does Macbeth bind himself by an oath to do the deed. Her determination displaces his anxiety, and ironically her image of dashing out the brains of her own baby prompts him to applaud her courage:

> Bring forth men-children only!
> For thy undaunted mettle should compose
> Nothing but males. (1.7.73–5)

The alternation in Macbeth between moral horror at the thought of murder and fulfilment of an idea of manliness in carrying it out is focused in the double significance of his soliloquy and vision of a dagger in the next scene. The sudden appearance of blood on the visionary dagger strengthens his resolve, and desire overcomes anxiety as he draws an actual dagger, aligns himself with the Weird Sisters in references to witchcraft and Hecate, and identifies himself with Tarquin. The vision of the dagger is replaced by a vision of himself acting out his role as rapist or murderer even as he moves slowly to the exit that will take him to Duncan: 'thus with his stealthy pace, / With Tarquin's ravishing strides, towards his design / Moves like a ghost' (2.1.54–6). Even as he goes, he cannot altogether shake off the sense of 'present horror' (line 59), and when he returns with the bloody daggers in his hands, his moment of achievement at the same time unmans him: 'I am afraid to think what I have done; / Look on 't again I dare not' (2.2.50–1).

Unmanned temporarily by his murder of Duncan, Macbeth recovers on the arrival of Macduff and Lennox to claim that his 'violent love' prompted him to kill Duncan's attendants in a display of 'courage' when he found them with their daggers 'Unmannerly breeched with gore'. The pun on 'unmanly' here is suggestive, and links with Macbeth's vision of a bloody dagger that pointed the way to Duncan. It is in effect another vision in words, this time of how the dead Duncan and his grooms appeared, for in fact it was Lady Macbeth who had the courage to stab the grooms, but who now faints, perhaps because she in turn is unmanned, and cannot bear to think what she has done. From this point on Macbeth alternates between a 'manly readiness' (2.3.133) to rid himself of those who stand in his way and a condition in which a 'torture of the mind' (3.2.21) unmans him. He can prate about 'manhood' (3.1.91, 102) to the murderers he hires, yet be 'quite unmanned in folly' by the apparition of Banquo's ghost (3.4.72). His fears and anxieties are shown in his recognition that he has his desire, the throne, 'without content', since he sees only enemies where he once had friends.

The process of recognition is brought home in the banquet scene, when his vision of more blood marking the 'gory locks' of the ghost of

Banquo seems to bring to life his earlier fear that pity would 'blow the horrid deed in every eye', for Macbeth thinks he has revealed his guilt in the murder of Banquo to all the court. In his last encounter with the Weird Sisters, when he sees the line of Banquo's descendants stretching out to the 'crack of doom' (4.1.117), the 'blood-boltered' ghost of Banquo returns, and, finally, this 'horrible sight' (4.1.122) drives him to seek again the 'manliness' of the battlefield, where there is no room for hesitation or feeling:

> From this moment
> The very firstlings of my heart shall be
> The firstlings of my hand. (4.1.146–8)

His agents butcher Lady Macduff, who has only the 'womanly defence' of innocence (4.2.77), and her children, and the news of this deed prompts Macduff to redefine manliness in terms of what Macbeth has lost, the ability to feel:

MALCOLM: Dispute it like a man.
MACDUFF: I shall do so;
> But I must also feel it like a man.
> I cannot but remember such things were
> That were most precious to me.
> > (4.3.220–4)

Macbeth, by contrast, has 'supped full with horrors' (5.5.13), literally at the banquet with Banquo's ghost in attendance, and metaphorically in that a consequence of his killings is that he has lost the ability to be moved, so that the death of his wife means nothing to him.

Tomorrow and tomorrow and tomorrow
Creeps in this petty pace from day to day
To the last syllable of recorded time,
And all our yesterdays have lighted fools
The way to dusty death. (5.5.19–23)

The future ('tomorrow'), the present ('creeps'), and the past ('All our yesterdays') collapse into the boredom of meaningless repetition ending in the prospect of death, as Macbeth discovers he has lost any reason for remaining alive.

Instead of Norwegian invaders as at the beginning of the play, Macbeth faces an English invading force, and it is ironic that he cannot simply carve out his passage, but avoids Macduff until he is forced to fight him. It is ironic, too, that in this war young Siward is praised for dying 'like a man' (5.9.9) in confronting Macbeth, who has brought about a situation in which an heroic concept of manliness centred on courage does, for the duration of war, again become valued. The end of the play returns to a condition like that at the beginning. Macbeth is first shown as a killer whose achievements are measured by his unrestrained violence on the battlefield. Ambition drives him to killings of a different kind, beginning with the murder of Duncan, killings that have to be planned, and which allow time for reflection. He has to meet a new challenge, overcome his moral scruples, and align himself with the powers of evil emblematized in the Weird Sisters. In freeing himself to do the deed, he becomes a slave to fear, to the sense that he will never be secure, and is not released from this fear until faced again with the prospect of battle against Malcolm and the English army. It is only the 'big wars / That make ambition virtue', as Othello puts it (3.3.352–3); what then is left for the hero to do whose prowess in defending Scotland against enemies led Duncan to say, 'More is thy due than more than all can pay' (1.4.21)?

Macbeth begins the play as a killing machine in war, and his growth seems to depend on finding out how far he can go in confronting further and more terrible images of death in deliberate murder. The play reveals the price he pays in achieving what he is driven to do, and also exposes the limitations and moral consequences of manliness that is rooted in violence. In the compressed poetry and visual images of the play, Shakespeare makes us respond to the inner impulses that Macbeth does not fully understand, and which drive him to overcome scruples and dare damnation. Macbeth takes us beyond ordinary moral boundaries and judgements, for in the end the play is less concerned with a murderer who deserves our moral condemnation, than it is with a great warrior who breaks through a fear-barrier in doing what he is good at, killing, only to find on the other side not the achievement and success he looks for, but rather a need to go on repeating himself in a desert of spiritual desolation.[19]

If Malcolm and his forces restore fertility symbolically in bringing on stage their 'leavy screens' and moving the forest of Dunsinane, they are forced to fight for their cause on the killing fields of another war. Macbeth has renewed the cycle of violence, and we are again asked at the end of the play to applaud in war that which fills us with revulsion in peace, as the head of Macbeth is brought onstage, replacing the head of Macdonwald, chopped off, as we are told in the opening scene, by Macbeth. As Macbeth literally carved up Macdonwald, so now he ends as 'this dead butcher' (5.9.35) in Malcolm's image. If this neat shaping of the action were all the play offers, it would not amount to much. Macbeth is so much larger than Malcolm's summing up, and one way to perceive this is to notice that it may be seen as another take on the Cain and Abel story. Macbeth is not Duncan's brother, but he is his kinsman, his 'valiant cousin' (1.2.24). In the play version, however, the defining act, the murder of Duncan, leads not, as Cain's act does, to founding a civilization or even a dynasty. Macbeth may destroy all the 'unfortunate souls' that 'trace' Macduff's lineage, but Malcolm and Donalbain escape his clutches, as does Fleance. Macbeth wears a 'fruitless crown' and wields a 'barren sceptre' (3.1.60–1). The killing of Duncan becomes a defining act in bringing Macbeth not to a sense of achievement, but only to a discovery that his life has lost meaning; instead of giving point to his career by making him king, he is forced to go on killing, which in the end makes everything pointless, as all his grand ambitions dwindle into a sense of himself as no more than a shadow, and of all he has done as 'signifying nothing'.

In this play Shakespeare also probes more deeply than before into the problem of violence in a society conditioned by war. Macbeth is a warrior whose courage and skill make him formidable in leading Scottish forces against tough external enemies: Norwegians, and against rebels: Macdonwald. Lady Macbeth makes it seem an easy matter for one so experienced to kill a sleeping old man, but the play brings out the discordances between open violence in battle and secret violence in murder. What appears to him simple turns out to be a nightmare of complications as Macbeth has to free himself from the virtues and scruples (loyalty, valour, service, kinship) that established him as a commander and carry out an act of treachery based on deception ('False face must hide what the false heart doth know'). Lady Macbeth is mistaken in thinking his courage fails him. In murdering Duncan Macbeth is divided against himself, has to repudiate the values that made him a leader, and the play explores the difference between violence practised openly with general approval, and violence practised covertly against a king, a mirror image of what Macbeth would like to become. Macbeth is restored to an exhausted and wan wholeness only when he can once again fight an enemy in open war in confronting an English army in the final scenes.

Shakespeare dramatizes another take on manliness and violence in *Coriolanus*, which has some close links with *Macbeth*. Lady Macbeth, who has no experience of killing, is easily transported in imagination beyond the present (1.5.55–7) into the warm glow of a future in which she and her husband rule Scotland. She can chastise Macbeth with the 'valour' of her 'tongue' (1.5.26), but has no anticipation of what it will mean to murder. Her efforts to 'unsex' herself succeed briefly, but evaporate at the moment when she faints and cries, 'Help me hence, ho!' after Macbeth describes what she in fact has done, that is, kill one of Duncan's grooms, in 2.3. Her collapse here visually dramatizes her weakness, and confirms that she cannot sustain her attempt to be manly, and is after all no more than a woman in a man's world. Macbeth works alone in plotting the death of Banquo, while Lady Macbeth ends by reliving nightly in sleepwalking the nightmare of the murder of Duncan. By contrast, Volumnia projects her fantasies of manliness on to her son in *Coriolanus*, and so can sustain them with a terrifying complacency. She boasts that she first sent her only son Martius as a youth to a 'cruel war' to prove himself a man (1.3.14–15); she rejoices when he returns from battle wounded and blood-stained, and she is charmed by Valeria's account of her grandson tearing a butterfly to pieces:

VOLUMNIA: One on 's his father's moods.
VALERIA: Indeed, la, 'tis a noble child.
                    (1.3.67–8)

'Mood' meant fury, and the women are applauding the boy for an act of wanton cruelty, so that they early on establish an ironic shadow over the word 'noble', a word that registers both the patricians' sense of the worth of Coriolanus, and the limitations of their idea of nobility as measured by arrogance, disdain of the common people, and prowess in war. Later on, when Coriolanus is angered by the tribunes and plebeians into a 'worthy rage', all these meanings come into play in the remark of Menenius, 'His nature is too noble for the world' (3.1.255).

In spite of his scorn for the people as 'rats' (1.1.161, 248), or as a disease (3.1.78), and his avowed readiness to kill his own countrymen as 'slaves' (1.1.198) or for refusing to follow him (1.4.40), Coriolanus is, paradoxically, what we would now call a celebrity when he returns victorious to Rome. Brutus describes the 'popular throngs' who fill the streets to catch a glimpse of him after his triumph at Corioles, and a messenger reports:

I have seen dumb men throng to see him, and
The blind to hear him speak. Matrons flung gloves,
Ladies and maids their scarfs and handkerchers
Upon him as he passed. (2.1.262–5)

In making a god of him – even the nobles bend to him as to 'Jove's statue' – the patricians and the people reinforce his basic isolation from them in his limited perception of the value of life as centred in war. They almost worship him as a superstar, and help thus to confirm his beliefs, overlooking for the time being all the signs he has given of being inflexible with his peers and merely contemptuous of the plebeians. If Volumnia first instilled in him this scorn for the people as 'woollen vassals, things' (3.2.9), the people themselves in their adulation of him as a hero paradoxically help to make him what he is. When he asks her, 'Would you have me / False to my nature?' (3.2.14–15), that 'nature' has been constructed and fostered not only by her, but by all in Rome. As Brutus knows:

> He hath been used
> Ever to conquer, and to have his worth
> Of contradiction. (3.3.25–7)

The last phrase suggests the way he confirms his worth or stature by contradicting or defying others. His prime loyalty is to the Achillean view that chooses a brave death (1.6.71) or a 'noble life before a long' one (3.1.153), where 'noble' again is equated with bravery in battle.

The people know Coriolanus only as superstar or idol, and he knows the people only as objects, things, animals, so that the tribunes can easily exploit that gap to force him into exile, into becoming openly a 'lonely dragon' (4.1.30) looking for death or a war to fight. It is ironic that being called 'traitor to the people' (3.3.66) makes Coriolanus 'sweat with wrath' again (1.4.27), as he did when the Volscians disdained him in battle. In spite of his appeal to 'love of country' when urging soldiers to follow him (1.6.72), his first loyalties are to his mother and to the ideal she has inculcated of a warrior-hero; his next is to the patricians, but he has no allegiance to any larger concept of Rome that would include the people. In the pursuit of that ideal, he can easily turn on his country, offer his services to the Volsci and threaten to destroy Rome. The brief 'marriage' between Coriolanus and Aufidius when they embrace each other in a male bonding as warriors with a mutual love of fighting ('Our general himself makes a mistress of him', 4.5.200) is shattered when Coriolanus rapidly takes over leadership of the Volscians, isolating himself much as he did in Rome. 'He is their god', says Cominius (4.6.91), and, as when he was in Rome, a brittle popularity encourages him to behave indeed like a god, and inevitably stirs enmity, this time in Aufidius and his followers. With Rome there for the taking, Coriolanus yields not for love of Rome or the patricians, but to the pleading of his mother, appropriately since she has embodied for him the values he lives by, and so he exposes himself once more to the charge that he is a traitor, this time to the Volscians.

The wrath of Coriolanus is overwhelmed by the rage of Aufidius and his conspirators, and all that remains is for Aufidius to say, 'Yet he shall have a noble memory'; but the word 'noble' has become so tainted in the play that it now points only to the one thing Coriolanus was good at, fighting.

When Aufidius begins to resent being overshadowed among his own people, he takes stock of Coriolanus, suggesting at the end of Act 4 three possible reasons why Coriolanus was cast out by Rome, namely, pride, defect of judgement, and the inability of a warrior to adapt to peace. All are relevant, but he learns something more when he sees Coriolanus yield to Volumnia, and discovers that the great warrior remains in some ways an adolescent, a boy, 'clucked to' and home from the wars by a doting mother. This is the knowledge he uses to bring about the death of his enemy, driving him into a rage by branding him a 'boy of tears'. The play reveals a fresh perspective on the figure of the violent warrior trained to kill. We know nothing of Macbeth's background as he emerges from the slaughter of the battlefield bloody and victorious early in the play, and we soon learn that doing what becomes a man on the battlefield is easy for him. It takes the goading of his wife to push him into turning his manliness against the king he served, and translate killing in war into murder in peace. *Coriolanus* is a play that reflects on the limits of manliness in a different way, by dealing with a protagonist whose conduct and attitudes are limited initially by what his mother has made of him, sending him to 'cruel wars' as a boy, and are confirmed by the adulation he receives when he returns victorious from those wars. Coriolanus is effective only when he is alone, for he is unable to see the people as human, or to contain his contempt for those from whom he differs, so that he has no larger loyalty, and it seems inevitable that he will become, in his own image, a 'lonely dragon'. Macbeth seeks to achieve dominance in society at the court of Scotland, but finds that the murder of Duncan isolates him, and makes him fearful of others as much as they fear him; he loses touch even with his wife, so that he, too, by a different process, ends as a lonely dragon. Both plays in their different ways explore the problem of violence in relation to the limits of what it is to be a man.

NOTES

1. E. A. J. Honigmann, Introduction to his Arden edition of *Othello* (Walton-on-Thames: Thomas Nelson, 1997), 32–3.
2. Made in a lecture in 1819; see *Lectures 1808–1819: On Literature*, ed. R. A. Foakes, *The Collected Works of Samuel Taylor Coleridge*, Bollingen Series LXXV (Princeton University Press; London: Routledge, 1987), II, 315.

3. Honigmann, Introduction to *Othello*, 34–6.

4. Cited by Elinor Shaffer, *Shakespeare Quarterly*, 19 (1968), 196.

5. Stanley Edgar Hyman, *Iago: Some Approaches to the Illusion of his Motivation* (London: Elek Books, 1971).

6. Honigmann, Introduction to *Othello*, 36.

7. Borrowing the title of Anthony Storr's book, *Human Destructiveness* (New York: Grove Weidenfeld, 1991); he argues that aggression is linked to self-preservation, self-assertion, and self-affirmation, and converts to hatred 'when self-preservation is threatened or self-affirmation denied' (25).

8. Honigmann, Introduction to *Othello*, 38.

9. See Joel Black, *The Aesthetics of Murder* (Baltimore: Johns Hopkins University Press, 1991), 73.

10. *Shakespearean Tragedy* (1904; New York: Meridian Books, 1955), 187; compare Hyman, *Iago*, 61–76.

11. In *The Aesthetics of Murder*, Joel Black comments on the way murder may be seen as artistic when 'the reader's focus is shifted from the point of view of the victim to that of the murderer' (60).

12. *Samuel Johnson on Shakespeare*, ed. H. R. Woudhuysen (London: Penguin Books, 1989), 222.

13. See Gary Taylor and Michael Warren, eds., *The Division of the Kingdoms: Shakespeare's Two Versions of King Lear* (Oxford: Clarendon Press, 1983), and *King Lear*, ed. R. A. Foakes, Arden Shakespeare, Series 3 (Walton-on-Thames: Thomas Nelson and Sons, 1997), 116–46.

14. Jonathan Dollimore, *Radical Tragedy* (Brighton: Harvester Press; Chicago: University of Chicago Press, 1984), 197–8.

15. Janet Adelman, *Suffocating Mothers: Fantasies of Maternal Origin in Shakespeare's Plays, Hamlet to The Tempest* (New York: Routledge, 1992), 116.

16. In Adrian Noble's production for the Royal Shakespeare Theatre in 1993; see the report of it by Peter Holland in *Shakespeare Survey*, 47 (1994), 199–202.

17. See Alan C. Dessen and Leslie Thomson, *A Dictionary of Stage Directions in English Drama* (Cambridge University Press, 1999), 33–4.

18. In his edition (Cambridge University Press, 1997), A. R. Braunmuller emends to 'chaps'.

19. I revise here some ideas I developed in 'Images of Death: Ambition in *Macbeth*', in John Russell Brown, ed., *Focus on Macbeth* (London: Routledge, 1982), 7–29; see also 'Poetic Language and Dramatic Significance in Shakespeare', in Philip Edwards, Inga-Stina Ewbank, and G. K. Hunter, eds., *Shakespeare's Styles: Essays in Honour of Kenneth Muir* (Cambridge University Press, 1980), 79–83.

CHAPTER 8

Roman violence and power games

In a series of plays set in ancient Rome, Troy or Greece that begins with *Julius Caesar* in 1599 Shakespeare explored fresh aspects of violence in relation to war, heroism, and the pursuit of power. In turning to pre-Christian settings he was able to move on from the troubling complexities of *Henry V* and the intractable issue of whether there can be a just war in Christian terms, or whether it is in its nature 'impious'. He also freed himself from any need to deal with the issue of succession, the sacredness attributed to kingship in English history, or the extent to which the sins of a monarch may affect his descendants. He was enabled to focus *Julius Caesar*, the first of these plays, directly on the political assassination of a ruler. In *Troilus and Cressida* the idea of heroism comes under scrutiny in the context of a war that, because it is not related to English history, can be seen in a new, satirical perspective. The later Roman plays, *Antony and Cleopatra* and *Coriolanus*, have a more seriously critical concern with war and violence in the context of the politics of empire and the pursuit of power.

JULIUS CAESAR, ASSASSINATION, AND MOB VIOLENCE

Julius Caesar has struck many commentators as having a simplicity and clarity that differentiates it from the earlier histories, but at the same time, it is a play that offers a fresh perspective on violence and war. Caesar is the first dramatic character to be assassinated on the public stage for political reasons. The assassin as a killer hired privately for payment was already an established figure in the drama,[1] but political assassination as a public course of action chosen deliberately for a cause is different in kind. Shakespeare has Macbeth refer to the killing of Duncan as 'assassination' in his only use of the word, the first recorded in the *OED* as meaning the taking of life by treacherous violence, and the term 'assassin' soon gained currency in the seventeenth century, but commonly with reference to the murder of a public figure for reward.

The name Caesar had long been available to signify an absolute monarch or emperor, as can be seen in Shakespeare's use of it in, for example, *Henry VI*, Part 3 where the King, wandering in disguise, laments his loss of power: 'No bending knee will call thee Caesar now' (3.1.18). If an English monarch could be equated with Caesar, then a play about Julius Caesar might have some topical connection with concerns in the late years of Elizabeth's reign about the legitimacy of rebellion.[2] Shakespeare, however, was innovative in his play in rejecting the common view of Rome as an empire under the sway of the Caesars, a view derived from Suetonius, in favour of a republican idea of Rome derived from Plutarch.[3] By Shakespeare's time there was a vast European literature offering opinions for or against Julius Caesar, appointed 'dictator' in Rome, who might be perceived as a tyrant, but also as the pattern for a benevolent monarch. Equally Brutus might be viewed as a lover of freedom, or alternatively as an example of a traitor, placed in the lowest circle of Hell in Dante's *Inferno*, whose death provided 'an evident demonstration, that peoples rule must give place, and Princes power prevail'.[4] Shakespeare achieves an extraordinary nuanced balancing act in his representation of both Brutus and Caesar.

Caesar's hesitations, his changes of mind, his falling sickness and deafness, his treatment of the senators as 'Good friends' (2.2.126), and his refusal to listen to Artemidorus ('What touches ourself shall be last served', 3.1.8), all help to moderate our sense of his personality, so that it seems in character that he refuses the crown offered him before the people by Antony. At the same time, Caesar is waited on as the man in power, admired by Antony, who is all obedience: 'When Caesar says "Do this", it is performed' (1.2.10). Caesar was above all famous as a warrior, and North's translation of Plutarch's life of him is devoted largely to his achievements in battle, including his invasion of England and his well-known message to Rome after his victory over King Pharnaces in Asia Minor, 'Veni, vidi, vici' [I came, I saw, I conquered].[5] Cassius tries to downplay this aspect of Caesar by boasting to Brutus that he rescued Caesar from drowning, carrying him on his back just as Aeneas carried his father Anchises from burning Troy. Later, in his funeral oration, Antony reminds the plebeians that the mantle on Caesar's body is the one he wore when he 'overcame the Nervii' (3.2.174). The idea of Caesar as warrior, as related to epic heroes, underlies the action of the play, but Shakespeare is concerned to emphasize the gap between the public image of authority earned by past achievements, and the present weaknesses and limitations of Caesar as a man. The senators look to him to conduct state affairs in the Capitol, and his authority and potential brutality are glimpsed in the violent punishment of the tribunes of the people, Marullus and Flavius, who are 'put to silence', according to Casca, suggesting they were executed for 'pulling scarves off Caesar's images' (1.2.281–2).[6]

Caesar also projects an image of himself as embodied in his name, an image of constancy and courage in authority: 'always I am Caesar' (1.2.209), a name that cannot be 'liable to fear'. So it is also understandable that Brutus should be anxious when the people appear to 'Choose Caesar for their king' (1.2.79). By the same token, Brutus could be seen as representing freedom: he is conscious of his descent from Lucius Junius Brutus who by tradition drove the tyrant Tarquin from Rome (1.2.157–9; 2.1.53–4), and he conspires to kill Caesar in the name of honour and freedom. With selective emphasis Caesar can be perceived as a dictator and Brutus as a republican idealist. The play was staged and read in the United States for decades after independence as embodying, in the words of the advertisement of the 1770 production in Philadelphia, 'The noble struggles for liberty by that renowned patriot, Marcus Brutus'.[7] The rise of fascism suggested a different take on the play. Rather than celebrating the heroism of Brutus, the remarkable production by Orson Welles in New York in 1937 presented Caesar as Mussolini, with blackshirted followers giving him Nazi salutes.[8] The play was subtitled 'Death of a Dictator', and its emphasis was on the ineffectiveness of Brutus and the libertarian ideal as they are overwhelmed by the forces of fascism.

Shakespeare's play may be adjusted to support such interpretations, but they diminish its complexity. Caesar is an ambiguous figure, not a tyrant, however much those around him seem to push him towards adopting that role; and Brutus is nudged by Cassius towards inventing for himself reasons for Caesar's overthrow, even as he acknowledges that 'the quarrel / Will bear no colour for the thing he is' (2.1.28–9). It is Cassius who reconstructs Caesar as a tyrant (1.3.92, 103), harping on the notion that Brutus and the conspirators are 'underlings' (1.2.139) or in bondage to Caesar (1.2.60, 96; 1.3.90, 113). Brutus worries that Caesar might be ambitious and might like to be crowned as emperor (2.1.12–16), but it is only when he has to show leadership and encourage the gathered conspirators that he adopts the language of Cassius and speaks of 'high-sighted tyranny' (2.1.118). Even then he urges on his companions as if they were going against an abstraction not a man. Brutus and the other conspirators think that by killing Caesar they have destroyed not a tyrant but tyranny itself, and can substitute for tyranny an alternative abstraction: 'Liberty! Freedom! Tyranny is dead!', cries Cinna, echoed by Cassius and then Brutus (3.1.78, 81, 110). Cassius, the instigator of what for him has been a plot against an enemy, is caught up in the general fervour as the assassination is successful, and imagines the conspirators will be known as 'The men who gave their country liberty' (3.1.118).

In all the build-up to the assassination of Caesar there is no mention of what is to happen after his death. By his insinuations that the conspirators are underlings, and that the name of Brutus will start a spirit as soon as Caesar's, Cassius works on his friend by implying that he would make as good a ruler as Caesar, but always the main emphasis is on achieving freedom from bondage. The question who is to exercise power, and by what means, is never directly addressed. Brutus remains blind to the conseqences of his actions, never more so than when he calls on his comrades to bathe their hands in Caesar's blood, and wave their red weapons while crying 'Peace, Freedom and Liberty'. The bleeding body of Caesar is onstage through much of Act 3, and his ripped and blood-stained mantle is displayed by Antony, a vivid emblem of the violence that mocks the conspirators' cry of 'Peace'. The question who is to ensure peace and freedom, who is to govern after Caesar, is not discussed by them, and it lies at the heart of the play. Its absence allows an interpretation of Brutus as acting for the 'common good to all', in Antony's words (5.5.72), though he is concerned only with the general idea or name of liberty in conspiring against the idea of tyranny, and has no concern for the common good. So he could be played as embodying a republican ideal in America, provided that the struggle for liberty excluded the mob, and the scene of the lynching of Cinna the poet (3.3) was omitted. In the reduced and much altered blackshirt version with which Orson Welles launched the Mercury Theater in New York in 1937, he restored this scene, which had long been omitted in productions designed to enhance the stature of Brutus. It is a brief scene of great power that shows a remarkable anticipation of modern interpretations of the psychology of crowds. In thirty-eight lines Shakespeare dramatizes the critical moment when a bunch of citizens becomes a mob: 'The most important occurrence within the crowd is the *discharge*. Before this the crowd does not exist; it is the discharge which creates it.' The 'discharge' here occurs not when Cinna begins to answer the questions put to him

Figure 7 *Julius Caesar*, Act 3, Scene 3, directed by Trevor Nunn, with John Barton, Buzz Goodbody and Euan Smith, Royal Shakespeare Theatre, 1972. The plebeians shouting 'Tear him, tear him!' as they surround and kill Cinna the poet.

by the plebeians, but is triggered when he reveals his name. At that point they cease to hear him, and join together in the cry 'tear him', as he becomes for them the embodiment of a hated name. As a mob, then, they finally rush off to set fire to the houses of the conspirators, to 'burn all': 'A crowd setting fire to something feels irresistible; so long as the fire spreads everyone will join it and everything hostile will be destroyed.' [9]

The violence of the killing of Caesar, displayed so vividly onstage by Brutus and the other conspirators when they coat their arms and swords in his blood, and when the funeral orations take place in the presence of his bloody corpse and his clothes covered in blood, indirectly produces the violence of the mob. The Mercury production began in darkness, and the lights came up to reveal Caesar, uniformed to suggest Mussolini, silencing everyone by speaking Casca's line (1.2.14), 'Bid every noise be still.'[10] Caesar's death brought an end to his ability to control noise, to keep crowds in awe, and the consequences of the assassination were brought home in the carefully orchestrated scene in which the poet

Cinna wandered onstage to encounter a group of men who ignored his offer of poems; he tried to withdraw, only to find his way blocked, as other groups surrounded him in an ever-tightening circle. They began to tear his poems, and finally united as a mob, daggers drawn, and Cinna disappeared, screaming as he was murdered.[11] Welles saw Brutus as a man of principle, but also as an ineffectual liberal, desiring reform, but having no idea how to bring it about. He reduced the play to ninety minutes of continuous action, cut out Octavius, and the scene where Caesar's ghost appears, and curtailed the part of Antony. The play, for him, effectively ended once Antony set mischief afoot by stirring up the plebeians at the end of 3.2. The following scene, in which the innocent poet Cinna is lynched, thus took on tremendous importance. Brutus deluded himself into thinking he could destroy Caesar's name or spirit by stabbing his body, and the mob's destruction of Cinna for the sake of his name enacts a horrifying parallel. Brutus bathed in Caesar's blood with no thought for his victim, but anticipating the re-enactment of the murder on the stage:

How many times shall Caesar bleed in sport
That now on Pompey's basis lies along,
No worthier than the dust? (3.1.114–16)

His cold-blooded triumph in the murder of Caesar is put in perspective by the violent death of Cinna.

Shakespeare's play completes the narrative of the rebellion, which is launched before dawn as the conspirators debate where the east lies (2.1.101–11), and is rounded off symbolically at the end of another blood-stained day with the death of Cassius:

O setting sun,
As in thy red rays thou dost sink tonight,
So in his red blood Cassius' day is set.
(5.3.60–2)

The violence of the assassination breeds other forms of violence. The mob's lynching of Cinna is the most terrible. The first concern of the triumvirate is to name and agree to execute all the supporters of the conspirators (4.1). Immediately after this scene the play jumps in time to the civil war that ensues. Shakespeare diverts us with the quarrel between Brutus and Cassius, the report of the suicide of Portia, and the appearance of the ghost of Caesar to Brutus. It is a fine sequence that eloquently establishes a sense that, however much they try to cheer themselves up,

Cassius and Brutus are troubled by an unspoken awareness that all has been in vain, and the mood is one of resignation. When Brutus promises his boy Lucius, 'If I do live, / I will be good to thee' (4.3.264–5), he knows as we know that he will not live.

The scene prepares for the final encounter with the forces of Octavius and Antony at Philippi. Once again the stage is stained with blood, as young Cato is killed fighting, while Cassius dies on the sword with which he stabbed Caesar, and Brutus runs on his own sword. It is only in death that Cassius and Brutus find the freedom they thought to achieve with the assassination of Caesar (5.5.54). The bodies of Cassius and Brutus lie onstage marking the end of the 'day' of rebellion. In a final irony, Titinius puts a crown on the dead Cassius (5.3.97), who had so objected to the idea that Caesar might accept a crown. Shakespeare's main interest, however, is not in the completion of the cycle of violence, which happens relatively swiftly, but in the originating act and its immediate consequences. He shows at length how Brutus can only condition himself to participate in the murder of Caesar by turning him into an abstraction, an embodiment of tyranny. Brutus has no substantial motive, but this 'noblest Roman of them all' can be seduced by a foggy idealism into killing one who loves him (1.2.309). This is the mystery Shakespeare explores, and the death of Cinna the poet is the central scene of the play, in showing how all the lofty talk of freedom from bondage by the conspirators leads after the murder at once not to liberty, but to chaos and an explosion of spontaneous random violence.

TROILUS AND CRESSIDA AND THE FUTILITY OF WAR

Most of Shakespeare's plays written after *Julius Caesar* deal in some way with primal scenes of violence. *Hamlet* is pivotal in this respect, and I comment at length on this play in Chapter 5. In *Troilus and Cressida* Shakespeare repeatedly stresses the triviality of the motives that drive the Trojan War. The Greek heroes spend their time inventing ways to trick Achilles into returning to the battlefield, while the Trojans knowingly debate and reject the law of nature and of nations that demands the return of Helen to her husband Menelaus, and keep her as a 'spur to valiant and magnanimous deeds' (2.2.201). That 'spur', however, cannot goad Troilus to go to the battlefield when Cressida summons, or stir Achilles to break his promise to his lover Polyxena not to fight. Keeping Helen is the 'cause' for which the Trojans, according to Hector, are fighting, but he proves indeed that to keep her is to persist in wrongdoing, so that there is truly no cause to continue a war in which the warriors march out from Troy to do battle on days when they feel like it, and return from the field at the end of the day, as in 1.2, having fought at random with whatever Greeks have chosen to appear. The war has been going on for years, with 'many a Greek and Trojan dead', as Hector says (4.5.213), and seems at once pointless and carried on by a kind of inertia. The idea of 'valiant deeds' is contaminated by the absence of any good cause, and by the lechery that plagues Achilles, Troilus, Patroclus, Paris, Helen, Diomedes, and Cressida. Thersites provides a chorus to point up the failings of the Greek heroes, while Pandarus, the archetypal go-between, dwindles into an embodiment of venereal disease at the end. High talk of policy or honour is continually undermined by what the warriors do, and the effect is to trivialize the whole idea of the Trojan War as having no rationale other than the potential for fame in time to come.

Troilus proposes keeping Helen because she is 'a theme of honour and renown' (2.2.200), but really she is only an excuse for prolonging the war. Women and love may provide an ostensible 'cause' for fighting, but, ironically, Hector alone issues a challenge on behalf of his 'lady' (1.3.274), but then fails to carry through his fight with Ajax. Cressida renders the lovesick Troilus unable to fight; Helen prevents Paris from entering the fray, 'I would fain have armed today, but my Nell would not have it so' (3.1.131–2); Achilles has sworn an oath to Polyxena that he won't do battle ('fail fame; honour or go or stay', 5.1.43); and Andromache and Cassandra do their best to keep Hector from the field. The direct influence of these women is to keep men from heroic activity in battle, except insofar as Diomedes may be said to fight for Cressida when he wears her sleeve on his helm, by which time she is a theme of dishonour and infamy. Hector, most upright of all the Trojans and Greeks, is tainted when he succumbs to the temptation of killing for the sake of a rich armour, and Achilles, seeking revenge for the death of Patroclus, arranges for him to be assassinated by his Myrmidons rather than met in fair fight. The play begins with Troilus, smitten with love or lust for Cressida, disarming, and ends with him rushing about the battlefield in mad pursuit of the hated Diomedes.

It might seem that this undermining of heroic ideals, together with the satiric voyeurism of Pandarus and Thersites, would validate critical readings of the play that emphasize incoherence and disorientation, and see it as anticipating the absurd theatre of the twentieth century.[12] However, Shakespeare wrote knowing how the Trojan War ended and well aware that fame had indeed canonized the Greek and Trojan heroes in Homer's epic. So he can play off our knowledge against the ignorance of the characters, who cannot see the future, and only know

> The end crowns all
> And that old common arbitrator, Time
> Will one day end it. (4.5.223–5)

Time is indeed a crucial factor in the play. The play begins in the eighth year of the Trojan War (1.3.12), and the action takes place in the space of a few days. In the opening scenes Trojan warriors go out to battle and return the same day. Aeneas brings Hector's challenge to the Greeks for a fight to take place 'Tomorrow morning' (2.1.123). In Act 3 Pandarus arranges an excuse for Troilus to miss supper at Priam's table and spends the night bringing him and Cressida together. Cressida is traded for Antenor the next morning (4.1). Later that morning the inconclusive fight between Hector and Ajax takes place. The Trojan visitors are entertained by the Greeks until night falls, and torches are called for in 5.1 and 5.2 to mark the lateness of the hour. The return to battle and the death of Hector follow on the next day. On this level the action is notable for its swift changes and reversals of fortune.

In the consciousness, so to speak, of the characters, time takes on a different meaning. The war has dragged on for seven years, and the passage of time seems slow to Troilus, who has to bear with patience the leisurely progress Pandarus is making in his suit to Cressida (1.1.1–26), and to Hector, who is bored with 'this dull and long-continued truce' (1.3.261). Cressida confesses she has loved Troilus 'for many weary months' (3.2.113). The Trojans and Greeks are concerned with the passage of time, both in the sense that nothing has been achieved 'After so many hours, lives, speeches spent' (Priam in 2.2), and in their awareness of time as the destroyer (*Tempus edax rerum*), a familiar idea celebrated most notably in the advice Ulysses gives to Achilles:

> For beauty, wit,
> High birth, vigour of bone, desert in service,
> Love, friendship, charity, are subjects all
> To envious and calumniating Time.
>   (3.3.171–4)

Well, yes, all things pass away, as 'Injurious Time' robs Troilus of Cressida after their one night together (4.4.41), and 'blind oblivion' will swallow up the very stones of Troy and other cities (3.2.184). The proverbial image of Time the Reaper with his scythe is brought to life in such lines, as time seems an agent in human affairs; 'The bitter disposition of the time / Will have it so', says Paris as Cressida is hauled off to the Greek camp.

Time is perceived also in a third way in the play, as a preserver, as embodied notably in Nestor, 'Instructed by the antiquary times' (2.3.255), who fought with Hector's grandfather and can evaluate Hector's prowess in relation to past heroic deeds. Hector sees him as a 'good old chronicle / That hast so long walked hand in hand with time' (4.5.201–2), a 'storehouse of memories',[13] but he was also reminding Shakespeare's audience and readers of their historical records such as Holinshed's chronicles. Hector's special heroism is thus related to a past history in the play, and also to a future in which his fame and that of the other heroes will be celebrated in 'time to come'. Their concern for fame overrides all other considerations in the Trojan decision to continue fighting. Shakespeare did not need to give much emphasis to the mythical status of figures drawn from a well-known great epic story, for the play inevitably appeals frequently to the legend of the Trojan War as established by time in the consciousness of his audience. He did take care to include those incorporated

Figure 8 *Troilus and Cressida*, Act 5, Scene 9, directed by Ian Judge, Royal Shakespeare Theatre, 1996. Achilles stands by as his Myrmidons butcher the unarmed Hector.

from medieval legend, Troilus, Cressida, and Pandarus, in this longer perspective of time, when they join hands at the end of 3.2 and appeal to 'memory' to register the truth about them.

The long perspective of memorializing time is something Shakespeare could exploit in his only play based on Homeric epic. *Troilus and Cressida* is also his only play that enacts a small part of a well-known legend, begins in the middle of it, and ends still in the middle, with the war continuing. The death of Hector leaves the action incomplete, for a literate audience would be aware that most of the play's characters, including Troilus, Achilles, and Paris, would be dead before the war ended with the fall of Troy. I think that what many have seen as a 'chaotic splintering' in the last act of the play,[14] a lack of structural coherence, can be explained as related to an action that is incomplete as staged, but which could be readily completed in the imagination of audiences familiar with the legend of Troy.[15] The open ending has helped to foster a variety of opinions about the play and its significance, but if it can be seen as demystifying the heroes of traditional epic, and inviting terms such as fragmentation and disjunction, Shakespeare could at the same time rely on us to see beyond the 'extant moment', and know, as Achilles does not, "What's past and what's to come'. Hector and Achilles have survived as archetypes of heroism in war, even if the play throws a cold light on the worth of such heroism. The play allows us a kind of double vision, in which resides much of its power.

Shakespeare's treatment of the Trojan War has its basis in Homer, who represents the Greek heroes as tribal leaders embroiled in quarrels among themselves, and who shows Trojans and Greeks alike as putting a selfish concern for glory above other loyalties. I think Shakespeare was fascinated by their culture of violence, which he reinterprets in contemporary terms. In the play the War has acquired its own momentum, and a chance of ending it is rejected by the Trojans in their concern for glory. The Trojans debate the matter as Elizabethans might have done, Hector showing his acquaintance with the moral laws of nature and of nations, defined by Hooker in *The Laws of Ecclesiastical Polity*, before tossing these aside in his concern for the 'joint and several dignities' of the warriors. The Greeks debate the speciality of rule and necessity for 'degree, priority and place' in terms that relate to Elizabethan concepts of government and order. So whereas in Homer violence is an unquestioned way of life for warriors habituated to the idea of heroic death in hand-to-hand combat and to the repeated destruction of cities, in *Troilus and Cressida* a gap is opened between the civilized understanding of issues possessed by both sides, and a barbaric addiction to fighting that defies reason and common sense.

The distancing established by this gap undermines the traditional idea of the hero derived from Homer as a kind of super-warrior. The Trojan War as depicted in the play is chaotic, and on the battlefield, '"blockish" Ajax' is as good as the next man. The fighting is pointless, since whatever rules policy or chivalry might encourage are ignored. The play marks a new departure in Shakespeare's treatment of war, one that echoes Hamlet's meditation on Fortinbras's expedition into Poland to fight over a worthless patch of ground 'for a fantasy and trick of fame'. Possibly Shakespeare was disenchanted with the wars in which England had been involved for years, and in writing *Troilus and Cressida* (?1602–3) had in mind the ongoing siege of Ostend that began in 1601 and lasted until 1604. There, soldiers drawn from the low countries, assisted by their supporters from England and elsewhere, defended the town, described later by William Camden as 'a barren plot of sand',[16] against Spanish forces. The first of several printed accounts of the siege was entitled *The Oppugnation and fierce Siege of Ostend* (1601), which could have suggested Shakespeare's coinage in Ulysses' vision of disorder; 'Each thing meets / In mere oppugnancy' (1.3.111).[17] *Troilus and Cressida* would have been topical, but perhaps unplayable in view of its scathing indictment of war at a time when patriotism was in demand, and this could help to explain why it surfaced only in 1609.

VIOLENCE, POWER, AND GLAMOUR IN *ANTONY AND CLEOPATRA*

From one point of view *Antony and Cleopatra* may be seen as developing further and on a grander scale the emasculation of the warrior-hero by his lust for a woman. The opening scene echoes Troilus' 'Call here my varlet, I'll unarm again' as Antony refuses to hear the ambassadors from Rome, preferring to devote himself to 'pleasure' with Cleopatra. From the beginning Antony is associated with Mars (1.1.4), the god of war, and with Hercules (1.3.85), his 'ancestor' (4.12.44), the god who leaves him before the battle of Actium (4.3). Both of these connections have significant reverberations in the play. Mardian, the eunuch who serves Cleopatra, imagines 'What Venus did with Mars' (1.5.19) as he watches his mistress with Antony, reminding us of legends in which Mars seduces or is seduced by Venus and disarmed.[18] Cleopatra remembers putting her clothes on the drunken and sleeping Antony (2.5.21–3), recalling the

enslavement of Hercules by the Amazonian Omphale, who compelled
him to spin with her women. In his anger when he thinks Cleopatra has
betrayed him, Antony is tormented as if with the 'shirt of Nessus', the
poisoned shirt sent to Hercules by his wife Deianira (4.12.43). Antony's
subjugation is most marked when he turns tail at Actium and blames
Cleopatra:

> You did know
> How much you were my conqueror, and that
> My sword, made weak by my affection, would
> Obey it on all cause. (3.11.65–8)

Troilus, who starts out 'weaker than a woman's tear' (1.1.9), is merely
one of the participants in a war that has become meaningless. Antony,
on the other hand, is ruler of half the world, and his association with
gods both magnifies and diminishes him.

Writing on *Coriolanus* in *Characters of Shakespeare's Plays* (1817), William
Hazlitt saw the nature of poetry and the imagination as anti-democratic:

> Kings, priests, nobles are its train-bearers, tyrants and slaves its executioners . . .
> Poetry is right-royal. It puts the individual for the species, the one above the
> infinite many, might before right.

Heroism for him is linked with 'The insolence of power'; 'the assumption
of a right to insult or oppress others' excites the imagination: 'We had
rather be the oppressor than the oppressed', since 'The love of power in
ourselves and the admiration of it in others are both natural to man.'[19]
A central concern with power differentiates both this play and *Antony and
Cleopatra* from *Troilus and Cressida*. *Antony and Cleopatra* may also be seen
as related to *Julius Ceasar*. Antony's power, like that of Caesar, excites
our imagination; in spite of their failings, both seem larger than life,
and have a glamour that enchants, like that of star athletes now. The
glamour of Julius Caesar stems from his place in history, focused in his
boast, 'Veni, vidi, vici' after his conquest of Syria,[20] so that he seems to
Cassius to 'bestride the narrow world / Like a colossus' (1.2.133–4). The
glamour of Antony is centred in his relationship with Cleopatra, and in
the gaudy, sensual pleasures of life in Egypt: 'I' the east my pleasure lies'
(2.3.39). Here are no potentially mutinous citizens, tribunes, or senators
to trouble Octavius and Antony; they have to put Pompey in his place,
but essentially the power they share over the known world is absolute and
unchallenged.[21] The difference between them lies in the uses to which
they put that power.

As Hazlitt pointed out, power is based on oppression. Octavius is characterized as a cool politician, calculating every move. He has appropriate scorn for the common people who favour Pompey (1.4.40–7), uses Lepidus in wars to put down Pompey, and then gets rid of his fellow triumvir (3.5.7–12). As Shakespeare depicts Octavius, he is a ruler who has read Clausewitz, and clears his way to world domination both by policy, and by war and violence as alternative forms of policy. He is even willing to push his sister into marriage with Antony, though he knows it will not do any good, 'for 't cannot be / We shall remain in friendship' (2.2.119–20). Consequently it is difficult to warm to him. The triumvirs are so secure that they can indulge in a grand feast to celebrate their accord with Pompey, though Octavius does not like it: 'Our graver business / Frowns at this levity' (2.7.119–20). We hear about feasts in Egypt, 'Eight wild boars roasted whole at a breakfast' (2.2.189), but the only one staged takes place on Pompey's ship near Rome, and is seen in a double aspect, both as a marker of social harmony, and as degenerating into an orgy of drunkenness. 'The third part of the world', Lepidus, overcome with wine, has to be carried out, and then Octavius leaves with a frown, but not before Enobarbus has made him link hands with Antony and Pompey to sing a song to Bacchus.

Octavius is perceived in terms of control, both self-control and authoritarian control of his share of the empire, and nothing is allowed to distract him from graver business. Antony is perceived in terms of relaxation, easily distracted from affairs of state. Octavius seems preoccupied with maintaining and enlarging his authority through agents who silence Lepidus and Pompey for him. Antony is seen as enjoying his power in a kind of careless security, so that what to Octavius are his 'lascivious wassails' (1.4.57) appear to the audience as a breathtaking mode of opulent living; Octavius takes, while Antony gives. His excuse for putting off Caesar's messenger sets the tone:

Three kings I had newly feasted, and did want
Of what I was i' the morning. (2.2.81–2)

Antony has such a superfluity of lands at his disposal that he can make Cleopatra Queen of Syria, Cyprus, and Lydia (3.6.10), and such an abundance of kings at his command that he can summon twelve named and more unnamed ones to levy armies for him in opposing Octavius (3.6.65–77). His generosity is dramatically emphasized in the way he instantly responds to the news that Enobarbus has deserted by sending his treasure after him. Dolabella may not believe Cleopatra's final vision

of Antony, but it sums up something valid in what we see of him; there
was no winter in his bounty, and it is true that

> In his livery
> Walked crowns and crownets; realms and islands were
> As plates dropped from his pocket. (5.2.89–91)

It is hard not to feel that the play in large measure endorses Blake's
dictum, 'Damn braces, bless relaxes'.[22]

The contrast between Octavius and Antony ensures that the former
is perceived as colder and more cruel, as in casually putting Alexas to
death, and placing the armies that have revolted from Antony in the
vanguard of the next battle against him. These acts are politically astute,
but also mark a kind of cold-blooded calculation. In Hazlitt's terms, it is
thus Octavius who seems associated with power as oppression. The play
concerns figures who are so well established in power that we are hardly
aware of the violence that keeps them there. It is brought home less in
the deaths of Lepidus and Pompey, which are merely reported, than in
the scene in which Ventidius enters in triumph after his victory over the
Parthians with the dead body of Pacorus. Lepidus was carried off 'dead'
drunk in the previous scene, so that an ironic visual contrast is made,
pointing up the extent to which Antony and Octavius 'have ever won /
More in their officer than person' (3.1.16–17). They are able to keep war
at a distance until the battle of Actium, after which Antony is forced to
fight and lead his soldiers in person in his penultimate battle. Here he is
at once reduced and enlarged in stature, as for all his diminished power
he shows that he has heroic qualities, which Octavius never displays –
never needs to display for that matter.

War is the normal condition of empire, fought at its borders, at a distance, and in the play its violence is brought home only in the scene of
Ventidius and then in Antony's last stand against Octavius, where individual heroics fail against the overwhelming forces of the Roman armies.
The violence foregrounded in the play is personal, notably Cleopatra's
beating of the messenger who reports that Antony is married (2.5), and
Antony's treatment of another messenger, Thidias, who is whipped for
kissing Cleopatra's hand (3.13). Cleopatra's outburst of anger is provoked
by bad news, and Antony's by the behaviour of Cleopatra – the messenger
suffers for what she has done. In both cases the violence is an immediate
emotional response, a spontaneous reaction, and seems more excusable
than the large-scale violence of war. The self-inflicted violence of the
suicides of Antony and then of Cleopatra also appears courageous since

it defeats Octavius' intentions to execute Antony and put Cleopatra on display like an animal in Rome. Octavius achieves world domination, but in a muted triumph, a pale shadow of the excitement generated by Tamburlaine or Henry V. Shakespeare emphasizes the sense of lost grandeur by devoting the final act to Cleopatra and Octavius' devious dealings with her. At the end she dresses up as Venus, as she did when she first met Antony: 'I am again for Cydnus' (5.2.227) is an implied stage-direction, recalling Enobarbus' description of her as 'O'er picturing that Venus' in her barge (2.2.207–11). Throughout the play Antony is associated not only with Hercules, but with Mars, Bacchus, and Jupiter, identified with war, feasting, and bounty. Antony and Cleopatra both have a glamour not given to Octavius, so that the story of his winning control of the world takes second place. The faults of both Antony and Cleopatra are evident enough from Philo's opening lines in the play, and are commented on frequently enough from a Roman perspective, but the moral judgements made by Octavius are undermined by his own use of deception and murder in achieving his political ends, and the play stops short of making a moral assessment of the protagonists. Octavius says:

> Their story is
> No less in pity than his glory which
> Brought them to be lamented.
> (5.2.359–61)

But in the play they have the pity and the glory; Octavius merely gets the empire.

CORIOLANUS AND THE HERO AS MACHINE

Coriolanus (?1608) has obvious links with *Julius Caesar* in that both plays dramatize a popular rebellion against tyranny, and both deal with a period when a significant shift was taking place in the government of Rome. The action of the earlier play turns on the offer of a crown to make Julius Caesar king or emperor, while in *Coriolanus*, which relates to a much earlier period in Roman history, roughly B C 495–2, the action is provoked by the establishment of tribunes of the people, which marked a move towards democracy. The Rome of *Coriolanus* is still a city state competing with other cities for control of territories outside the 'gates' through which Martius is expelled at the end of Act 3. This older world has recently emerged from the tyranny of the Tarquins, and Martius himself at the age of sixteen (so Shakespeare; being but a stripling in North's Plutarch)

took part in the battle that drove out Tarquinius Superbus. Shakespeare
adds that which is not in Plutarch: 'Tarquin's self he met / And struck
him on his knee' (2.2.94–5), so that in the play Martius begins his career
identified as the liberator of Rome.[23] Within a short time the anger of
the plebeians at various harshnesses of patrician rule led to the appointment of tribunes of the people. Shakespeare focuses on one grievance,
the shortage of corn, and on Martius as the leader of those senators
who were prepared to starve the tribunes and plebeians into submission. So, ironically, Martius has become the enemy of the people by
the time the plays opens with the First Citizen crying 'Let us kill him'
(1.1.10).

According to Plutarch, Martius grew up 'inclined to the wars', neglected his education, and from his childhood exercised himself in handling weapons. In the play Martius is brought up to fight by his mother,
who wanted him to be famous, and sent him off as a youth to 'a cruel
war' (1.3.14). The difference is important. In the opening scene it is the
pride of Martius, not his addiction to fighting, that is ascribed by the
Second Citizen to his natural inclination: 'What he cannot help in his
nature, you account a vice in him' (1.1.40–1). Plutarch's account suggests
that Martius was by nature dedicated to fighting, whereas in the play his
passion for war is shaped or constructed by his mother. Volumnia, indeed, seems to embody an ancient Roman idea identifying, in the terms
of North's Plutarch, 'Virtus' in Latin with 'valiantness'.[24] Shakespeare
remembered this phrase in Cominius' praise of Martius:

> It is held
> That valour is the chiefest virtue and
> Most dignifies the haver. (2.2.83–5)

Effectively Martius is bred up 'loaded with precepts' to make him feel
invincible (4.1.9–11) and behave like a hero in epic, for whom war is an
end in itself, as the means to honour and fame. In this respect he has
connections with the warriors in *Troilus and Cressida* and, behind that play,
the *Iliad*. Shakespeare thus situates a kind of epic hero, whose horizons
are limited to war, in a society that is for the first time being forced to
acknowledge and share power with the plebeians. The play thus offers
another perspective on war and violence, not distanced as in *Antony and
Cleopatra* behind the glamour of empire achieved, but foregrounded in
the context of political change.

The other Greek and Roman plays end in war; *Coriolanus* begins with
conflict between the Romans and the Volscians, establishing in the first

act a dramatic world in which war is an accepted state of affairs. Martius
has fought seventeen battles since he defeated Tarquin (2.2.100), and
bears the scars of twenty-seven wounds (2.1.155). He has fought five times
with Aufidius (1.10.7) in personal combat, and yet another war with the
Volscians comes conveniently to put a temporary end to the threat of
rebellion by the plebeians in the first act. Menenius wittily exploits an
ancient concept of the state as an organic body in order to calm the mob,
disingenuously arguing that the belly (the people) receive the 'flour of all'
(punning on 'flower') leaving the patricians with the bran (1.1.144). The
analogy of the state with the body[25] is touched on in imagery elsewhere in
the play, for instance in the voices required for election, in the description
of the tribunes as the tongues and mouths of the people, in the idea of
Martius as a disease, a gangrened foot (3.1.294–307), or of the people as
'the bowels of ungrateful Rome' (4.5.133). In Plutarch the fable is serious
and credible, but in the play Menenius is enjoying himself tricking the
citizens with a story he does not believe, as is seen when he ends by
saying 'Rome and her rats are at the point of battle' (1.1.161). Images of
the people as animals are yet more common in the play.

As against the organic image presented in his fable, Menenius begins
by telling the citizens that they waste their time challenging the state:

> For your wants,
> Your suffering in this dearth, you may as well
> Strike at the heavens with your staves as lift them
> Against the Roman state, whose course will on
> The way it takes, cracking ten thousand curbs
> Of more strong link asunder than can ever
> Appear in your impediment. (1.1.65–71)

Here the state is imaged as a machine, as if the plebeians might be linking arms to stop the progress of a tank that destroys chains (curbs as
chains linked to a horse's bridle) and crushes everything in its path. As
Philip Brockbank suggested, 'The description of the Roman state is a
proleptic invocation of Martius. The body-politic is here the Achillean
body, a war-machine, a destructive, neutral, advancing thing, yielding to
no human obstacle.'[26] Martius becomes this war-machine when he enters the gates of Corioli alone, and comes off 'mantled' in blood (1.6.28),
and appearing as if he were 'flayed' (1.6.22). Masked thus, Martius is seen
as 'a thing of blood, whose every motion/Was timed with dying cries'
(2.2.109–10). He ran 'reeking o'er the lives of men' (119) at Corioli, just
as later in attacking Rome he seems to Cominius 'like a thing/Made by

some other deity than Nature' (4.6.91–2). Menenius compares him to an 'engine', meaning an engine of war, a battering ram, and there is a hint of what might be some robot out of science fiction: 'He is able to pierce a corslet with his eye, talks like a knell, and his hum is a battery' (5.4.20–1) – his merest interjection sounds like guns going off. In war, when he is most himself, Martius becomes a killing machine, prepared equally to destroy Volscians or Romans, like a butcher killing flies (4.6.96). Martius is Shakespeare's final depiction of an epic hero, 'bred i' the wars' (3.1.319), as one who prefers 'a noble life before a long' (3.1.153). He is compared to Hector by his mother (1.3.41–4), and also by Aufidius (1.8.11). Like Hector, he has a faithful wife, but unlike the Hector depicted in *Troilus and Cressida*, he is quite unable to reconcile his warrior's addiction to blood and violence with either a domestic scene in which, as an emblem of pity, his graciously silent wife weeps in the only way she can communicate with him, or with the political scene, in which compromise and negotiation are demanded.[27]

The inadequacies of the virtues of Martius are exposed in the opposition between his implacable will and the 'absolute shall' (3.1.89) of the tribunes and the people, who also behave like a machine for violence when roused into a mutinous mob willing to cast Martius from the Tarpeian rock. Aufidius, out of envy and emulation, determines to 'potch' at Martius by craft (1.10.15), but sees more clearly than any other the nature of his enemy. He identifies pride, defect of judgement, and an inability to adapt from war to peace as faults of which Martius has 'spices' (4.7.46), but recognizes, too, that these do not explain him:

> He has a merit
> To choke it in the utterance. So our virtues
> Lie in th'interpretation of the time,
> And power, unto itself most commendable,
> Hath not a tomb so evident as a chair
> T'extol what it hath done. (4.7.48–53)

This difficult passage summing up Aufidius' account of Martius suggests that the merits of Martius are discredited in speaking of them, and virtues are perceived as such according to what suits the time, differing in peace and war. Thus power, which always thinks itself most worthy of praise, is never more likely to be overthrown than when it is extolled in public, that 'chair' being the rostrum for a formal oration (such as that from which Antony delivers his funeral oration over Caesar's body in *Julius Caesar*, 3.2.74). Here the lines refer back to the oration delivered by Cominius to the senate in 2.2 after the victory of Martius at Corioli, a speech that leads his hearers to attempt to give Martius, now named Coriolanus, power as consul. The ultimate effect of the oration is to rouse the plebeians, who rightly think the virtues of Martius are not suited to peace, and thus to force him into exile, and bring about his death. It is, of course, ironic that Martius absents himself rather than hear his praises sung by Cominius, and that it is Volumnia's wish rather than his own that he should seek power ('I had rather be their servant in my way / Than sway with them in theirs', 2.1.203–4). It is also ironic that the only time Coriolanus boasts of his feats is when he is taunted by Aufidius at the end, so that his own words provoke the conspirators to kill him.

A psychological accounting for the shaping of the character of Martius might take account of his dependency on his mother, and on the extent to which he is caught between two worlds at a time when authority maintained by force is giving way to government by diplomacy; but no such accounting can fully explain him.[28] He can only think of violence as a fitting way of living, so that he remains a figure whose vision is blinkered, as is brought out in the telling moment when his family come as suppliants to him outside the besieged Rome, and, after he has kneeled to his mother, he greets his own young son (who noticeably does not kneel until Volumnia orders him to do so):

> The god of soldiers,
> With the consent of supreme Jove, inform
> Thy thoughts with nobleness, that thou mayst prove
> To shame invulnerable and stick i' the wars
> Like a great sea-mark, standing every flaw
> And saving those that eye thee! (5.3.70–75)

This is Shakespeare's addition to his source-material in Plutarch, de-signed to show that Martius has not changed: 'nobleness' is won on the battlefield as equated with fame, and he wants his son to be like himself, a soldier others look to, immovable in war, like a great rock or landmark, impervious to every gust of wind (one sense of 'flaw') and to every weakness. He is to be 'to shame invulnerable', incapable of shame-ful deeds, or do the words mean incapable of feeling shame? Even as Martius speaks these lines to his mother, Valeria and Virgilia are about to 'shame him' with their knees (5.3.171) into making peace. It is only in this way that he learns he cannot 'stand / As if a man were author of himself' (5.3.35–6); misbehaving in the eyes of his mother alone makes Coriolanus feel shame. Even then, the speech with which he yields to his mother's pleading is 'an evasion of self-awareness',[29] and to him an 'unnatural scene' (5.3.187) as marking what his warrior code utterly denies, the possibility of surrender.

Coriolanus is magnificent in embodying an heroic ideal, and appalling at the same time in exposing the limitations of that ideal. The play contains Shakespeare's most powerful critique of the heroic code and of war. It sets Coriolanus' single-minded passion for fighting in the context both of the fickle allegiances of plebeians easily manipulated by their tribunes and of the deviousness of patrician politics, so that there is no clear sense that peace is preferable to war. The servants at the house of Aufidius on the whole prefer war to peace in 4.5, because in peace men have less need of one another. If the heroic code can turn men into killing machines like Coriolanus, and blind them to other values and loyalties, the servants also remind us that peace can make 'men hate one another' (4.5.237) and so trigger renewed violence, as seen in the hostility beween the plebeians and the senate. Violence is revealed as part of the human condition, which is why, as Hazlitt put it, 'the love of power in ourselves and admiration of it in others' are natural to human beings. It is also the reason why Coriolanus remains curiously sympathetic as a character, in spite of his tantrums, his delight in tearing wings off butterflies, and his lack of feeling for others.

In these Roman plays Shakespeare was released from any need to invoke Christian values, and the absence of this perspective makes possible the creation of dramatic worlds in *Antony and Cleopatra* and especially *Coriolanus* in which values and virtues are relative, not absolute. In *Timon of Athens* Shakespeare sketched in Alcibiades another soldier who is banished and returns to besiege his native city, Athens in this case. Unlike Coriolanus, Alcibiades has no ideals, no dedication, even to war. He is a character who adjusts his values and ideas of virtue to the interpretation of the times. He is banished for trying to persuade the senators to bend the laws and excuse a murderer; he is accompanied by prostitutes when leading his army; and when the 'lascivious' city of Athens yields to him, he promises that only his own and Timon's enemies will be punished. In the fine scene in which he confronts the corrupt senators who have failed to help Timon or do anything about usury, but who now take a firm stand on the death penalty for murder, Alcibiades presents himself as a humble suitor to their 'virtues / For pity is the virtue of the law' (3.5.7–8). He claims the killer, his friend, a man of 'comely virtues', acted in rashness, not in cold blood, and though what he did was wrong, he should be let off because all men behave like that: 'To be in anger is impiety; / But who is man that is not angry?' (3.5.58–9). Who, indeed? In his flexible notions of virtue, and in implying that anger is natural to men, Alcibiades raises issues that are more fully explored in *Coriolanus*, a play in which violence is shown as inseparable from human aspirations, ideals, and even the desire for peace.

NOTES

1. See Martin Wiggins, *Journeymen in Murder: the Assassin in English Renaissance Drama* (Oxford: Clarendon Press, 1991), and above, p. 31.
2. David Daniell, Introduction to his edition of *Julius Caesar*, Arden Shakespeare, Series 3 (Walton-on-Thames: Thomas Nelson and Sons, 1998), 28–9.
3. As argued by T. J. B. Spencer, 'Shakespeare and the Elizabethan Romans', *Shakespeare Survey*, 10 (1957), 27–38, cited in Daniell, 47.
4. Geoffrey Bullough, *Narrative and Dramatic Sources of Shakespeare* (London: Routledge; New York: Columbia University Press), v, 24 (citing Appian, 1578).
5. The Latin phrase was added by the French translator Jaques Amyot, and taken over by Sir Thomas North in his English version; see note 20 below.
6. According to Plutarch, they were imprisoned by Caesar's followers, and Caesar deprived them of their offices.
7. Cited by Daniell, Introduction to *Julius Caesar*, 105.
8. See *ibid.*, 110.
9. Elias Canetti, *Crowds and Power*, transl. Carol Stewart (London: Gollancz; New York: Viking Press, 1962), 17, 20.
10. Frank Brady, *Citizen Welles* (New York: Charles Scribner's Sons, 1989), 123.
11. Brady, *Citizen Welles*, 125.
12. David Bevington, Introduction to his edition of *Troilus and Cressida*, Arden Shakespeare, Series 3 (Walton-on-Thames: Thomas Nelson and Sons, 1998), 78–9.
13. Bevington's gloss at 4.5.203.
14. Bevington, Introduction to *Troilus and Cressida*, 79.
15. The legendary founding of London as Troynovant or New Troy was popular, and was celebrated, for example, in Thomas Heywood's *Troia Britanica* (1609), published in the same year as Shakespeare's play. In it Heywood narrates the progress of the Trojan War and ends by tracing the ancestry of James I back to Brutus, a grandson of Aeneas who gave his name to Brutain. Other versions may be found in George Warner's *Albion's England* (1584), Spenser's *Faerie Queene*, 11, x, and Michael Drayton's *Polyolbion* (1612).
16. *Annals* (1635), IV, 198–9, cited in Nick de Somogyi, *Shakespeare's Theatre of War*, 238.
17. de Somogyi, *Shakespeare's Theatre of War*, 238–43.
18. One is the story told in the *Odyssey* of Venus and Mars being caught in bed together by her husband Vulcan and trapped in a net; the other, told by

Lucretius, *De Rerum Naturae*, 1, 29–40, describes Mars, overcome by love, lying disarmed in the lap of Venus. For the mythological allusions in the play, see John Wilders, Introduction in his edition of *Antony and Cleopatra*, Arden Shakespeare, Series 3 (London and New York: Routledge, 1995), 64–9.

19. William Hazlitt, *Complete Works*, ed. P. P. Howe, 21 vols. (London: J. M. Dent and Sons, 1930), IV, 214–15.
20. Bullough, *Narrative and Dramatic Sources*, V, 75.
21. See Alexander Leggatt, *Shakespeare's Political Drama*, 175–6.
22. From William Blake's, 'Proverbs of Hell', in *The Marriage of Heaven and Hell* (?1793).
23. See Sir Thomas North's translation of Plutarch in Bullough, ed., *Narrative and Dramatic Sources of Shakespeare*, V, 507.
24. *Ibid.*, V, 506.
25. This is altered in the play from the account in North's translation of Plutarch; in the play the belly is more fully personified as a 'grave' voice, and does not laugh at the folly of the citizens, as in Plutarch. Also the idea of the belly's 'audit', claiming it is left only with the bran, is entirely Shakespeare's. See Bullough, *Narrative*, V, 510.
26. Introduction to *Coriolanus*, Arden Shakespeare, Series 2 (London: Methuen, 1976), 40.
27. Lee Bliss, editor of *Coriolanus* (Cambridge University Press, 2000), 63, observes that the final image of Coriolanus killed by Aufidius and his 'conspirators' echoes the slaughter of Hector by Achilles and his Myrmidons in *Troilus and Cressida*. As Coriolanus is associated with Hector, so Aufidius turns into an Achilles.
28. In the Oxford edition of *Coriolanus* (Oxford: Clarendon Press, 1994), 48–55, R. B. Parker gives a psychological acount of Volumnia's relations with her son, with reference to Freud, Lacan, and Janet Adelman.
29. Bliss, Introduction to *Coriolanus*, 59.

CHAPTER 9

Violence and the late plays

In the late romances Shakespeare takes further his exploration of violence. These plays touch in various ways on all his earlier concerns, but treat them in a new way.[1] Human violence is related to the violence of nature, to storms and tempests (as in *King Lear*), to the dangers of sea-travel, and to natural forces such as the bear that kills Antigonus in *The Winter's Tale*. The violence associated with war, as in the Roman plays and in *Macbeth*, is given a new perspective in *Cymbeline*, as victors yield and defeat becomes a kind of victory. In psychological and political terms violence seems in these late plays to erupt suddenly in bursts of anger for which there is no adequate explanation, as if picking up on the question Alcibiades asked, 'who is man that is not angry?' This is most marked in the anger of Leontes and Prospero. Whereas his previous plays brought home the tragic consequences of deeds of violence, Shakespeare's late plays accept violence as an inescapable part of the natural world and of human society, and are more interested in ways to moderate, control or atone for it. *The Tempest* receives most attention here because it seems to me that it gains much of its depth as a culmination of the dramatist's exploration of issues connected with violence; in it Shakespeare moves finally from a concern with the expression and effects of violence to a study of the precarious possibilities for controlling it in a dramatic world where violence continually threatens to break out.

FORTUNE, NATURE, AND VIOLENCE IN *PERICLES*

The travels and adventures of Pericles, his wife Thaisa, and daughter Marina, take place in a world of unpredictable and sudden forms of violence, both among humans and in nature. Shakespeare had used storms at sea and shipwrecks to separate twins and launch plays of comic mistakings in *The Comedy of Errors* and in *Twelfth Night*, but in these works the storms appear as little more than part of the machinery to start in motion the complications of the plots. The storm dramatized in *King Lear* functions in much greater depth at the centre of the action, as an extension of the turmoil in Lear's mind, as a symbolic embodiment of the confusion and discord in the kingdom, and potentially as an expression of the anger of the gods. It also seems to spring from the violence Lear has unleashed in his kingdom, and to gather up and reflect in its fury the cruelty those in power inflict on others. In *Pericles* storms take on yet another aspect, as manifesting the unpredictability of life in dramatic worlds where Fortune rather than human intention predominates, as in romance. But Shakespeare exploits storms for a deeper purpose in relation to human violence.

The opening of the play must have been startling when it was first played, with the Chorus, Gower, who sets the scene in ancient times, drawing attention to a row of severed heads displayed onstage, a sight that would have reminded spectators of the heads of executed traitors and criminals mounted on London Bridge. As so often in Shakespeare's plays, the ancient is interwoven with the contemporary. The heads serve as emblems of human cruelty; Pericles also finds in them a lesson to himself to know his 'frail mortality':

For death remembered should be like a mirror
Who tells us life's but breath, to trust it error.
(1.1.46–7)

If life cannot be trusted, as subject to chance, then the actions of the many who have risked their lives in an attempt to solve the riddle of Antiochus in order to win his daughter as a bride become more understandable. Yet in accepting the challenge Pericles himself subscribes to the violence and oppression he condemns in Antiochus:

The blind mole casts
Copped hills towards heaven, to tell the earth is thronged
By man's oppression; and the poor worm doth die for't.
Kings are earth's gods; in vice their law's their will.
(1.1.101–4)

Pericles seems to be represented by the blind mole in this confused image, in contrast to King Antiochus the oppressor, but the suitors whose heads are displayed willingly chose to face death if they could not solve the riddle. In solving it, Pericles turns Antiochus into an oppressor indeed, who must try to prevent his vice becoming generally known, and who hires Thaliard (who is armed anachronistically with a pistol) to kill Pericles.

Pericles expects Antiochus to make war on him at Tyre or plot against his life, and it is to avoid 'this tempest' (1.2.98) that Pericles accepts the advice of his counsellor Helicanus to move on, only to encounter another kind of tempest at sea, and be cast ashore as sole survivor from his ship in 2.1. Man's oppression seems matched by that of nature, though we are not allowed to dwell on the sailors Gower tells us perished in the wreck, any more than on the executed suitors whose heads were displayed by Antiochus. The fishermen who establish the idea of a coast grieve for the 'poor souls' who lost their lives in the shipwreck, but Pericles himself makes no mention of the crew or his companions, and only laments for himself, until he is cheered by finding that the prized armour his father gave him has by chance been cast on shore. Although the changes of fortune that afflict Pericles occur at intervals during what is notionally a long stretch of time, they are crowded into the action or into the dumbshows that interrupt Gower's choric speeches. A year has passed by the time Pericles is recalled to Tyre, but the tempest that causes a second shipwreck follows in the action soon after the first. The changes of what Gower calls 'fortune's mood' (Act 3 Chorus, 46) appear inexplicable, and from Act 3, in dialogue that is more characteristically Shakespearean than the first two acts, the nurse Lycorida begins to sound a note that reverberates at the end of the play in calling on Pericles to be patient (3.1.19, 26).

In this second terrible storm ('never was waves nor wind more violent', 4.1.59), Marina is born and, as Pericles supposes, Thaisa is drowned, birth and death occurring at the same time, matter for joy and for tears. Marina grows up in the space of a choric speech, and soon finds herself at the mercy of a hired murderer, when she is 'saved' by the intervention of pirates, so that she has good and bad fortune at the same time. The violence intended against her springs, according to Gower, from Dionyza's envy that Marina outshines her own daughter, but we never see this daughter, only Dionyza in the act of hiring Leonine without further explanation to do the deed. Her desire to kill seems to arise as naturally as tempests do in nature. Human violence is evidenced from the opening scene in the grisly heads mounted on stage, in Pericles' willingness to risk losing his life, and in Antiochus hiring a murderer to pursue him; but it is also implicit in the lust that leads to incest. This mode of violence is not in itself life-threatening, but the scenes of Marina in the brothel at Mytilene, comic as Boult and the Bawd are, play continually with the idea of rape and venereal disease, with both of which she is threatened. Marina only escapes because she has other accomplishments with which she can earn more money than as a prostitute.

Throughout the action there are occasional appeals to the gods, but no explanation for what troubles Pericles:

> O you gods!
> Why do you make us love your goodly gifts,
> And snatch them straight away? (3.1.22–4)

So although the play ends with the triumphant reunion of Pericles with his wife at the temple of Diana, where her preservation seems a 'great miracle' wrought by Cerimon, through whom 'the gods have shown their power' (5.3.58, 60), it is a conventional comic resolution like that in *The Comedy of Errors*, and does not follow out the logic of the narrative. The emotional climax is, of course, in the reunion of Pericles and Marina, whose 'wayward fortune' (5.1.90) brings her to him when, in his grief, he seems to be at the point of death, and she appears to him as the very figure of Patience, 'smiling Extremity out of act', come to renew his acceptance of life. In the epilogue Gower tells us we have

> In Pericles, his queen and daughter, seen,
> Although assailed with fortune fierce and keen,
> Virtue preserved from fell destruction's blast,
> Led on by heaven, and crowned with joy at last.
>
> (lines 3–6)

The gods may *seem* to preserve virtue, and to punish wickedness in the case of Antiochus and his daughter, struck by lightning, and Cleon and his wife, burned in their palace by the citizens of Tharsus, but do they exist? It appears rather that fortune, the violent impulses of humans, and the violent forces of nature shape the destinies of the characters, and there is no reason why Pericles should have been singled out for the suffering he endures. Only in retrospect do arbitrary events that occur by fortune or accident and natural disasters become assimilated into the idea of a divine dispensation.

MORTAL ACCIDENTS IN *CYMBELINE*

Pericles is overstuffed with action and incident, with spectacle, fighting, dancing, tempests, shipwrecks, attempted murders, and pirates. There isn't time for much emotional involvement before the late scenes of Marina in the brothel and of Pericles restored by her. In his next plays Shakespeare developed more refined ways to create dramatic worlds in which fortune and violence are controlling factors. In *Cymbeline* the violence is less prominent, and characters are more fully developed; and instead of a choric figure to remind the audience they are listening to an old tale, the dramatist incorporates an overt self-conscious theatricality, constantly reminding the audience they are watching a fiction, yet at the same time claiming that in some sense it is true. Though less melodramatic than *Pericles*, *Cymbeline* has an even more intricate story-line that leads to an extended series of revelations in the bravura final scene; and, like the earlier play, its action affords a continual variety of accidents and coincidences so that we are led to accept unexpected shifts and flagrant improbabilities as an aspect of a dramatic world in which chance and fortune predominate. The opening dialogue sets the tone, as a knowledgeable gentleman explains to an incredulous visitor that the King's two sons were stolen twenty years previously and have remained untraced ever since:

> Howe'er 'tis strange,
> Or that the negligence may well be laughed at,
> Yet is it true, sir. (1.1.65–7)

The sense of strangeness, or estrangement from ordinary expectations, is important throughout the action in establishing the perspectives that guide our understanding of it, notably in relation to the violence in the play.

One of the strange features of the play is Shakespeare's use of Holinshed's account of ancient Britain, which is a mixture of myth and history. Cymbeline (Cunobellus) reigned when Augustus was Emperor in Rome, and during the period when Christ was born, though no mention is made of this event in the text. Perhaps for an audience that might not be familiar with ancient legend, the play includes a kind of history lesson in 3.1, when the Queen, Cymbeline, and Cloten explain to Lucius, the Roman general, what he must already know, the story that Cymbeline was descended from Mulmutius, the first king of Britain, and from Lud, who made Lud's-town his capital (3.1.33), later called London, and was also the nephew of Cassibelan who defeated Julius Caesar, but afterwards submitted to him. The connection between Rome and Britain goes back to the legend of Brutus, descended from Aeneas, founder of Rome, who in turn founded New Troy (Troynovant), later to become London. The matter that provides a frame for the action is Cymbeline's refusal to pay tribute to Rome, which is borrowed from Holinshed's account of Guiderius. Many commentators have tried to make topical sense of such historical references in the play, but without much success. I think this scene (3.1) may function in quite another way in the action.

In response to the demand of Lucius that the promised tribute be paid to Rome, the most boastful rhetoric comes from the mouths of Cloten and the Queen. Cloten, whose name is linked to 'clotpole' (4.2.184), is first seen in 1.2 sweating from the 'violence of action' in which he has been fighting with some unnamed opponent, and there is something of the foolish braggart soldier about him. In 3.1 his cheeky retorts to Lucius might seem momentarily to recall the patriotic tone of speeches in the early history plays, such as those of the Bastard Faulconbridge in Act 5 of *King John*, though they do not in the same way boast of English military prowess ('Come the three corners of the world in arms, / And we shall shock them', 5.7.116–17). Cloten does boast of his readiness to fight, and literally cocks a snook at the Romans:

> Britain's a world
> By itself, and we will nothing pay
> For wearing our own noses.
>   (3.1.12–14)

The Queen joins in with her tale of Cassibelan making Britons 'strut with courage', and Cymbeline follows up by saying his 'warlike people' should shake off the yoke of Rome. Their combined challenge provokes Lucius to promise 'war and confusion' in retaliation. In its threats of war and violence this scene has links not only with Cloten's desire to fight in 1.2, but also with Posthumus, who, as we learn in 1.4 on his arrival in Rome, meets a Frenchman who intervened to prevent him fighting a duel to the death merely to 'prove' his boasts about the beauty and virtue of Imogen.

The scene with Lucius also chimes with the move to Wales that soon follows, when we first encounter Belarius, who has brought up Cymbeline's sons to despise the idea of the court and the 'city's usuries' (3.3.45), and to admire courage in battle. They think of themselves as beastly, 'Like warlike as the wolf', since all they know is hunting, and they long to fight men, and to be able to say, as Belarius can about his feats in battle against the Romans, 'Thus mine enemy fell' (3.3.91). All this talk of violence comes to a head in the battle scene, in which Posthumus describes how Belarius, Guiderius, and Arviragus, by 'strange chance' (5.3.51), hold back and defeat the entire Roman army in a lane dammed with the dead. The desire of Arviragus is satisfied:

> What thing is this that I never
> Did see man die, scarce ever looked on blood
> But that of coward hares, hot goats, and venison!
>   (4.4.35–7)

He thinks of fighting as that which brings fame, and is ashamed to have remained so long 'a poor unknown'. The violent urges of the young males produce a satisfying outcome in the defeat of the Romans, but this is not the whole story.

In the court and the city another kind of violence operates, as seen in Jachimo's famous visual rape of Imogen in her bedchamber in 2.2, where he invites comparison with Tarquin's rape of Lucrece. Even more disturbing is the reaction of Posthumus when he believes Jachimo's report and rejects Philario's appeals to patience, for he re-enacts in words the rape he imagines took place in bestial terms, in the image of a 'full-acorned boar' mounting Imogen (2.4.168). Posthumus has idealized Imogen as a paragon of beauty and goodness, so that she has been for him a kind of trophy to boast about, and his image of her is all too easily destroyed. In his willingness to believe the worst of her we see the worst of him as he orders Pisanio to murder her. In the event, it is Cloten who comes near to acting out the fantasies of Jachimo and Posthumus, as he sets off in Act 4 to rape Imogen and kill Posthumus. It is appropriate that the clothes of Posthumus fit him just as well, for he is a mirror-image of the hero, possessing his worst attributes without his redeeming features. The violence related to sex in the play is healed and rejected in the ceremonial obsequies both for Cloten, whose headless body symbolizes the death of lust, and for Imogen, who 'dies' only to return to life. Her moving aria on the theme 'Our very eyes / Are sometimes like our judgements blind' (4.2.301–2) is also a comic extravaganza on a missing head as she mistakes the body of Cloten for that of Posthumus, whom we know to be alive and ready for what now must be the outcome, their happy reunion.

The violence expressed in the urge to fight and kill, and in war, comes to its climax in the battle between the Britons and the Romans in Act 5. Guiderius and Arviragus at last get their fill of fighting and survive the 'slaughter' (5.3.8–13, 48–51, 78) in which many die on both sides. The outcome is a matter of luck, turning on the arrival of Belarius, Guiderius, and Arviragus, as Lucius, taken prisoner, points out to Cymbeline who threatens to execute him:

Consider, sir, the chance of war, the day
Was yours by accident. (5.5.75–6)

Cymbeline's attention is diverted by his half-recognition of Imogen, now clothed as the page of Lucius, and the series of revelations that ensue lead to reconciliation, and finally to Cymbeline's renewed submission to Augustus Caesar. As the funeral ceremonies for Cloten and Imogen that begin with 'Solemn music' (4.2.186 SD) exorcize the spirit of lust, so the 'Solemn music' (5.4.29 SD) that heralds the apparitions that entertain Posthumus in jail, and then the descent of Jupiter, exorcize the spirit of physical violence. The descent of Jupiter sitting on an eagle is another serio-comic moment, with all the fun of an unexpected bit of self-conscious theatrical contrivance, yet at the same time, a display of supernatural power and violence, as he 'throws a thunderbolt' (5.4.92 SD) to frighten the apparitions, who 'fall on their knees'. His message, however, is to promise peace and harmony, and leave a prophecy that Britain will 'be fortunate and flourish in peace and plenty' (5.4.144).

The witch-like Queen who likes to mix poisons and plot murders conveniently dies in despair before the end, and the dramatic skill with which all the intricacies of the plots are resolved is justly celebrated. There remain two deeds of violence that challenge interpretation. One is the death of Cloten, which is treated so casually by Guiderius when he takes on Cloten's challenge, kills him offstage, and returns as victor carrying the head of his enemy. The King's Men had property heads which were often used for grotesque effect, as in *Measure for Measure*, *Pericles*, and *The Revenger's Tragedy*. Is there something inherently comic in a severed head being treated like a ball? As the head expresses the person, the identity, and feelings of a human being, so the reduction of it to a plaything is horrifying on one level, and a reminder of the fragility of life:

Golden lads and girls all must
As chimney-sweepers come to dust.
          (*Cymbeline*, 4.2.262–3)

We have to laugh at such knowledge, at the byplay with skulls in the graveyard in Act 5 of *Hamlet*, and at Guiderius swinging the head of Cloten as he goes off to 'throw 't into the creek'. It is a way of keeping death at bay, recognizing its presence, yet carrying on with zest for life, mourning for the passing of those we love, and half-enjoying the spectacle of those we do not care about being destroyed in accidents on the roads or in shoot-outs daily on television or in films. It is only with a measure of disrespect for death that we can follow the advice of Jupiter, 'Be not with mortal accidents oppressed' (5.4.99), where 'mortal' means both 'human' and 'deadly'.

The other act of violence occurs when Posthumus strikes and knocks down Imogen as she tries to stop him blaming himself for causing her death, as indeed he did seek to murder her. 'She' (a boy-actor) is in disguise still as a boy, of course, but even so, his violence in treating her

as making fun of his passion, 'Shall 's have a play of this?' (5.5.228), is
unprovoked and shocking, a grown man and a hardened fighter striking
a boy playing a girl disguised as a page. Even with the coming of peace
and the general reconciliations of the final scene, this one deed reminds
us that violence may erupt out of nothing, that all are capable of such
acts, even the noblest men. In probing further the problem of violence in
this play, Shakespeare makes light of the death of Cloten, who seeks the
fight in which he is killed, and whose death can be treated with casual
humour, but stages the equally casual violence of Posthumus towards
Imogen as distressing and disturbing. To say we are not invited to care
for Cloten, but do sympathize with Imogen is not enough to explain our
ability to switch so readily between casual disrespect for decapitation and
horror at a blow that is soon forgotten; is it because we know intuitively
that violence happens and could afflict any of us unexpectedly that we
can maintain this double vision? Mortal accidents are bound to occur in
a world where the gods seem allied to Fortune, and the eyes of even the
best may be as blind as their judgements.

EXPLOSIONS OF VIOLENCE IN *THE WINTER'S TALE*

The Winter's Tale turns on three notable eruptions of violence. Many
have sought explanations for the sudden change in Leontes in the opening scene, when, having pressed Hermione to encourage Polixenes to
prolong his visit to Sicily, he is overwhelmed with jealousy so violent
that he seeks to have Polixenes murdered; but no attempt to account for
the behaviour of Leontes in psychological terms or to establish motives
seems convincing. In the opening dialogue between Archidamus and
Camillo, Shakespeare emphasizes the longstanding affection between
the two kings, brought up together in childhoood. It is Leontes who goes
out of his way to urge Polixenes to stay at the end of a visit of nine months,
and then pushes Hermione into helping his efforts. Moreover, Hermione
is presumably vividly pregnant, for we are told in the next scene that she
'rounds apace' and is spread 'Into a goodly bulk' (2.1.16–20). If Polixenes
may be supposed the father of the child she is carrying, he must, implau-
sibly, it seems in this scene, have committed adultery with her shortly
after he arrived at the court of Leontes. Later Emilia says Hermione is
'something before her time delivered' (2.2.25), but still it makes no sense
that Leontes would suddenly become jealous after such a length of time.

This scene appears to develop more intensely and powerfully the incident that triggers the opening of *Cymbeline*, where, in an unexplained

fit of anger, Cymbeline banishes Posthumus and imprisons his daughter Imogen. The action of Leontes is so shocking precisely because it is in-explicable, a spontaneous outburst of violence made convincing by the brilliantly tortured syntax of Leontes' speeches, summed up in his most memorable lines here:

Affection! Thy intention stabs the centre;
Thou dost make possible things not so held,
Communicat'st with dreams. – How can this be? –
With what's unreal thou coactive art,
And fellow'st nothing: then 'tis very credent
Thou may'st co-join with something. (1.2.138–43)

Leontes knows he is communicating with dreams or nightmares, and creating something out of nothing, yet his language suggests he cannot help himself. The destructive idea that haunts him is focused in the phrase 'stabs the centre', an image that calls into play not only the potential violence of sexual desire with hints of rape, but also the wounding of the heart or feeling, and the sense of a deathblow to the 'rooted...affection' (1.1.23) that existed between Leontes and Polixenes.

After Polixenes and Camillo escape, Leontes becomes obsessive, talks of justice, but seeks to have Polixenes murdered, and directly equates justice for Hermione with death (3.2.90–1). His behaviour towards Hermione is attributed to madness or sickness by Paulina, and his anxi-ety to have Hermione, Paulina, and his own daughter burned as if they are witches (2.3.7–8, 95, 113, 133, 140, 155) points up the strangeness of his conduct as something to be wondered at. It is possible to relate the condition of Leontes here to obsessive compulsive disorder or other psychological illnesses that modern analysis has defined. His initial vio-lent outburst, however, that launches the action of the play comes out of nowhere, and is paralleled by the second equally sudden and unex-plained moment of violence when Antigonus is caught in a storm, and also becomes hunted by a bear that is being hunted by men. In the 'savage clamour' of the tempest and the hunt he makes his exit, famously pur-sued by a bear. Since the 'bear' has to perform a similar run at him in each performance, I think it must always have been played by an actor dressed in a bear-skin, so that it would have been grotesque, comically entertaining, and frightening at the same time. Such a reaction is ex-pressed by the Clown, the Shepherd's son, as witness of the death of Antigonus and of the wreck of the ship that brought him to Bohemia with the loss of all its crew:

And then for the land-service, to see how the bear tore out his shoulder-bone, how he cried to me for help and said his name was Antigonus, a nobleman. But to make an end of the ship, to see how the sea flap-dragoned it; but first, how the poor souls roared, and the sea mocked them; and how the poor gentleman roared, and the bear mocked him . . . (3.3.93–9)

The deaths of the ship's crew and of Antigonus are enjoyed as spectacle by the Clown, who gawps at them, much like the drivers who slow down to a crawl on motorways to stare at the carnage caused by a gruesome accident. For him and his father it is in any case a 'lucky day' as they find the infant Perdita and riches of 'fairy gold'.

'Things dying' demand only brief attention as spectacle, and are sup-planted by 'things new-born'. Dying is distanced emotionally and re-duced to a relatively insignificant place in the larger perspective of time, as Shakespeare points up for us by immediately (or possibly after an interval in the theatre) bringing on the choric figure of Time, probably costumed in the traditional symbolic garb as a winged old man carrying a sickle and hourglass. His immediate function is to mark the gap of sixteen years between the first three and last two acts of the play, but he serves a more fundamental and important purpose in the perspective he establishes on the action. What he makes clear is that in the long view, *sub specie aeternitatis* as it were, he is indifferent to humanity:

I that please some, try all; both joy and terror
Of good and bad, that makes and unfolds error.

(4.4.1–2)

He makes no moral distinctions, can create and destroy, and presents himself as 'witness to / The times that brought them in', the times, that is, that have brought in the present action, 'what is now received'. His is the eternal eye, and he is an aloof beholder of the fortunes and misfortunes of people. It is from this perspective that we are invited to understand the action. The shift to Bohemia, all flowers and festival, with its sunny atmosphere contributed to even by the song-and-dance routines of Autolycus, whose thieving never impoverishes anyone, seems to promise happiness, until Polixenes suddenly penetrates the disguise worn by Florizel, and breaks out in violent anger and cruel threats against Perdita ('I will devise a death as cruel for thee, / As thou art tender to 't' 4.4.442–3) and the old Shepherd. On a smaller scale this echoes the sudden outburst of Leontes in the first act; so Time brings joy and terror.

The human violence in the play erupts suddenly, appears spontaneous, and seems analogous to the violence of nature that destroys Antigonus and his ship. The persecuted Hermione quibbles at the idea of grace in Act 2, Leontes consults the sacred Oracle at Delphi, and in the last act beats his breast and denounces himself as a sinner against 'The blessed gods' (5.1.167–72), now blaming himself for the death of Mamillius as well as for his cruelty to his queen. Yet there is no sign that the heavens have any concern for humanity. The power of the statue scene springs in part from the indifference of the gods who may or may not exist for all the effect they have. Paulina, something of a control-freak, creates the moment when the statue of Hermione comes to life, as a play within the play, staged in an imaginary chapel, with the statue perhaps suggesting a sculpted memorial to the dead. She prepares her audience by saying, 'It is required / You do awake your faith' (5.3.95), but what kind of faith? Is it a faith in her powers as a conjurer or artist? If there is a larger faith implied, it is created by Paulina. She has ensured that the 'good' queen and Leontes learn to be patient, 'Rejoicing in hope, patient in tribulation' (Romans 12.12), and that Leontes is conscious of having sinned (5.1.171). The penitent Leontes, it is true, pays respect to the gods, and the final scene, set in 'the chapel' (5.3.86), evokes a mood of quasi-religious awe as Hermione proves to be alive, and invites us to share in the 'notable passion of wonder' (5.2.16–17) Camillo and Leontes feel when they discover the Shepherd's daughter is, in fact, Perdita. It is wonder at the mystery that Fortune, Florizel's 'enemy', and Time can at last bring joy. So the whole business is contrived to seem a miracle, and constitutes the final triumph of the union of art and nature, a statue that is living. Paulina is a projection of the dramatist, anticipating Prospero, who constructs by her art and by what seems 'magic' (5.3.39, 110) a satisfying resolution to events that were not felt as they occurred to be part of a providential dispensation, but rather happened at the mercy of time, fortune, and accident. Three sudden and unexpected explosions of violence shape an action in which death and disaster are taken for granted as an inevitable part of life, and religion is invoked to console and help humans to cope with what they cannot control or understand.

There has been much anger and suffering, but if 'Fortune, visible an enemy', as Florizel puts it (5.1.215), can bring disaster and frustrate human plans, the Oracle, it turns out, speaks true, and it appears finally to the characters that some higher powers may have a concern for human affairs. But if so, their influence can only be perceived in retrospect in Shakespeare's romances, which, in the way of this genre, have happy endings. It seems that for Shakespeare in these plays final reconciliations are linked to an invocation of the gods, to a sense of religious possibilities that satisfy an immense nostalgia for pattern and purpose in life. As events take place, they are subject to chance and are inexplicable, while the future remains inscrutable. Religion looks to the past, to ancient texts and rituals, for ways of explaining and coping with what humans cannot control or understand in the present and future, and especially with acts of violence that erupt in human society and in the natural world. Christian apologists in Shakespeare's age liked to claim that 'Fortune is a mere fiction', a fancy and vain conceit,[2] and that things done by God are ascribed to Fortune. In Shakespeare's romances Fortune is in control, and it might seem rather that things done by Fortune are in the end ascribed to the gods, but through human contrivance, as when Paulina brings a statue to life.

Shakespeare's last comment on Fortune and the Gods comes in the final, violent scene of the play he wrote in collaboration with John Fletcher, *The Two Noble Kinsmen* (1613). The cousins Arcite and Palamon, caught fighting in contravention of the laws of Athens, are allowed to fight one another for the hand of Emilia, and seek the support of their preferred god. Arcite seeks the favour of Mars, and a 'clanging of armour, with a short thunder' is heard, which the knight takes to be an auspicious sign. Palamon prays to Venus, and then 'music is heard; doves are seen to flutter', so that he too believes he has a favourable token of her support. It is not clear what either of the signs means. In the event, Arcite overthrows Palamon, who is thereby doomed to die; but Arcite, trotting in triumph into Athens on a horse given to him by Emilia, is thrown off and killed when the horse stumbles. So Palamon lives to have Emilia, and Duke Theseus has the last word:

> Never Fortune
> Did play a subtler game. The conquered triumphs;
> The victor has the loss; yet in the passage
> The gods have been most equal. (5.4.112–15)

The gods, he says, have been impartial; but it is not clear that they have intervened at all, and it is Arcite's misfortune that he falls off his horse and is killed. How can the gods and Fortune be distinguished?

VIOLENCE, FREEDOM, AND SLAVERY IN *THE TEMPEST*

The Tempest seems an appropriate sequel to *The Winter's Tale* to the extent that Prospero as orchestrator and magus takes over, so to speak, from Paulina. The opening scene dramatizes the terrifying violence of a shipwreck in a storm, witnessed by Miranda, who suffers with the 'fraughting souls' she sees drowned as the ship splits. Although Prospero at once assures her 'There's no harm done' (1.2.15), the storm and shipwreck are much more affecting being enacted onstage than those described by the Clown in *The Winter's Tale*; he enjoys the sight of Antigonus being eaten, whereas Miranda weeps at the 'direful spectacle' (1.2.26), which has taken all her attention as well as that of the audience. It forces our participation in what is at once a representation of natural violence, and at the same time is contrived by Prospero's art, exemplifying his powers as a magician, and also the potential for violence in him. It is an appropriate beginning for a play in which a barely suppressed violence threatens always to break through the veneer of civilization. Prospero, a duke 'for the liberal arts / Without a parallel' (1.2.73–4), has rescued Ariel from the foul witch Sycorax, only to make him a 'slave' (1.2.270) and threaten him as punishment for disobedience with tortures worse than those Sycorax practised. Prospero cannot speak to Caliban without abusing him as a 'poisonous slave' (1.2.321), having, as colonial ruler, failed to impose his moral code, and again threatens him with torments merely for answering back in language that he has learned from his master. Prospero's threats are reflected in Caliban's curses, and mark the difficulty he has in controlling the violence that erupts in his language.[3]

This proneness to violence is a feature of the hierarchical society from which Prospero has been exiled. The terms in which he treats the island of which he has made himself 'lord' (1.2.459) and the social and moral order he establishes there are imported from Milan (or more immediately, London), even as his aim is to return home and regain his former status as duke. This is to say that power relations are at the heart of the play. He treats Ferdinand as a usurper who has come to take the island from him, even if, as it turns out, his plan is to test his worth as a partner for Miranda. Most of those who come to the island see opportunities for power. Caliban, who was king of it and himself (1.2.344) has been displaced by Prospero as ruler, and the Italian aristocrats and the others who are cast up on it think of gaining control. As Antonio seized the dukedom of Milan from Prospero, and Prospero took the island from Caliban, so Antonio and Sebastian plot to make Sebastian King of Naples by murdering Alonso; and Caliban, Stephano, and Trinculo have ideas of killing Prospero so that Stephano can be king and the others viceroys (3.2.109–11) in the island. Even Gonzalo's vision of his ideal commonwealth begins from the idea of colonization ('Had I plantation of this isle', 2.1.145), with himself as governor. Gonzalo's vision differs from what is practised on the island in its utopian abolition of work, laws, commerce, weapons, and other trappings of civilization as it is commonly conceived, but still, as Sebastian mockingly observes, 'he would be king on 't' (2.1.158).

The desire to be king, to claim possession and gain power, that affects so many of the humans in the play is related to two concepts that are highlighted in the action, namely slavery, or servitude, and freedom. Prospero, book-lover, magician, artist, imagines the height of civilization, manifested in the masque he creates to mark the betrothal of Ferdinand and Miranda. This 'majestic vision' (4.1.118) combines poetry, dance, song, and spectacle in celebrating love, peace, and plenty, and in creating images of the gods, a sense of religion. It lasts a short time as a 'vanity' of Prospero's art (4.1.41), but establishes an idea of the power of the imagination, the reaches of the mind. At the same time, it is dependent on the constant vigilance of Prospero and Ariel in maintaining his control of the island and those on it; and Prospero's rule is in turn dependent on maintaining Caliban and Ariel in a state of servitude. Caliban is necessary as a slave to fetch in wood (1.2.314) and do menial tasks, while Ariel also is needed as a 'slave' (1.2.270) to keep the humans on the island under surveillance. Power for those who rule necessarily requires subservience in the ruled, as is marked in the irony of Caliban shouting 'Freedom, high-day!' when he exchanges his old master for a new one in Stephano (2.2.184).

The idea of servitude operates at a deeper level in the play in relation to the culture to which Prospero and the Italian aristocrats stranded on the island belong. Although cast ashore in a shipwreck, their clothes hold 'their freshness and glosses, being rather new-dyed than stained with salt water' (2.1.66–7), and they are presumably dressed in current London court fashion, which, around 1610, had reached something of a peak in elaboration of hats, doublets, ruffs, matching cuffs and hose, breeches, and decorated shoes.[4] Antonio remarks 'look how well my garments sit upon me', meaning his clothes as ruler of Milan in place of Prospero, and the group are wearing the rich garments they put on to attend the wedding of Alonzo's daughter Princess Claribel to the King of Tunis (2.1.71–3). In other words, they are dressed in costumes that identify them as courtiers, and are armed with swords as a sign of authority. Their power-dressing signals their hierarchical status and restricts their behaviour accordingly. The ruffs or stiff standing collars that set off their heads, the elaboration of cuffs and hose, the decorative roses on high-heeled shoes, and the management of the rapiers that were signs of

Figure 9 The well-dressed aristocrat. Portrait of Dudley, Baron North, 1614–15,
artist unidentified.

Figure 10 Power-dressing at the Jacobean court. Portrait of George Villiers, Duke of Buckingham, attributed to William Larkin, about 1616.

masculinity to counterbalance an almost effeminate abundance of satin
and lace in doublets and feathers in hats, all proclaimed the status of the
wearers. At the same time their clothes inhibited them from ordinary
physical activity, and functioned as display, showing them as men of
power, requiring to be served, not to do anything themselves.

Prospero has a 'magic garment' (1.2.24) that is necessary to his exercise
of power as a magician, until the end of the play, when he removes it,
and sends Ariel for the 'hat and rapier' that will help to re-establish
himself as Duke of Milan. Prospero has, of course, been, in effect, for
long a prisoner on the island, and in returning to Milan he joins the other
aristocrats as prisoners of their roles, of the relationships of power and
dynastic rivalries that will be resumed in Italy. Sebastian and Antonio
are notoriously left unscathed at the end of the play, in spite of their
momentary desperation when Ariel appears like a harpy to require of
them 'heart's sorrow / And a clear life ensuing' (3.3.81). Prospero himself
joins them in the corridors of power, anxious to resume his role as duke.

What then of the idea of freedom? Slavery is maintained by forms of
violence, as in Prospero's threat of penning Ariel in an oak for twelve
years, or the imprisonment and hard labour inflicted on Caliban:

> Here you sty me
> In this hard rock, whiles you do keep from me
> The rest o' th' island. (1.3.344–6)

Yet Caliban, usually played as naked or nearly naked, has a measure of
freedom lacked by the courtiers, since he is unconstrained by their court
clothes and their concern for rank and status. Like him, Ferdinand is
humiliated and sentenced to hard labour, heaving logs, and, paradoxically, it is the scene where (stripped down to his shirt and unconstrained
by his courtier's clothes?) we see him pitied by Miranda that defines both
the limits of Prospero's power and the richest idea of freedom in the play.
Miranda disobeys her father in revealing her name to Ferdinand, and,
more startlingly, in offering marriage to him, 'I am your wife if you will
marry me' (3.1.83). Ferdinand endures his 'wooden slavery' for her sake:

> The very instant that I saw you did
> My heart fly to your service; there resides
> To make me slave to it; and for your sake
> Am I this patient log-man. (3.1.64–7)

The idea of slavery or subjection is here transfigured, for in this higher
voluntary 'service' of love true freedom is to be found, echoing the Collect

for peace in the order for Morning Prayer in *The Book of Common Prayer*, 'O God... whose service is perfect freedom'. Miranda will be Ferdinand's 'servant' whether he will or no, and he accepts her offer 'with a heart as willing / As bondage e'er of freedom'. The willing acceptance of the service of love and bond of marriage constitutes an elevated concept of freedom, and her behaviour startles Prospero, who desired this outcome, but could not control it, and is 'surprised with all' (3.1.93).

In this log-bearing scene I assume both Ferdinand and Miranda are costumed appropriately, which is to say casually, in, as we might now say, work-clothes. When they are revealed to Alonso and the rest in the final scene, they must surely be in formal dress like the others, playing the game of chess that traditionally emblematized the give and take of aristocratic courtship. With its trade in knights, bishops, castles, kings, and queens, the game also symbolizes power-relations, as in Thomas Middleton's play *A Game at Chesse*, an overtly political play. It is, I think, going too far to find here in the tableau of Ferdinand and Miranda a 'brief game of love and war that seems to foretell in their lives all the ambition, duplicity and cynicism of their elders',[5] hinted at in Miranda's 'Sweet lord, you play me false' (5.1.172). Ferdinand denies this, and a kinder interpretation might see them both as learning the rules. But certainly their appearance here aligns them with Alonso, Prospero, and the other Italians, who are all about to return to the political intrigues and power-relations of Naples and Milan.

The final entrance in the play is that of Caliban, Stephano, and Trinculo, driven in by Ariel, 'in their stolen apparel'. In a parody of the plot of Sebastian and Antonio to kill Alonso in order to make Sebastian King of Naples, Stephano, prompted by Caliban, is prepared to kill Prospero to make himself king of the island:

Monster, I will kill this man. His daughter and I will be king and queen – save our graces! – and Trinculo and thyself shall be viceroys. (3.2.108–10)

In order to be exercised power has to be evident, and just as Prospero puts on court trappings to show himself as he was 'sometime Milan', which is to say he has to wear the right clothes to be recognized as duke, so Stephano and Trinculo need clothes that will embody their new status. This explains why Prospero can so easily distract them with the garments he orders Ariel to hang on a line. The stage-direction calls for 'glistering apparel', which may be 'trumpery' to Prospero, but appears to Trinculo grand, even as he knows it 'belongs to a frippery' or pawnshop: 'O King Stephano! O peer! O worthy Stephano! – look what a wardrobe here is for thee!' (4.1.222–3). The word 'wardrobe' commonly signified the office at court charged with the care of clothing, and in order to become a king, Stephano has to look like one. The gowns and jerkins on the line, no doubt borrowed from the company's stock, seem to offer the right clothes. Prospero has set this up without making the connection between their seduction by tawdry finery and his own need to dress the part of duke. Is there any essential difference between the desire they have for splendid clothes and Prospero's need to display himself as ruler?[6] All the costumes in the play, including those of Prospero's masque of Ceres, are another kind of trumpery, contributing to an 'insubstantial pageant', as they all are finally part of a theatrical wardrobe.

When Trinculo, Stephano, and Caliban are driven in, tormented with 'dry convulsions' (4.1.259) and cramps (5.1.287), Ariel is ordered to set them free, but their freedom is to return to a condition of servitude, allowing them to be mocked as 'things' by Sebastian and Antonio (5.1.264). Their brief enjoyment of a kind of political freedom occurs when they are drunk, while Gonzalo's commonwealth and the masque of Ceres celebrate an ideal of harmony, of peace, prosperity, and love that can only be imagined as a 'majestic vision' (4.1.118). In actuality the play restores the old hierarchies and political structures that confine people into their assigned roles as aristocrats and servants. Only Ariel is freed at the end to 'the elements', to dwindle into a minute, solitary figure, a spirit with nothing to do; but perhaps spirits don't need to do anything. Humans do, to define the parameters of their short lives. Prospero renounces his 'rough magic', which he uses to torment his enemies as well as to bring about his return to Milan, and also famously renounces vengeance in favour of 'virtue' (5.1.27–8), yet in the end sees something of himself in Caliban: 'this thing of darkness I / Acknowledge mine' (5.1.275–6). The phrase carries much weight; it reminds us that Prospero gave Caliban knowledge and taught him how to curse. It also reminds us of the similarities between the latter's curses and Prospero's threats of torture in Act 1; Prospero has just called Caliban a 'demi-devil', and devils were associated with darkness. In this acknowledgement Prospero thus sees a reflection of the darkness that is in himself, that destructive urge in the exercise of power that he has on a number of occasions in the play suppressed with difficulty. If he can renounce the 'rough magic' that has, by his own account, enabled him to call up violent storms, set war between the sea and sky, create earthquakes, open graves, and raise the dead, as well as control and torment his enemies (5.1.41–50), Prospero is not able to rid himself of the potential for violence that is a characteristic of humans in the play and of the structures of society that constitute their civilization. The darkness is in everyone.[7]

This may seem a strange assertion in relation to Prospero's epilogue, which ends with a specifically Christian appeal that echoes the Lord's prayer, and perhaps the general confession in the service of morning prayer, 'Spare thou them, O God, which confess their faults. Restore thou them that are penitent.' The epilogue also apparently plays in its last line, 'Let your indulgence set me free', on the specifically Catholic meaning of 'indulgence' as remission of the punishment for sin. As in the other late plays, there is a good deal of religious colouring in *The Tempest*; but the action is largely contrived by Prospero's art, and there is little sense of a Christian agency at work. Prospero tells Miranda that 'Providence divine' brought them to the island (1.2.159), but it might just as well have been the 'accident' or 'bountiful Fortune' (1.2.178) that he says brought his enemies to the same shore. The 'devils' seen by Ferdinand as his ship split (1.2.214) were created by Ariel to bring the crew to 'desperation'. The spirits that torment Caliban, like the 'ministers of Fate' (3.3.61) that make Alonso, Sebastian, and Antonio briefly desperate, are created by Prospero and Ariel. Ferdinand claims that Miranda is his 'by immortal Providence' (5.1.189), though it is Prospero who has arranged for their marriage in Italy, and for the tableau that presents them to Alonso and the others. Christian religion is marginalized, for Prospero as theurgist on his island is the controller and worker of miracles. I suspect Shakespeare thought he might have gone too far in this play, and added an epilogue in which Prospero seeks release from the bonds of the stage, so that he can be a Christian, asking for forgiveness for his faults, faults that include acting as if he were God.

POWER-DRESSING AND AUTHORITY IN *THE TEMPEST*

Perhaps the most intriguing aspect of Shakespeare's treatment of power and violence in *The Tempest* has to do with costume as a sign of status and authority. James I, as is well known, liked to emphasize his godlike authority, as when in an address to Parliament he said, 'Kings are justly called Gods, for that they exercise a manner or resemblance of Divine power upon earth',[8] and Prospero's renunciation of his authority in the epilogue could have been written for the performance of the play at court in November 1611.[9] James liked to be portrayed in the full panoply of majesty, and his liking for elaborate dress may have influenced court fashion. I think another influence may have been the abandonment of the sumptuary laws that remained in effect throughout the reign of Elizabeth, but were repealed when James came to the throne. This repeal permitted tradesmen and merchants to ape aristocrats in their dress. The ruff, for instance, became so fashionable that in 1617–18 the Wardrobe accounts for the Royal Court record the purchase of 27 ells of cambric and 359 yards of lace to make twelve suits of ruffs, or ruffs with matching cuffs for the wrists. Ruffs, like the modern tie, were useless except to show off the head as identifying authority, and it is hard to imagine how people (they were worn by men and women) managed, for example, to eat and drink while encumbered by them. Webster and Dekker make a joke of the problem in their satiric play *Westward Ho!* (1607), in which one character, Mrs Honeysuckle, says to a friend at 1.2.200, 'I was yesterday at a banquet, will you discharge my ruff of some wafers?' If commoners were adopting such fashions, it may help to explain why aristocratic costumes became so richly elaborate and extravagant during this period.

It may also help to account for Shakespeare's evident interest in exploiting costumes in his late plays. In a pattern begun with Edgar in *King Lear*, a young royal or aristocratic protagonist is reduced to something like beggary. Pericles is shipwrecked and cast up naked on a shore where fishermen provide him with a 'gown' (2.1.78). Posthumus in *Cymbeline* throws off his elegant Italian clothes to appear as a 'Britain peasant' (5.1.24), before resuming his courtly costume in 5.3. In *The Winter's Tale*, Florizel dresses as a 'swain' in order to woo Perdita, and later exchanges clothes with Autolycus at Camillo's behest in order to escape from Bohemia; then he seems to take on something of the nature of Autolycus when, still oddly costumed, he deceives Leontes into thinking he has come from Libya with his 'wife' Perdita (5.1.158–67). Ferdinand is made a slave by Prospero, and forced to stack logs for him before recovering his princely role and, I believe, his princely costume for the betrothal masque in 4.1. In each case the change or loss of clothes marks something like a rite of passage, as each character is temporarily deprived of the status and authority conferred by rank and appropriate costume, and each displays his common humanity. Clothes do not, of course, make the person; Perdita's grace and charm are evident in spite of her apparent low rank, and for Camillo she is 'The queen of curds and cream' (4.4.161). Dressed as the goddess Flora, she feels her robe changes her disposition (4.4.134), but it only expresses the royalty to which she is entitled. Dressed as a courtier Autolycus instantly becomes a 'gentleman born' (5.2.135) which seems to mean for him a licence to get drunk whenever he likes. Guiderius and Arviragus grow up as peasants, but, educated by Belarius, their 'royalty' is shown in their behaviour.

In these late plays Shakespeare was much concerned with the ways in which clothes can make, conceal or confuse identity.[10] Dressed in the clothes of Posthumus, the body of Cloten is taken for that of her husband by Imogen. His head is, of course, missing, but all the same she is, as in effect she acknowledges, misled by her eyes, which take the garments for the man. In the general joy at the finding of Perdita in *The Winter's Tale*, all distinctions of rank and person are lost and 'There was casting up of eyes, holding up of hands, with countenance of such distraction that they were to be known by garment, not by favour' (5.2.47–50). Here garments alone identify the king and the shepherd. Earlier in this play Camillo persuaded Perdita to conceal her face: 'Dismantle you, and (as you can) disliken / The truth of your own seeming.' (4.4.654–5). He wants to conceal her from prying 'eyes', but she is conscious of pretending to be someone else, 'I see the play so lies / That I must bear a part.' What is the relation between truth and seeming (or appearance) in the context of a play in which each actor is bearing a part?[11] Shakespeare teases his audience, especially in the late plays, by the enigmatic variations he orchestrates on this theme.

It is in *The Tempest*, however, that clothes become centrally important in the concept of the play, the courtiers' costumes representing what is now called power-dressing. In the early years of the reign of James satirists liked to comment on the importance of appearance for 'farmers' sons' and their like who aspired to leave working, 'wash their hands and come up gentlemen' (*Revenger's Tragedy*, 2.1.21), and would sell their lands to buy finery in order to show off in London. William Camden writes of a nobleman who sold a manor and 'came ruffling into the Court in a new suit saying: *Am not I a mighty man, that bear an hundred houses on my back?*'[12] Lavish expenditure on costumes was a feature of the court masques that could be seen as festal embodiments of the concept of monarchy promulgated by James I. Stephen Orgel relates *The Tempest* to masques such as *Oberon*, in which Prince Henry, playing a 'medieval knight and Roman emperor combined', tames rough satyrs and enters in a chariot from a scene of wild rocks as it is transformed into a palace. The palace symbolizes order, and there he accepts 'homage to the British court' (line 253), appropriately in the Palladian banqueting house at Whitehall, where the masque was performed.[13] Orgel sees Shakespeare's play in similar terms, as an expression of Jacobean political ideology, with Prospero as a 'royal illusionist' producing in his masque of Ceres 'an essay on the power and art of the royal imagination'.[14] He thinks the court audience 'saw the masque, with its scenic illusions and spectacular machines as models of the universe, as science, as assertions of power, as demonstrations of the essential divinity of the human mind'.[15] Ben Jonson may have had such a vision, as in his image of the dance at the climax of his masque *Pleasure Reconciled to Virtue* (1618) resolving the maze of human actions into measure and proportion:

> For dancing is an exercise
>   Not only shows the mover's wit,
> But maketh the beholder wise,
>   As he hath power to rise to it;
>
> (lines 233–6)

but the masque could at best be an image or emblem of harmony and order, expressing an unattainable ideal. Ceres and Juno may bless Ferdinand and Miranda, anticipating their marriage, but what Orgel sees as a 'majestic vision' ends uncertainly as the dance of nymphs and 'sunburnt sicklemen, of August weary' closes abruptly in discord with a 'strange hollow and confused noise'. This noise returns us to the 'real' world of Caliban, Stephano, and Trinculo with its plots of murder and political ambitions.

An alternative interpretation of the masque could have occurred to the most ardent Neoplatonist. From a platonic perspective, as Thomas Carlyle later put it, 'the thing Visible, nay the thing Imagined, what is it but a Garment, a Clothing of the higher, celestial Invisible?'[16] At the same time another point of view would show humanity as a 'botched mass of tailors' and cobblers' shreds', or in Swift's words, 'a forked straddling animal with bandy legs'. Swift was echoing Lear's comment on Poor Tom, 'Unaccommodated man is no more but such a poor, bare, forked animal as thou art' (3.4.106–7). Shakespeare evidently shared Carlyle's double perspective on clothes, and saw too that 'Robes and furred gowns hide all', and provide a cover for viciousness. The splendid costumes the players no doubt wore for the masque, Iris in rainbow colours, Juno descending drawn in a car by peacocks, are at once set against the trumpery hung on the line to distract Stephano and Trinculo. Grand costumes reappear as frippery; disembodied they become mere cloth, which, as Caliban perceives, 'is but trash' (4.4.221–4), just as the masque itself is a 'vanity' of Prospero's art.

An attention to Shakespeare's material concern with clothes in the play qualifies an idealist view of the masque and the play. Peter Greenaway seems instinctively to have recognized this in his film *Prospero's Books*, in which he costumed the aristocrats in especially extravagant courtly costumes as men of power, all sporting enormous white ruffs round their necks.[17] The dominant colours were white and black, corresponding to the most common colours in the Jacobean court, so that even the variations in ornament did not entirely dispel the sense of a court uniform. Greenaway was influenced by the large ruffs seen in Flemish paintings later in the seventeenth century, but the effect he created was, I think, true to the spirit of Shakespeare's play. Central to the concept of the film are Prospero's lines informing Miranda about their escape from Italy:

A noble Neapolitan, Gonzalo
Out of his charity, who being then appointed
Master of this design, did give us, with
Rich garments, linens, stuffs, and necessities
Which since have steaded much; so, of his gentleness,
Knowing I loved my books, he furnished me
From mine own library with volumes that
I prize above my dukedom. (1.2.161–8)

In the film Prospero is clothed in rich garments indeed, in a magnificent magic cloak, or, when relaxing in his library (which recalls Michelangelo's Bibliotheca Laurenziana in Florence), as a Renaissance potentate or Doge, possessor of books that embrace all the culture of the age, and that symbolize his desire to return to the source of that culture in Italy. In the play Prospero ends by prizing his rich garments and status in Milan above his books. The last we hear of his library is his intent to bury his 'book' (of magic spells presumably), 'deeper than did ever plummet sound' (5.1.56).

In the film Prospero's spirits, including Ariel and 'all his quality' (1.2.193) and Caliban are almost if not quite naked. On the stage, too, Caliban in particular has usually been played with a minimum of clothing, symbolizing freedom from the social and political constraints of the age. A sense of the significance of the contrast with the aristocrats was revived in 1988 when Tony Haygarth played Caliban at the National Theatre in London as naked except for a kind of box covering his genitals, a contraption that has been interpreted as an 'artificial phallus',[18] but could just as well be thought of as Prospero's control mechanism for subduing Caliban's sexual energies. After a command performance the actor was introduced to the present Queen Elizabeth, who was dressed in an elegant court gown. The contrast may have prompted some there to link Caliban with the 'savages' John Smith encountered in Virginia, as drawn by John White, who represents them as wearing skimpy loincloths at most. Accounts of *The Tempest* often used to 'listen exclusively to

Prospero's voice'[19] as spokesman for the play, and treat Caliban, with whatever gesture towards his poetry, as a morally 'savage and deformed slave' in accordance with the description someone attached to his name in the list of characters in the First Folio. More recently new historicist and materialist readings of the play have located it within colonialist discourse in an effort to expose its ideological implications by stressing Prospero's authoritarian ways in dispossessing Caliban of the island, and in claiming that the reconciliations of the ending are a sham.[20]

The play is fundamentally concerned with the exercise of power, and keeps reminding us of a range of issues connected with rule, subjection, and freedom, and, to grasp the complexity with which these are treated, an understanding of the function of costume in the action is necessary. For the indications of costume in the text relate to the play's deepest levels of significance and irony. In his account of the play, Stephen Orgel understandably resists accepting the superficial neatness of the conclusion, but is puzzled to comprehend why Shakespeare 'was unwilling to have Antonio repent'. He thinks the play's 'genre' points to an answer, as Shakespeare found 'the promised restorations and marriages of comic conclusions inadequate to reconcile the conflicts that comedy has generated'.[21] I think Shakespeare was in full control of his dramaturgy, and that the ending is implicit in the overall structure of the play. It is true that in forgiving his enemies Prospero, so to speak, blanks out from his own speeches in Act 5 the nastiness of Alonso, Sebastian, and Antonio, and indeed stops Alonso from bringing up the past with his remark, 'Let us not burden our remembrance with / A heaviness that's gone' (5.1.199–200). He is supported by Gonzalo, who congratulates all on finding themselves 'When no man was his own'. Prospero goes further in diverting attention from the aristocrats on to the misdeeds of Stephano, Trinculo, and Caliban with his lines:

These three have robbed me, and this demi-devil –
For he's a bastard one – had plotted with them
To take my life. (5.1.272–4)

But in allowing Antonio and Sebastian to come through unscathed, and by including them in Prospero's editing out of past misdeeds by courtiers, Shakespeare was in effect transforming the genre by a characteristic innovation. The ending is made strange not so much because Antonio and Sebastian seem unchanged, but rather because Prospero joins them in the corridors of power, anxious to return to Milan in order to secure the future of his dynasty by the marriage of Ferdinand and Miranda, and ready to resume his subordinate relationship to Alonso, whom he now addresses as 'my liege' and 'your highness' (5.1.245, 302).

The elisions by Prospero and Gonzalo of political violence, of usurpation by Antonio, and attempted murder by Sebastian and Antonio, disturbingly redefine the civilization Prospero has envisioned, in the masque of Ceres and elsewhere, as the source of morality, music, poetry, dancing, art, and high culture generally. In effect Shakespeare returns us to the courts of Milan and Naples as centres of power, where courtiers are all dressed alike in the costumes of authority, a style of dress that imprisons them in their roles, and provides a concealment for their vices, hatreds, and machinations. Antonio and Sebastian take their corruption back with them to Italy, where they may find further opportunities to gain Milan by violence, or to 'come by Naples' (2.1.292–3). Prospero and all the aristocrats are released at the end from their confinement on the island only to return to a worse kind of confinement, symbolized in the clothes worn by courtiers. The power that nearly all the characters have sought turns out finally to be constraining rather than a means to achieve freedom, and especially for Prospero. He began by expressing his scorn for Antonio, who, in usurping Milan, agreed to do homage to Alonso, King of Naples,

To give him annual tribute, do him homage,
Subject his coronet to his crown, and bend
The dukedom yet unbowed. (1.2.113–15)

The shift from this condemnation of Antonio to his own humility towards Alonso in the final scene marks Prospero's willing return from his island of order and art to the intrigues and jostlings for power that have characterized the courts of Italy. In the end Prospero needs to provide for Miranda and to be reabsorbed into a social nexus where he will no longer be able to control the impulses to violence in others or perhaps the darkness in himself. In its way *The Tempest* turns out to be Shakespeare's most considered exploration of the human proneness to violence in relation to political power, servitude, and freedom.

NOTES

1. For interesting discussion of issues relating to power and politics in the late plays, see the essays collected in Gordon McMullan and Jonathan Hope, eds., *The Politics of Tragicomedy. Shakespeare and After* (London and New York: Routledge, 1992) and in Gillian Murray Kendall, ed., *Shakespearean Power and Punishment* (Madison, N.J.: Fairleigh Dickinson University, 1998).

2. Citing William Gouge, *God's Three Arrows* (1631), 379–80.
3. In *Repositioning Shakespeare* (London and New York: Routledge, 1999),
   Thomas Cartelli relies on the African novelist Ngugi wa Thiongo's perception of Prospero as analogous to Conrad's Mr Kurtz in his *A Grain of
   Wheat*; Prospero's brutality, he observes, operates 'out of an assumption of
   highmindedness that differentiates itself from the brutality of an Other'
   (101).
4. For the value and importance of clothes in Shakespeare's age, see Peter
   Stallybrass, 'Worn Worlds: Clothes and Identity on the Renaissance Stage',
   in Margreta de Grazia, Maureen Quilligan, and Peter Stallybrass, eds.,
   Subject and Object in Renaissance Culture (Cambridge University Press, 1996),
   289–320. The 'theatrical companies accumulated costumes' (302), including the cast-off clothing of aristocrats and used masquing costumes, and
   could rent from pawnbrokers such as Philip Henslowe, much of whose trade
   was in valuable cloaks, doublets, and gowns. Thomas Platter observed in
   1599 that 'The actors are most expensively and elaborately costumed.' See
   also Andrew Gurr, *The Shakespearean Stage*, 3rd edition (Cambridge University Press, 1992), 193–200, and Karen Newman, *Fashioning Femininity and
   English Renaissance Drama* (Chicago: University of Chicago Press, 1991),
   108–27.
5. Stephen Orgel, Introduction to *The Tempest* (Oxford Shakespeare, Oxford
   University Press, 1987), 29.
6. See Stephen Orgel, *Impersonations* (Cambridge University Press, 1996), 104–
   5, on 'the widespread conviction in the culture' that such robes confer
   authority rather than merely confirming it.
7. In considering the play's relation to James I and contemporary politics,
   David Scott Kastan points out that the marriage of Ferdinand will 'accom-
   plish precisely what the "inveterate" hatred (1.2.22) of Alonso for Prospero
   attempted: the dissolution of Milanese sovereignty into Neapolitan dynastic
   rule'; see *Shakespeare After Theory* (London and New York: Routledge, 1999),
   197. It is only by ignoring such aspects that the play can still be read as a 'tale
   of reconciliation and reunion', as by Robin Headlam Wells, 'An Orpheus for
   a Hercules: Virtue Redefined in "The Tempest"', in Wells, Glenn Burgess,
   and Rowland Wymer, eds., *Neo-Historicism: Studies in Renaissance Literature,
   History and Politics* (Cambridge University Press, 2000), 240–62.
8. *The Political Works of James I*, reprinted from the edition of 1616, with an
   introduction by Charles Howard McIlwain (Cambridge, Mass.: Harvard
   University Press, 1918), 307.
9. This is the earliest record of a performance; see Orgel, ed., *The Tempest*, 62.
10. See Stallybrass, 'Worn Worlds', 308–10, where he comments especially on
    the use of costume in *Cymbeline*.
11. On 'seeming' and truth in Shakespeare's plays, see Philip Edwards, '"Tender
    and True Pay": Representing Falsehood', in Grace Ioppolo, ed., *Shakespeare
    Performed: Essays in Honor of R. A. Foakes* (Newark: University of Delaware
    Press, 2000), 122–30.

12. William Camden, *Remains of a Greater Work* (1605), 221.
13. Stephen Orgel, *The Illusion of Power: Political Theater in the English Renaissance* (Berkeley and Los Angeles: University of California Press, 1975), 67.
14. *Ibid.*, 45.
15. *Ibid.*, 58.
16. Thomas Carlyle, *Sartor Resartus* (serialized 1833–4; first American edn, 1836; first English edn, 1838; ed. Kerry McSweeney and Peter Sabor, World's Classics (Oxford University Press, 1987), 52.
17. The effect can be seen in *Prospero's Books: A Film of Shakespeare's The Tempest* (New York: Four Walls Eight Windows; London: Chatto & Windus, 1991).
18. M. C. Linthicum, *Costume in the Drama of Shakespeare and his Contemporaries* (Oxford: Clarendon Press, 1936), 159.
19. Francis Barker and Peter Hulme, 'Nymphs and Reapers Heavily Vanish: the Discursive Con-texts of *The Tempest*', in John Drakakis, ed., *Alternative Shakespeares* (London and New York: Methuen, 1985), 204.
20. Sensitive discussion of colonialist issues in the play may be found in Peter Hulme's *Colonial Encounters: Europe and the Native Caribbean, 1492–1797* (London: Methuen 1986, reprinted 1992), and the introduction to Orgel's edition (1987), 31–9. Colonialist readings in turn have come under attack, and seven of them are criticized by Ben Ross Schneider, Jr, '"Are We Being Historical Yet?": Colonialist Interpretations of Shakespeare's *Tempest*,' *Shakespeare Studies*, 23 (1995), 120–45. Schneider emphasizes the influence of Seneca and Montaigne in claiming that the play is concerned with Prospero's effort to 'gain freedom by maximising his power' (137), freedom being the ability to contemplate death.
21. Orgel, ed., *The Tempest*, 55.

CHAPTER 10

Afterword

The problem of violence, especially as represented in random or point-less murders, is more acute now than in Shakespeare's time, not least because of technological advances in methods of killing, which made possible the terrible destruction of the World Trade Center in New York on 11 September 2001, with massive loss of lives. Terrorism appears to be a special manifestation of the human propensity to violence, occurring when men who feel in some way alienated or deprived of a role in society identify with a political or religious cause to the point where they become willing to carry out killings for the cause, and to die for it themselves. A cause is not the same as a motive; terrorists may have no idea which or how many people they will kill. Such men are represented, for example, by anarchists in the late nineteenth century, and now by some disaffected Muslims in the Middle East and by some Catholic nationalists in Northern Ireland.[1] The wide availability of guns has also made it possible for socially marginalized or deprived people, usually men, to display their anger by indiscriminate killings of others, often former associates in the workplace, but sometimes, shockingly, schoolchildren. American culture is said to support 'aggressive responses among young males as a legitimate expression of *self-help* in confrontations with others, especially other young males', as such behaviour contributes to the construction of ideals of masculinity.[2] The film-maker who is the central character in Ben Elton's black comic novel, *Popcorn* (1996), says at one point 'Being a killer is a career option in America, like teaching or dentistry', and such a career is symbolized in the figure of the hitman, who crops up again and again in fiction and in films.

The most intriguing and compelling image of violence at the present time, however, is embodied in the serial killer, a male who looks 'normal', that is to say, like other people, and kills perfect strangers, and whose violence is unmotivated, except that there may be a 'nearly consistent gendering: a male violence that is anti-female and anti-homosexual'.[3]

People are fascinated by such figures in life (Geoffrey Dahmer, for instance), and in fiction (Hannibal Lecter, for example). The serial killer who carries out motiveless murders seems to be a modern phenomenon, associated perhaps with what Mark Seltzer calls a 'machine culture' of mass replication, so that one typical location for serial violence is a motel or hotel, as in Alfred Hitchcock's film *Psycho*.[4] Seltzer criticizes the notion that such murders are motiveless, 'a renovated version of motiveless malignity. There is a sublime circularity in such an understanding of the motive for killing as the drive to kill: nothing, in effect, drives the drive.'[5] There is circularity only if one assumes that a murderer must have an identifiable motive, and our desire to understand, to explain, certainly encourages us to attribute motives to murderers. It may be true that 'Pure murder is a thoroughly unmotivated, disinterested act, a supreme fiction that is only possible in the realm of art',[6] but the serial killer and mass murderer, whose activities have been made possible by the technology of modern travel and weaponry, fascinate because there is no obvious explanation for what they do. In the absence of any moral accounting for serial killings, we relate to them aesthetically, in Joel Black's words, as 'an involved, but secure, observer',[7] watching films or reading about them. It was at the beginning of the machine age in 1827 that De Quincey jokingly considered murder as 'One of the Fine Arts', and hailed Cain as a genius and the inventor of murder.

Machines replicate the same action or procedure, and the repeating revolver, rifle, and then machine gun and sub-machine gun made possible mass killings in war and in peace. The use of aeroplanes loaded with fuel to destroy buildings and the people in them is an extension of this exploitation of machines for murder. It is paradoxical that the development of civilization has led simultaneously to the ready availability of machines for killing, and hence the emergence of modern serial killers and terrorists, and also to the abandonment of many traditional forms of aggression. The potential for aggression, as I argued in the Introduction, I take to be present in everyone as a genetic inheritance from the primates and primitive man. In this way it is possible to explain why the desire to assert individuality is so common, and why the construction of masculinity is based on a maintenance of status. Male self-esteem and honour have traditionally demanded active defence, while female honour has more often been associated with passivity. In this gendering of honour men have usually fought, while women have been more likely to suffer rape and to redeem their honour by suicide, as Lucretia did. It is not long since duelling was in vogue and 'male honor depended on a reputation for violence and bravery';[8] but as prosperous societies emerged in Europe and the United States, and as women have successfully competed for positions of authority, physical violence has given way to other, more subtle, kinds, the most obvious form being verbal violence.

A sharp tongue has always been a means for a woman to fend off unwanted attentions by men or keep a husband in order. Now words have become one of the means by which professional and business people may maintain status and gain respect. Gaining the upper hand in argument, as well as ways of humiliating others, of putting people down, can be involved in competing for superiority. In the replacement of physical by other kinds of violence, display can also contribute to the establishment and preservation of status, for example: in dress, the well-cut suit; in appurtenances, the Rolex watch, the larger office, the grander house, and car. Display in the sense of performing a threat of violence is common among chimpanzees and other primates, and human beings, too, may seek to settle differences and establish pecking orders in the same way. It is obviously safer and less likely to result in harm if a threat displayed, or a hint of terrible consequences, has the effect of causing others to back off and accept a lower standing. Both in the development of machine weapons, and in the refinement of non-physical forms of violence, our society is very different from that of Shakespeare's age; but if the forms in which violence is expressed have changed, the basic problem remains the same.

Let me reformulate the problem: assuming that a potential for violence is natural to human beings in instinctual urges including those to defend the self, family, or tribe; to retaliate when attacked; to assert individuality; and to claim status or respect; how should we relate to and seek to mitigate or control the recurrent outbreaks that seem inevitable? The problem cannot be resolved into one of good versus evil, for it is most disturbingly seen in the many instances of good men who commit acts of violence, as in that most enduring of examples, Hamlet. The law can only act in retrospect to punish after a crime has been committed, and religion promotes violence as much as it heals the suffering. Moreover, those instinctual drives may be manifested in acts of violence that seem unmotivated and inexplicable, and so cannot be foreseen. Audiences now are fascinated by stories of violent criminals, sometimes indistinguishable from violent police, and of serial killers who murder without hesitation, not relating to their victims in any way.[9] The current vogue for ultra-violent movies was preceded by other kinds of crime and gangster films, and these in turn by Westerns in which violence was 'less a means than an end in itself – less a matter of violating another than of constituting one's physical self as a male'.[10] All these are related to our 'machine culture', but also to a long history of forms of fiction that return in some of their most powerful expressions to what lies behind current obsessions, namely a recognition that human history is bound up with and in some way dependent on unpremeditated, spontaneous acts of violence. Our history begins, so to speak, with Cain's killing of Abel, and we are all descendants of Cain.

Before the machine age and before Darwin the biblical story of the beginning of the world was widely held to be literally true, and the problem of violence was likely to be seen in relation to the problem of the origin of evil, an issue that deeply troubled Samuel Taylor Coleridge. He was dismayed by the bloodshed and atrocities associated with the French Revolution and the wars that followed, and he was perplexed by the disparity between advances in civilization and the way in which great leaders such as Pitt and Napoleon could sanction or participate in the destruction of thousands of people in fighting wars or in tolerating the slave trade. How could men, differentiated from other creatures by having reason and responsibility, behave like animals? Coleridge's broodings on such matters led him to contemplate writing with Wordsworth a short epic on the theme of Cain and Abel, a project soon abandoned, and 'The Rime of the Ancient Mariner' was written instead. In the 1798 version of this poem the mariner shoots the albatross for no reason, and the crew, who see the bird as a good omen, regard the act as hellish. Later versions of the poem and the gloss added in 1817 nudge the reader towards interpreting the poem as dealing with the mariner in terms of sin, guilt, and penance, and Coleridge surely conceived the poem intending some religious escape route for the mariner in his return to society and a 'goodly company' walking to church. The first version, however, is ambiguous, and leaves us, too, with an image of the mariner as an eternal wanderer given strange powers to dominate and cast a spell over others. The mariner is also Cain *redivivus*, committing an act that differentiates him from others, a self-defining that marks him as special, and, like Cain, he is preserved to pass from land to land to retell his story, while the rest of the crew perish. Coleridge created a figure that has continued to haunt readers ever since, not because of the moral tacked on at the end, 'He prayeth best who loveth best', but because it imaginatively focuses on the issue of a good man who commits a terrible crime, apparently for no reason.[11]

Another classic version of a gratuitous act of murder is the subject of Dostoevsky's *Crime and Punishment* (1866).[12] The hero, Raskolnikov, like Coleridge, is troubled by Napoleon, and has written an article arguing that exceptional men may be justified in overstepping convention. He murders an old woman because he 'wanted to become a Napoleon' (428), to dare to step over moral barriers: 'I had to find out then, and as quickly as possible, whether I was a louse like the rest or a man' (433). Raskolnikov explains this in his confession to Sonia: 'He who dares much is right – that's how they look at it. He who dismisses with contempt what men regard as sacred becomes their law-giver, and he who dares more than anyone is more right than anyone' (431). The murder was for Raskolnikov an act of self-definition, confirming his status as a man, his freedom from the restraints others accept. In the end he is 'saved' by the ministrations of Sonia, and finds a new kind of 'freedom' in prison (552); the novel concludes with him finding a copy of the New Testament under his pillow. The novel richly explores Raskolnikov's predicament from many angles, and he interprets what he has done in a variety of ways as his moods swing between exhilaration and depression. As an extended meditation on the problem of violence the novel anticipates existentialist representations of murders as gratuitous or absurd, as in Albert Camus's *L'Etranger*, or, more recently, John Banville's *The Book of Evidence* (1989). As A. D. Nuttall has argued, the implication in *Crime and Punishment* that murder might be an authentic act of freedom 'survives the completion of the book', and suggests an existentialist position that is incompatible with Christianity.[13]

At the end of his book Nuttall links Raskolnikov and Hamlet: 'Thus Raskolnikov is Hamlet turned inside out. Hamlet, surprised to find an abyss within himself, delays. Raskolnikov, to demonstrate his independence of all reasons, carries out a *premature* crime.' Hamlet, he says, fits smoothly into 'the existentialist's account of human nature'.[14] This is to leave out of account Hamlet's self-defining act in his killing of Polonius, which may be compared with Raskolnikov's murder of the old woman; the two are more closely connected than Nuttall suggests. Like Dostoevsky, Shakespeare was deeply interested in the fundamental problem of coping with human violence. Their investigations continue to speak to us because the problem remains as acute as ever, and more difficult to deal with, if only because violence is no longer pretty much confined to the murder of one person by another, since modern weapons make possible mass murders on a scale hitherto undreamed of.

I have sought in this book to show how Shakespeare's treatment of violence changed and developed from his early histories to his late romances. In his early plays he imitates and outdoes the representations of violence for its own sake that excited Marlowe's audiences, apparently enjoying the challenge to find new ways to match the Rose spectaculars. His history plays led him into a deeper consideration of violence in relation to power and to wars, civil and foreign. The unresolved tensions and contradictions in the presentation of Henry V seem to me to reflect Shakespeare's growing uneasiness about violence even as he was finishing his studies of English rulers with a patriotic surge. The Chorus to Act 5, 30–4 expresses the hope that Essex would return triumphant from his expedition to put down 'rebellion' in Ireland in 1599, a hope soon disappointed. The failure and disgrace of Essex implicated Shakespeare's patron, the Earl of Southampton, and may have affected the dramatist's turn away from English history at this point. In *Julius Caesar* Shakespeare reverted to ancient history to deal with assassination and with the violence of the mob. *Hamlet* followed, a play in part growing out of *Julius Caesar*, with its allusions to this play, its use of Roman character names, and scene of mob violence. *Hamlet* is central in Shakespeare's developing concern with violence in its creation of a protagonist who meditates on the urge to revenge his father's death in the context not only of the conflict between classical heroic and Christian values, but also in the context of the control or release of violent impulses.

The later tragedies and Roman plays raise other issues relating to violence. Iago and Macbeth anticipate the aestheticization of murder as an art by De Quincey and others in the nineteenth century, and the glorification of the great criminal as suspending moral laws. *King Lear* portrays the terrible consequences that are brought about by the unthinking habit of violence on the part of the old king, and lead to civil war, war with France, and the deaths of all three of his daughters. In *Macbeth* and *Coriolanus* Shakespeare is much concerned with the construction of manliness and its relation to violence. The focus in *Antony and Cleopatra* is on power and the violence that is taken for granted as a means of controlling the Roman empire, power that in the end is made to seem empty and devalued in relation to human love. These plays all explore violence in relation to human agency and responsibility, but in the late plays Shakespeare's perspective changes, as violence is represented as common to nature and man, an unpredictable and inescapable part of human experience that has to be accepted. Natural violence is represented in storms and tempests, shipwrecks, and the bear that kills Antigonus, but also in the sudden and unexplained anger or hatred or lust that erupts in a character's behaviour. This is exemplified, for instance, in the effort by Posthumus to have Imogen murdered by Pisanio, and in the sudden rejection of Hermione by Leontes, and his attempt to have Polixenes killed. Accident, fortune, and the efforts of Paulina and

Camillo help to work out a solution that restores harmony; an oracle confirms what everyone except Leontes knows in *The Winter's Tale*, and gestures are made to the gods who appear in dreams or masques, but who have little or no effect on the world the characters inhabit. In *The Tempest* most of the human characters who come to the island want power and are willing to kill to obtain it, but in yet another shift of perspective Shakespeare focuses on Prospero's attempt as ruler and magus to control his own violent impulses and those of others, leaving uncertainty as to how far his success in the play's action may be sustained.

In his plays Shakespeare explores in increasingly complex ways many aspects of violence that bear on present-day concerns. In particular he came to appreciate that impulses to violence may be natural to humans. In *Richard III*, *Othello*, and *Macbeth* he enabled audiences to see how insight into the internal drives and feelings of his great villains might elicit sympathy for them and question the validity of applying to them simple categories of right and wrong, good and evil. He showed an understanding of the psychology of mob violence in dramatizing Jack Cade's rebellion and the death of Cinna. He was concerned in his history plays with the violence of warfare in relation to rule, and whether there could be a just war. In his Roman plays he explored the construction of masculinity in relation to both power over others and self-control. Finally, in the late plays, human violence is shown in relation to violence in the natural world, and both are shown as aspects of a world subject to chance and accident, uncontrollable by humans. In a last variation the Italians who are shipwrecked in *The Tempest* bring their impulses for violence and desires for power to an island controlled by a magus who can barely keep in check his own violence and whose rule is maintained by slaves. The reconciliations of the ending leave open the possibility that violence will break out again, and suggest that harmony is at best precarious, glimpsed in visions like the masque of Ceres and the betrothal of Ferdinand and Miranda. Shakespeare could not imagine the kinds of terrorism made possible by machine-age technology, but his plays provide an incisive commentary on the more general problem of the human impulse to violence.

NOTES

1. See John W. Burton, *Violence Explained* (Manchester University Press, 1997), 1–31, and Arthur F. Redding, 'Violence and Modernism', chapter 4 in *Raids on Human Consciousness. Writing, Anarchism, and Violence* (Columbia: University

of South Carolina Press, 1998), 117–59. Women, too, are capable of extreme violence, though much less prominently than men; see Kerrigan, 'Medea Variations', chapter 13, *Revenge Tragedy*, 315–42.

2. Citing Peter Spierenburg, ed., *Men and Violence. Gender, Honor, and Rituals in Modern Europe and America* (Columbus: Ohio State University Press, 1998), 68; see also Lee Clark Mitchell, *Westerns* (University of Chicago Press, 1996), chapter 6, 150–74.

3. Mark Seltzer, *Serial Killers. Death and Life in America's Wound Culture* (New York and London: Routledge, 1998), 67.

4. *Ibid.*, 33.

5. *Ibid.*, 134.

6. Joel Black, *The Aesthetics of Murder*, 92.

7. *Ibid.*, 73.

8. Spierenburg, *Men and Violence*, 6.

9. See Carlos Clarens, *Crime Movies* (New York: Da Capo Press, 1997), 294: 'The public may have grown tired of cinematic sex, but its tolerance for violence seemed undiminished.'

10. Lee Clark Mitchell, *Westerns*, 169.

11. See my essay, 'Coleridge, Violence and "The Rime of the Ancient Mariner"', *Romanticism*, 7 (2001), 41–57.

12. Page references are to the translation by David Magarshack (Harmondsworth: Penguin Books, 1951).

13. A. D. Nuttall, *Crime and Punishment. Murder as Philosophic Experiment* (Edinburgh: Scottish Academic Press, for the University of Sussex Press, 1978), 72–3.

14. *Ibid.*, 121.

Index